IDEOLOGY AND COMMUNITY IN THE FIRST WAVE OF CRITICAL LEGAL STUDIES

In *Ideology and Community in the First Wave of Critical Legal Studies* Richard W. Bauman presents a fresh, rigorous assessment of some of the key ideas developed by writers aligned with the early critical legal studies movement. This book examines several of the movement's major themes and arguments in its first decade, in the period dating roughly from the mid-1970s to the mid-1980s.

Heterogeneous and progressive, the critical legal studies movement inspired a variety of leftist re-examinations and critiques of the dominant liberal assumptions underlying the law and legal institutions. Bauman offers an exposition and assessment of the radical challenge to several central tenets of legal and political liberalism, including the values associated with individualism, moral scepticism, and state neutrality. He maintains that radical critics associated with early critical legal studies misunderstood many of the important assumptions and commitments of contemporary political liberalism and tended to misconstrue liberalism as relying on specific, deficient metaphysical underpinnings. Although the quest therefore might have failed, the early critical legal studies movement did succeed in sharpening discussions about the politics of law and legal interpretation and in providing a stimulus to other types of radical, contemporary critique.

RICHARD W. BAUMAN is Professor of Law, University of Alberta.

Ideology and Community in the First Wave of Critical Legal Studies

RICHARD W. BAUMAN

UNIVERSITY OF TORONTO PRESS
Toronto Buffalo London

© University of Toronto Press Incorporated 2002
Toronto Buffalo London
Printed in Canada

ISBN 0-8020-4803-X (cloth)
ISBN 0-8020-8341-2 (paper)

Printed on acid-free paper

National Library of Canada Cataloguing in Publication Data

Bauman, Richard W.
  Ideology and community in the first wave of critical legal
studies
  Includes bibliographical references and index.
  ISBN 0-8020-4803-X (bound).   ISBN 0-8020-8341-2 (pbk.)
  1. Law – History.   2. Law – United States – History.   I. Title
  KF380.B38 2002   340'.11   C2002-900010-6

This book has been published with the help of a grant from the Humanities
and Social Sciences Federation of Canada, using funds provided by the
Social Sciences and Humanities Research Council of Canada.

University of Toronto Press acknowledges the financial assistance to its
publishing program of the Canada Council for the Arts and the
Ontario Arts Council.

University of Toronto Press acknowledges the financial support for its
publishing activities of the Government of Canada through the Book
Publishing Industry Development Program (BPIDP).

My ways of life are natural to me: in forming them I have never called in the help of any erudite discipline; but when I was seized with the desire to give a public account of them, weak as they are, I made it my duty to help them along with precepts and examples, so that I could publish them more decorously. I was then astonished myself to find that, by sheer chance, they were in conformity with so many philosophical examples and precepts. Only after my life was settled in its activity did I learn which philosophy was governing it! A new character: a chance philosopher, not a premeditated one!

Michel de Montaigne, *Essays*
(trans. M.A. Screech)

Contents

Acknowledgments

I wish to thank those who have read this book in whole or in part: Ronald Dworkin, Robert W. Gordon, Nicola Lacey, and Neil MacCormick, all of whom helped me by pointing out egregious errors, dubious arguments, and various inanities and infelicities, by suggesting fruitful lines of inquiry, and by providing in their own work fine models of scholarship. Despite their assistance, it should not be assumed that any of these kind individuals agrees with the contents of this book. For the imperfections and errors that remain, I take sole responsibility. As W.H. Auden versified about Oxford in 1937, the university and its denizens 'challenge our high-strung students with a careless beauty / Setting a single error / Against their countless faults.'

During the period of this book's preparation, I have also been deeply grateful for the intellectual camaderie and unstinting support of colleagues closer to home, among whom I single out especially Donna Greschner, David Schneiderman, and Bruce Ziff. I am indebted to Virgil Duff of the University of Toronto Press for his admirable patience. The referees who read the manuscript for that press also made numerous helpful suggestions.

Many of the themes of this book were initially worked out and appeared – in embryonic form – in an article contained in volume 33 (1989) of the *McGill Law Journal*. For permission to reprint that material here in revised form as Chapter 5, my thanks are due.

IDEOLOGY AND COMMUNITY IN THE
FIRST WAVE OF CRITICAL LEGAL STUDIES

1

Introduction

His reform of the system would have begun in the lecture-room at his own desk. He would have seated a rival Assistant Professor opposite him, whose business should be strictly limited to expressing opposite views. Nothing short of this would ever interest either the professor or the student; but of all University freaks, no irregularity shocked the intellectual atmosphere so much as contradiction or competition among teachers. In that respect the thirteenth-century University system was worth the whole teaching of the modern school.

Henry Adams, *The Education of Henry Adams*

Over the past twenty-five years, overtly ideological challenges to conventional forms of legal theory and legal scholarship have enlivened the atmosphere of many law schools, particularly in the United States, where, for some scholars, theoretical subscription or orientation has become a matter of passionate commitment. Proponents of liberal views on the importance of rights, on the role of courts as guardians of fundamental values, and on law's potential as a vehicle of incremental social progress have come under attack for both their flawed conception of human nature and their misguided efforts to promote individualistic principles at the expense of other moral values. Attacks on these lines have been launched from both the right and the left, from various groups of feminists, and from writers who view the law as an obstacle on the road to achieving justice for racial and other minorities. For legal academics in some institutions, the intensity of the debates has been discomfiting: commentators have attributed to the resulting tensions a decline in both the civility and the reputation of such traditional citadels of legal education as Harvard Law School.[1] Other law teachers, welcoming the opportunity to engage in a political free-for-all, have used the debates to espouse a conception of the law they believe should inform any polity worth belonging to. For the latter, the new climate in the law schools has been invigorating.[2]

Some of the most notorious opponents of the direct and indirect influence of liberalism on the shaping of legal concepts and legal doctrine have been associated with the Conference on Critical Legal Studies.[3] Members of this movement have self-consciously set themselves apart from orthodox legal academics. Although affiliated with other groups working for social change through the law, these critics have staked out a distinctive, comprehensive approach to the analysis of legal theory and doctrine.[4]

The story of the critical legal studies movement's genesis and growth has not yet been definitively told.[5] The original Conference, which assembled in Madison, Wisconsin, in 1977, involved a small cluster of law teachers who had, primarily through a complex personal network, discovered a common interest in re-examining legal thought and legal institutions in light of progressive social and political theory.[6] During its first few years, the Conference operated on a small scale, with membership essentially by invitation only. The leading figures were drawn from the law schools at Harvard, Buffalo, Wisconsin, and Stanford.

By the late 1970s, after the appearance of work that would become germinal in the development of the movement, the Conference changed character. No longer a coterie, it had opened up and become a loosely knit organization to which any individuals interested in radical legal change could subscribe. To use the scheme recently developed by Malcolm Gladwell to describe how 'cool' ideas catch on, the 'innovators' in critical legal studies, those who adventurously claimed to have invented new ways of thinking about the law, gave way to 'early adopters' who used the techniques to gather fresh insights into legal doctrines and practices.[7] Within a few years, gatherings held under the aegis of critical legal studies attracted more than a hundred participants.[8] The movement thus became widespread, and it expanded beyond the United States to gain adherents in other common law countries and in Europe.[9] To the first generation of Conference members, who have since come to hold senior positions at U.S. law schools, has been added a new wave of younger academics who have both built on the work of the original members and developed the radical critique in new directions.

The founding figures in critical legal studies – one might almost say the founding fathers, since very few women were initially involved – have remained dominant voices in the movement. They are prolific writers whose work continues to unearth and redefine the political content of traditional legal materials. In some cases, particularly that of Duncan Kennedy, radical criticism has taken a sinuous path. Identifying the principles and appraising the strategies of the movement generally are tasks made difficult by the changes in style and methods marking the development of critical legal studies. In addition, any assessment must contend with the problem presented by the prodigious quantity of published work that might be characterized as reflecting critical legal topics, principles, assumptions, or methods of argument. The list of such works now exceeds a thousand articles and several dozen monographs.[10] Readers of this book will include legal academics chagrined that their work is not discussed prominently, or perhaps not cited at all. As connoisseurs of the practice of authoritative annotation, they are liable to read in such under-valuation or lacuna a polemical intention on my part, an unforgivable *damnatio memoriae*.[11] By confining my discussion largely to the period when critical legal publications were still fresh, however, I have avoided poking a stick at a wasp's nest – namely, the problem of classifying many academics of the past generation as more or less 'radical,' with all the attendant implications of drawing up a list of persons more or less subversive. Not all legal academics who have published a critical piece of work – and who among us takes pride in lacking rigorous standards or in being non-judgmental? – would be pleased to be associated with the critical legal studies movement.

Although there is no doubt about the significance of critical legal work in recent legal scholarship, its continued vitality has been questioned. According to some commentators, the movement has exhausted its store of once-fresh ideas. Conceptual fatigue has set in and critical legal writing, it is claimed by some outsiders, has become predictable and arid; like legal realism before it, critical legal studies has reached a dead end.[12] Readers interested in radical critique with compellingly novel insights might prefer feminist or racial critiques of legal and political theory or a syncretism of elements of each of them.[13] Without necessarily endorsing this dismissal of critical legal work as outmoded or supplanted, my discussion in the following chapters will sum up in significant ways the original direction of critical legal studies as an avowedly 'radical critique.' While it was by no means the only form of radical critique of law to appear in the last quarter of the twentieth century, critical legal studies was certainly notorious, and it both attracted and repelled legal scholars and law students.[14] My discussion will also provide some clues as to the enduring potential of critical legal studies as a form of sustained criticism of existing legal systems in liberal democratic societies. Using techniques of analytical philosophy, I investigate fundamental claims, assumptions, and modes of theorizing made on behalf of critical legal studies, particularly in the literature published in the decade after 1975. It was during this period that the formative pieces of critical legal scholarship, as well as some of the first attempts to defend liberal commitments against the sceptical jurisprudential projects of the left, appeared. As the vast majority of this discussion took place in literature published in the United States, my assessment will primarily (and perhaps arbitrarily, though unapologetically) concentrate on American manifestations of critical legal studies.

My interest in this project has been kindled by three sorts of questions. First, is liberalism, as described and evaluated by its critical opponents, indeed as theoretically unsound and impoverished as the critique implies? Many liberal thinkers and legal academics have either ignored or dismissed critical legal challenges, sometimes with considerable vehemence, so it seems worthwhile to review which charges brought against liberalism are telling and which have missed the mark.[15] Second, one might ask what difference to law, and to the relationship between law and politics, adopting the critical perspective would make. Does critical legal work contain insights that can truly release all citizens from their ideological blinkers when it comes to making, observing, and justifying the law of their society? What kind of difference would critical legal work make in a specific legal context – say, the rules surrounding the assessment of contractual liability? Finally, I have been tempted to ask whether critical legal writers are even interested in projecting a concrete alternative that translates their insights into legal structures and practices.

Each of the foregoing questions requires careful exposition and even-handed analysis. This book also brings into the foreground ideas that crucially affect the critical legal challenge to mainstream theory and institutions. While some authors have tried to defend liberalism as a political theory against its critical legal challengers, concentrating on, for example, the concept of the rule of law, their attempts have addressed only a thin or a murky version of some of the critique's key concepts of legal consciousness and doctrinal experimentation.[16] Other defences against the radical critique have not been conducted on the abstract plane of jurisprudence, but have tried instead to defend certain doctrinal principles and adjudicative practices against the withering allegations of indeterminacy and incoherence. The object of this book is to provide a rounded assessment of critical legal work at both the theoretical and doctrinal levels.

Each of the following chapters deals with a key element of the radical critique. Chapter 2 considers the attack on liberalism as a system of political and legal values. The discussion focuses on basic claims and arguments made by such leading figures in the critical movement as Roberto Unger, Duncan Kennedy, Karl Klare, and Mark Tushnet. I survey various attempts to define the constitutive principles of liberalism and to show their pervasiveness in legal theory and legal doctrine. Although several pieces of critical legal work attempt a comprehensive account of which ideas arguably obstruct desirable social changes, these need to be arranged into a tableau that makes clear the point of the critical version of liberalism. The purpose of Chapter 2 is to reconstruct the critical legal case against liberalism and to address the pivotal question of whether critical legal versions of political, economic, or legal liberalism accurately reflect multifarious types of historical or contemporary liberal theory. The radical critique has sought to expose the underpinnings of liberalism and the structural limits it places on legal discourse. I argue that the portrait of liberal principles presented by these radical authors is simplistic and tendentious: they capture only imperfectly the range of liberal ideas in political and legal philosophy. Liberals are not necessarily committed to such notions as the subjectivity of values, radical individual autonomy, or the superiority of experience in the private realm over that in the public realm. Moreover, the structural analysis deployed by early critical legal literature, designed to exhibit the supposed internal contradictions of liberal theory, has outworn its usefulness.

Chapter 3 examines critical legal work as a radical new interpretation of the view that legal ideas and institutions ideologically delude citizens of democratic communities, preventing them from imagining the range of fundamental social transformations. An influential strand of early critical legal writing developed a typology of different modes of 'legal consciousness,' understood as shared beliefs and assumptions that frame any thinking about the law. Each mode, it has been argued, exemplifies a different period of modern legal history. Different senses of legal consciousness are used in these accounts: the term can refer either to professional indoctrination or to a more widespread sense of popular understanding and enculturation. My purpose in Chapter 3 is to clarify and evaluate the claims made on behalf of such an explanatory system. A particular type of consciousness is supposed to shape law, legal practices, and legal doctrine. By isolating and criticizing particular modes of consciousness, including the conceptual filter associated with legal liberalism, early critical legal writers have tried to illuminate the conditions under which such consciousness might change. The so-called emancipatory aims of critical legal studies are tied to this prospect of conceptual revolution. In my view, this approach is analytically problematic and lacks explanatory power. The resort to explanations based on the consciousness of a legal era appears to address two of the inveterate problems raised by orthodox leftist accounts of the relationship between law and society. One of these problems is the degree to which law can be a relatively autonomous phenomenon, the other is the role of, and scope for, human agency in legal change. I conclude that reliance by early critical legal authors on the notion of consciousness raises more questions than it resolves. It remains unclear whether the kind of ideological critique practised by these critics is aimed at a body of beliefs that misrepresents social reality, or whether it abandons the notion of false consciousness in favour of something less robust. The major flaw in the theory of legal consciousness is that it erroneously attributes a uniform consciousness to everyone in a specific society, regardless of the particular identities of individuals. According to my account, the early critical legal account of social progress on the basis of changed consciousness is beset by problems that cannot be repaired without dramatically relinquishing several of the theory's major claims.

Chapter 4 shifts the discussion to the context within which most critical legal writing is found. That chapter offers a sustained analysis of a particular critical legal contribution to doctrinal discussion. The area chosen is contract law. This legal subject is particularly apt, for extensive treatments of the philosophical basis of contract doctrine have been provided by such radical critics as Duncan Kennedy, Roberto Unger, Clare Dalton, Elizabeth Mensch, and Jay Feinman. Studying an individual area is especially helpful in testing the claims made by early critical legal authors about the pre-modern history of doctrinal principles, as well as the alleged incoherence and manipulability of legal doctrine generally. I conclude from my examination of the radical literature in this area that the sceptical critique of contract law misconceives the form judicial reasoning actually takes and, in addition, adopts a standard of coherence that is inappropriate to legal reasoning. The main principles underlying contract doctrine, while they might give rise, because of historical circumstances, to competing lines of authority, are not fundamentally contradictory, nor do they create an overall scheme that is embarrassingly indeterminate. Judges are engaged in a rationally defensible exercise of practical deliberation when they adjudicate disputes over contractual liability. I argue that the very features of common law development in this doctrinal area depreciated by critical legal authors are essential to the growth and adaptability of the law.

Chapter 5 scrutinizes the political and institutional implications of early critical legal writing, in particular the 'communitarian' prescriptions that follow from the critique of legal liberal institutions. In contradistinction to the alleged assumptions of liberal ideology, particularly its asocial individualism and its priority of the right over the good, early critical legal writing tended towards a different theory of the self and of moral value. By deploying a series of communitarian tropes and images, early critical legal writing sketched several possible frameworks for a revamped social and political order. These attempts at reconstruction are set out and evaluated and I identify several problems that emerge. In particular, I identify two paradoxes in the critical treatment of institution building. The first I refer to as the paradox of engagement: though early critical legal authors called for an appreciation of the law as deeply political, they largely refused on principle to disclose in any detail their substantive political views. The second paradox I call the paradox of postponement. This arises out of the critical legal disinclination to prescribe institutions and procedures, for fear of imposing unnecessary and unwanted limits on the subsequent debate. Though law is viewed as essentially a matter of political choice, the radical critic is supposed to refrain from recommending the particular values that ought to shape a legal regime: the selection and adoption of values must be left to a future process involving a radically transformed, that is, post-liberal, society. In Chapter 5 I chart the efforts of critical legal writers to adumbrate a post-liberal polity, and in the end, I question whether the prescriptions for political reconstruction are either meaningful or effective. One of the significant ironies found in critical legal contributions to legal philosophy is that critical legal writers are remarkably agnostic with respect to which normative choices are defensible.

If an observer of the contemporary scene in legal theory were looking for explanations of the fragmentation of the leftist, radical critique of law in the United States into new forms, some of which rub against the grain of the critique as it existed a decade earlier, he or she would find it useful to re-examine the themes covered in this book. First, liberalism has proved remarkably resilient. One weakness of early critical legal writing was its general failure to address the most sophisticated versions of liberal theory then current. There was too great a tendency to construct a generic type of liberal political and legal theory, one that did not correspond with the polyvocal scene in actual liberal debates. There is no single, classic liberal perspective that warrants the kinds of generalizations critical legal writing was once disposed to offer.

Second, advances in leftist political theory have made the deployment of a theory of consciousness itself both simplistic and redundant. The theory exaggerates certain features (the political background of law) and misapprehends others (the blanket effects of a particular consciousness). Other radical critiques of law, based on feminist concerns or race issues, have been transfused with the energy originally associated with early critical legal studies.

Third, the radical critique of legal doctrine, where it does not simply revive legal realist insights into the nature of adjudication and doctrinal development, fails to describe accurately the difference that competing principles make to legal development. After the critique has been offered, the best examples of doctrinal writing associated with critical legal studies have achieved what good scholarship has always done. They have helped normatively weigh the assumptions underlying legal rules or principles, causing scholars and judges to rethink the premises of any conventional approach. But the critique has not transformed legal reasoning into an open-ended political contest, nor has the criticism of doctrine proved a fertile site for revolutionary activity.

Finally, the programmatic aspect of critical legal writing has been disappointing. Although the radical critique once inspired some legal academics to believe that they could play a role as agents for significant social change (while others feared that their colleagues would assume this role), the overall effect of the critique has been to render the courts and law schools livelier but not fundamentally changed institutions. The more modest tasks of early critical legal studies, including the opening up of academic discussion to a greater range of ideological opinion and the increased use of normative literature and arguments from outside traditional legal sources, have been beneficial to legal theory and legal education generally. The radical critique has also been significantly modulated into new forms of theory, such as neopragmatism and postmodernism (and other styles of thinking that connote novelty and supercession), to which many early critical legal writers have become notable contributors.[17] The surviving forms of the original critique, along with the new influences and models that have changed the terms of radicalism in Anglo-American law schools, are ripening to the point that they could eventually form the topic for another book, one that tries to make sense of the cacophonous milieu of current theoretical debates and to distinguish those writers who exhibit a jittery, fin-de-siècle disquiet from those who embrace an upbeat millennarianism, in which sound laws and good government are just around the corner.

The book I have written constitutes a cooler, more detached discussion. While I am not unsympathetic to the goal of making theoretical learning and the revisability of our conceptions central to the formation of lawyers, I am conscious all the same of the virtues in getting the exposition of the radical critique right by testing its generalizations and exploring its consequences. I am certainly not indifferent to the issues raised by the first wave of critical legal writing: as the subsequent discussion makes clear, I believe that central, urgent problems of political and legal philosophy formed part of that original agenda and they are worth caring about. I have my own views about the most plausible and defensible answers to those perennial problems; in greater or lesser relief these views are revealed throughout the text, even if they do not steal centre stage. I am a liberal – a hopeless case or hapless one, take your pick – convinced that liberalism, in a sophisticated and supple form, has survived the critical legal onslaught and that, like a sapling in the buffeting wind, it is now stronger for enduring such rough treatment. I also believe it was a mistake from the beginning for critical legal theorists to see the law school as an incubator for irresistible and enlightened social change. Their hubristic faith in the influence of the law teacher is touching but unrealistic. In my opinion, too, the heyday of critical legal studies has not been succeeded by a period of internal correction, rebalancing, or regrouping. Its formative figures did not put on a solid footing a comprehensive, robust theory that could underwrite widespread changes in practice. Sprightly though it was in its criticisms, the movement has lacked a firm foundation. The 1990s saw the emergence of radical perspectives that simply outflanked critical legal attacks on traditional theory and doctrine. A decade and a half ago, critical legal authors might have boasted that they ran 'the only game in town,' and that this fact raised the stakes accordingly. In retrospect, that boast would be misleading – though the demimonde image was, while it lasted, flattering. The game or 'action' offered by critical legal theory has not been improved or transformed. It is merely less patronized, less frequented, less stimulating overall.

Some readers will wonder whether I have not, as if emulating a tale by Jorge Luis Borges, conjured up for literary amusement a fabulous school of thought, endowed with a thousand lifelike details, and then ceremoniously dismantled it, premise by imaginary premise. In particular the tone of my remarks might seem outlandishly abstract and excessively ironic. All I can say is that such is the nature of philosophical analysis, the kind that often sets the teeth of working lawyers and judges on edge. On occasion during the writing I, too, winced at the degree to which my engagement was largely over abstractions. I have found confidence and reassurance, though, in a recent, roughly analogous work by Hanna Fenichel Pitkin.[18] The manner in which Pitkin, critically but without hostility, dissects the problematic uses of key concepts in Arendt's political theory is to me the epitome of academic responsibility. She provides exegesis and evaluation of the highest order. It is instructive that Pitkin can express disagreement or perplexity without standing vaingloriously over her materials like a victor. A similar tone, inquisitive rather than gladiatorial, is what I have striven for in the following chapters.

A few readers of this book in manuscript urged me to thrust daggers instead of probing fastidiously with lancets, to lower poleaxes rather than drawbridges to understanding. I can appreciate the purpose of their advice. They would like the book to make a resounding splash. By contrast, I am satisfied to canvass my topic earnestly, avoiding flamboyance. To get ahead these days, not everyone has to engage in stand-up theorizing in the manner of, say, Stanley Fish.

2

Writing on a Slant: The Construction and Critique of Liberalism

In a warm room, as I recall, without books,
without admirers, but there you are for them,
resting your brow on your palm,
you will write about us on a slant.

Joseph Brodsky
(trans. Roberta Reeder)

From the perspective of many theorists who have spent the past quarter-century criticizing the weaknesses and failures of liberal conceptions of justice and law, the resurgence in the popularity of political and economic liberalism after the events in central and eastern Europe since 1989 must seem strangely ironic. The demise of socialist regimes in these regions has been accompanied by what some writers have hailed as a 'liberal revolution,' with the adoption in many of these countries of a market economy, protection of civil liberties, and democratic styles of governance.[1] Attempts have been made to revive liberalism in other contexts as well, including Nancy Rosenblum's reconstruction of a neo-romantic tradition, in which personal and aesthetic experiences are used to recast liberal political theory.[2] These changes have occurred despite a deep sense of disaffection among some academics, including some academic lawyers, with both the ideas and practices of contemporary liberalism.[3] The *bête noire* of writers who work in the vein of critical legal studies has been liberalism, whether in its classical or revisionist forms. This is not to say that these radical critics, who view themselves on the political left, do not also object to the conservative thinking that has gained ascendancy in a number of Western democracies since the start of the 1980s. But at the time the Conference on Critical Legal Studies was founded, its charter members viewed liberalism as the dominant framework for legal and political theory. Anti-liberalism, which has a history stretching back at least as far as the period immediately after the French Revolution, gained a foothold in legal scholarship with the arrival on the scene of critical legal studies.[4]

Within the literature of critical legal studies there is no single, canonical formulation of what liberalism means. To capture all of the facets of political liberalism in a single description and then hope to command the approval of every critical legal author is simply impossible. The movement is too heterogeneous. Nor has critical legal writing typically derived its definition of liberalism from what liberal theorists themselves have said. Instead, critical legal analysis has often taken as its point of departure a statement of what might be called the core of liberalism, as framed by critical legal writers rather than liberals themselves. In the first part of this chapter, I canvass the work of several leading critical legal authors who have sought to reduce liberal thinking to relatively few premises and assumptions. The explanations I survey also seek to establish links between the philosophical foundations of liberalism and those kinds of economic and political institutions, such as capitalist forms of production and consumption or the legal protection of an individual's basic rights and liberties, associated with modern liberal democratic societies. Most importantly for our purposes, critical legal discussions connect liberal ideology with the basic features of modern, Anglo-American systems of common law; radical critics ambitiously attempt to prove that fundamental jurisprudential concepts, such as the rule of law, constitutionalism, and judicial review, are intertwined with liberal ideology. One striking claim made in critical legal theory is that mainstream theorists tend to define these crucial ideas in liberal terms, without realizing that alternative conceptions are possible and, from a critical legal point of view, perhaps even desirable.

Ideological critique lies at the heart of critical legal studies and distinguishes critical legal thinking from its sceptical forerunner, legal realism.[5] U.S. legal realists in particular expressed serious doubts about the theoretical adequacy of claims that law was composed primarily of determinative rules that neutral experts, trained in legal reasoning, could objectively ascertain and apply. Critical legal writers, respecting legal realism for its attack on formalistic models of adjudication, have viewed their own brand of scepticism as more profound and robust. One way of looking at critical legal work as an heir of legal realism is to see contemporary radical critics as having followed through on the corrosive project that realists began, but from which they eventually recoiled.[6] Part of the political upshot of legal realism was the lesson that the shape of government and the processes of politics should be reformed by the enactment, for example, of progressive regulatory and welfare legislation. Realism, as a shaping force in many law schools and within the legal profession, led to numerous political reforms during the New Deal.[7] At least at a rhetorical level, critical legal writers have been less interested in merely reforming legal regimes. The standards of what counts as progressive political imagination have changed. Instead of calling for moderate legal reforms at an incremental pace, critical legal accounts envision economic and political transformation – a total reorganization of society according to a post-liberal plan.[8]

After reviewing the way in which critical legal writers have presented various forms of liberalism, I assess the cogency of the arguments that underlie their portrait. I will call attention to problems with the consistency of various critical accounts, and in addition ask whether the radical critique takes into account the most sophisticated types of liberal political and legal theory. In order to grasp the point of these theories, one needs to recall the social and historical background against which liberal theories have been offered. Contrary to what critical legal writers have claimed, liberal theorists do not ground their arguments on naive assumptions about the subjectivity of values, radical personal autonomy, or the superiority of the realm of private experience over the political sphere. I also argue that the radical critique ignores much of the work of leading theorists concerned with issues of justice. Critical legal accounts of liberalism are often deficient because they fail to acknowledge the progressive possibilities of at least some versions of contemporary liberal theory. My argument, though it does not itself uncritically accept all major liberal tenets, concentrates primarily on whether the critical legal construction of central liberal ideas (setting aside questions about the truth of those ideas) has misapprehended their rich variety and distorted some of them into a form few liberals would recognize.

A Radical View of the Constitutive Principles of Liberalism

It takes little more than a brief acquaintance with the vast range of critical legal literature to realize that liberalism is treated within that literature as a diffuse pattern of ideas and arguments. Critical legal authors have used the term to denote a comprehensive framework of assumptions and beliefs that has analogues in many different types of disciplines. Liberalism can be found as a guiding paradigm in fields of inquiry other than political theory. For example, Roberto Unger's influential attempt to adumbrate the central ideas of modern liberalism, as they have emerged from roughly the sixteenth century forward, includes claims that there are liberal types of metaphysics, epistemology, theories of human personality, and law, as well as political and social theory.[9] This tendency to join together the foundations of different forms of knowledge will be referred to as the totalizing feature of critical legal discussion. At the root of the totalizing tendency is the assumption that certain metaphysical postulates form the basis for each political ideology and that, if the metaphysics can be discredited, the ideology must be discarded too. Critical legal writers have tended to perceive liberal theory as a unified body (or, in Thomas Heller's expression, a 'fundamental paradigm') of abstract insights common among different forms of discourse.[10]

A succinct attempt to spell out the salient features of political liberalism is found in Karl Klare's discussion of the origins of modern labour law in the United States.[11] According to Klare, the most important themes of the 'classical liberal political tradition' include the following. First, liberals believe that each individual holds values subjectively. Those values reflect that person's own desires or appetites. Second, ethical claims can be made only by resorting to 'instrumental terms.' Presumably, Klare is here restricting liberal morality to one model of utilitarianism, in which the rightness of behaviour is supposed to be judged by the consequences of the actions in question. In other words, Klare, unlike other critical legal authors, does not seem to allow a deontological understanding of ethical questions, which would involve reference to rights or duties rather than to consequential value. This position is probably explained by Klare's conception of liberal motivation strictly in terms of desire. Third, on Klare's model, liberals assume that a political society is an 'artificial aggregation of autonomous individuals.' Fourth, liberal ideology distinguishes public interests, which are properly the domain of the state, from private interests, which arise and are satisfied in the institutions of civil society. By 'civil society' Klare would appear to include institutions relating to family, employment, religious belief and practice, recreation, and fellowship. Finally, Klare claims that liberalism is committed to a conception of justice that is 'formal or procedural' rather than 'substantive.'[11]

Klare himself characterizes each assumption on this list as 'metaphysical.'[12] It is difficult to discern in what sense he is using this epithet. Klare appears to be drawing attention to what he views as interrelationships among different aspects of political liberalism, including its ethical orientation; its theory of individual and group behaviour; and its understanding of the role of the legislature, courts, and other, less official agencies of governance and association. Liberalism for him connotes an ideological structure that depends on a philosophical anthropology or a theory of the person. Against this background of a tightly interwoven ideology that predominates in modern Western democracies, Klare deals with his more immediate concern: a critical reinterpretation of the rise and operation of collective bargaining statutes. The legal doctrine is opened to re-examination in light of the critique Klare offers of the political theory that, regardless of which party has assumed power, framed law-making in the United States in the twentieth century.[13]

We should also note that Klare attributes the liberal themes identified to a tradition deriving from Thomas Hobbes, John Locke, and David Hume. He is not the only critical legal writer to claim that liberalism has a pedigree that stretches back to Hobbes. Other radical critics, including Unger, Duncan Kennedy, and Mark Tushnet, cast Hobbes as a formative figure in the history of liberal theory.[14] They extrapolate at least part of the meaning of liberalism from those earlier philosophers, even though the intervening centuries have given rise to a great variety of democratic ideas and constitutional developments.

Kennedy has spelled out his views on the primary features of liberalism in the process of discussing 'individualism.' 'Individualism' and what Kennedy calls 'altruism' are the two conflicting 'attitudes' or basic orientations towards the structure and content of the common law and the proper role for judges.[15] On Kennedy's scheme, individualism is generally associated with liberalism, though he does not think this association is based on a necessary connection or practical implication. Indeed, Kennedy is less willing than Unger to concede that there is any logical connection between the fundamental premises of individualism and an actual liberal legal order. In his description of the individualist social order, Kennedy reveals a great deal about what he considers the constituent elements of liberalism to be. Among these is the radical independence of each person. As Kennedy expresses it, individuals are assumed to be motivated by their own unique and incorrigible desires, 'without acknowledging any interdependence whatever as moral beings.'[16] There is no need for members of a society to agree among themselves on what values should be honoured or what collective ends should be pursued. Thus, Kennedy claims that liberal theory ties together the radical subjectivity of the members of the group with the arbitrariness of values or ends. The mechanisms used to maintain social order in a liberal society have to be tailored accordingly. For example, Kennedy argues that the use of formally realizable rules, to be applied by judges as if the only matter in dispute were factual rather than evaluative, is consistent with liberal political ideals. Thus, rules of property law, which function to respect and preserve the autonomy of individual owners, cohere with the liberal ideal of social life. Similarly, contractual rules are predicated on notions of individual self-interest. The system of contract doctrine, formulated largely at common law, helps separate individuals to engage in mutually beneficial transactions. Kennedy attempts to reveal the extent to which entire bodies of law embrace individualist principles of the highest order of generality. By means of the reconstruction of legal doctrine under the aegis of particular concepts, he illuminates what he calls a 'utopian' scheme for liberal justice. Kennedy also argues, of course, that polar principles can be identified and used to reshape legal doctrine. A 'counter-program,' equally utopian though not without some faint resonance in the established doctrines of the common law, can be generated from his description of altruist principles. In the latter case, a legal order is likely to be shaped by moral norms shared among citizens; the moral agnosticism associated with individualism will not be found in an ideal altruist society. In the altruist scenario he constructs, Kennedy imagines that judges would be less concerned with rules than with legal standards. On Kennedy's account, legal argument conducted in various forums, including the courts and classrooms, can be analysed to reveal the bipolar structures around which policy choices are made. Like Klare, Kennedy wants to claim that the attitudes, tendencies, or biases he discovers in the workings of common law adjudication are ultimate elements or particles. Individualism and altruism form, in his words, 'flatly contradictory visions of the universe.'[17] Again, this argument has a metaphysical ring to it. It implies that liberalism and its ideological rivals have underlying visions or deep structures that help determine legal responses to concrete human disputes.

Another ground on which liberalism has been criticized is the failure of legal liberals to grasp the relationship between justice and human needs. Peter Gabel, for instance, has taken to task theorists such as Ronald Dworkin for addressing issues of distributive justice in unduly formal, abstract terms.[18] From Gabel's perspective, advising a judge to discover existing rights and obligations of the parties before her, in light of principles of institutional morality, is a hopelessly circular way in which to think about justice. It simply authorizes the judge to find reasons for upholding and legitimating the status quo. Like William Simon, another early proponent of a critical legal perspective, Gabel would prefer legal reasoning that recognized and focused on litigants' daily lives, including their work, their material resources, and their social relationships.[19]

Among critical legal authors, one of the most influential and frequently cited presentations of the central propositions of liberalism is that of Roberto Unger. A large portion of Unger's *Knowledge and Politics* is devoted to building a grand synthesis of his understanding of liberal theory.[20] While this work is often referred to within critical legal literature, it has rarely been elaborated on by other radical critics or incorporated in any detailed way into their analyses. Unger's general insights have stood on their own as a sweeping attempt to reconceive liberalism as a coherent ideology that pervades modern thinking.[21] Few other critical legal writers have shared his aspiration to demonstrate the unity of political, social, economic, and legal theory. Most have relied on Unger's work as if it were an accurate and complete reconstruction of the rise and development of liberalism and treated Unger as the master surveyor of this topic. As the sheer volume of references to his work shows, Unger's portrait of liberalism helps set the terms on which the radical legal critique has been conducted.

Not all of Unger's discussion is used by fellow critics. For example, his complex analysis of the 'antinomies' of liberal reasoning has not had the same impact on critical legal writing as his discussion of the elements of liberal politics.[22] Another feature that separates Unger from the main currents of critical legal studies is his emphasis on the residual value of liberal ideas. In most examples of critical legal writing, the reverberating theme is the replacement of liberalism with more progressive foundations. Unger appears to be different. There are grounds for considering him not merely as a critic of liberalism, but as a theorist ultimately bent on retrieving or redeeming liberal values. His more recent work on political and legal philosophy reveals institutional recommendations which, he himself avows, could be seen as an attempt to perfect liberalism.[23] With these considerations in mind, it would be a mistake to treat Unger's *Knowledge and Politics* as a critical legal manifesto that illuminates all the relevant connections between law and liberalism. Though it is useful as a source of critical legal views of liberal ideology, that book should be interpreted cautiously.

Unger's distillation of liberal principles requires an investigation into both what he calls an 'unreflective' view of society and also the view that dominates specialized social studies. On either account, Unger claims that several principles lie at the 'core of the classic political theory of liberalism.'[24] The first of these principles he calls the principle of rules and values. In a liberal society the members cannot agree on a conception of the good that can be used to resolve conflicts; social peace thus requires the adoption of 'artificial limits' in the form of rules prescribing actions that persons are permitted or commanded to do and those they are prohibited from doing.[25] On Unger's description, values and rules are 'opposites' in the sense that they reflect two different ideas about the source of law and the ways in which freedom and social order might be established.[26]

Unger's second principle of liberal theory states that all values are individual and subjective. With liberalism's emphasis on human autonomy, each person is treated as an independent moral agent who is moved either by practical reason or by passion to adopt a certain course of conduct.[27] The limits to a person's action are set by the possibility of conflicts between that action and the interest of another individual. In situations of conflict, the basic liberal value of personal 'liberty' is incapable of determining which individual's interest should prevail. All interests and autonomously chosen values of the members of a society are accorded equal validity. There is no scale by which to measure the rank or importance of one individual's actions against another's. They are, in principle, incommensurable. All values are subjective, originating in the judgment of individual persons. Therefore, according to Unger, liberal theories do not acknowledge any social conditioning or interiorization of prevailing or traditional norms honoured in a particular society.[28]

It should be noted that Unger's use of the concept of subjective values merges two different ideas. Subjectivity for him primarily connotes the capacity of each individual to make moral choices. It also has another meaning, for which 'noncognitivism' might be a better term. Unger claims that, for liberals, morality is not a matter of knowledge, but rather one of predisposition. In other words, liberals do not think that normative debate can ever lead to complete agreement within a society on the highest good, at least so far as that conception of the good represents some sort of objective value that can be known for certain. In Unger's formulation, political liberalism depends on a conception of society that treats the personal judgment of its members as of primary importance and accords no political weight to communal ends or values. Each individual chooses values that reflect unique wants and interests. These will inevitably conflict with the wants and interests of others. Like other political theorists who claim to have exposed the ontological or metaphysical assumptions at the heart of liberal political theory, Unger construes liberalism as committed to a type of atomism, in which a society is seen as an aggregate of separate persons.[29] On Unger's depiction of the psychology underlying the liberal world-view, individuals are egoistic, struggling beings concerned primarily with advancing their own material welfare. Unger believes that liberal thinkers presuppose that human character is given to each person by virtue of a capacity for independent existence. That is, each person is born with a nature, rather than acquiring one with maturity.[30]

Unger compares these assumptions about the formation of human character and the radical isolation and selfishness of the pre-social person with the 'state of nature' as imagined by Hobbes.[31] Among critical legal writers, Unger is not alone in his tendency to invoke the horrors vividly described by Hobbes to illustrate conditions of psychological and political atomism.[32] He also treats political liberalism as if it were committed to explaining the rise of political societies through the device of a social contract.[33] The Hobbesian war of all against all can only be alleviated through a general peace treaty in which warring individuals agree to join together in some form of social union.[34] They willingly adopt constraints on their behaviour for the sake of security and peace. This agreement does not imply that human nature is thereby altered. The impulse towards entering into a social bond is prudence. The individuals involved would look to self-preservation as their guiding value, rather than anything less egoistic, such as an emerging sense of love, fellowship, or sympathy.[35] The instinct to compete and yet not to perish is assumed to be stronger than these more tender-hearted dispositions. The resultant union remains a treaty among separate parties. Those individual parties do not necessarily merge, as a result of their agreement, into a higher-level collectivity. The separate identity of each person is conserved; so, too, are the instinctively adversarial drives of each.

In Unger's reformulation of political liberalism, these assumptions about the consent of rational individuals to political rule explain the rise of political societies and the creation of political and legal obligation.[36] According to Unger, a liberal society once established reduces the potential for uncontrolled conflict by creating a mechanism through which individuals can calculate the intensity of their wants vis-à-vis those of other individuals. The forum chosen is the market. Through this form of regulated exchange individuals are able to barter for goods and resources they possess in unequal portions. In Unger's account of liberal thinking, the market becomes the primary institution for the distribution of wealth in a society.[37] The theory assumes that people are motivated to maximize their own utility, and the market permits the proper blend of freedom and security. Individuals are assured freedom to enter bargains with others who already own desirable resources. The liberal system also creates the means to enforce freely entered bargains. Legal sanctions are required to maintain the integrity and usefulness of markets. The rise of the market and its adoption in different social settings to assist trade in a wide variety of commodities have made possible the triumph of capitalist modes of business. For both historical and theoretical reasons, critical legal writers view capitalism as inextricably tied to the ideology of the market.

Unger claims that liberal political ideology does not require, as a condition for entering the social contract, that individuals relinquish all rights to whatever resources over which they might have established possession or control. Rather, under the terms of a liberal scheme of political obligation, each person is accorded protection for those resources when the social union is formed. Those who were wealthy in the state of nature have this advantage reinforced on consenting to join society. Any entitlement to an advantageous position is treated by classical liberal writers, such as John Locke, as well as by contemporary libertarian philosophers, as a matter of 'right.'[38] The work most often cited in critical legal literature on this point is that of C.B. Macpherson.[39] According to Unger, the paradigmatic use of rights discourse is made in the context of protecting possessory interests of the better-off parties to the social contract. Consequently, property rights become fundamental to the system. On some liberal accounts, they become 'natural' rights that provide the model for later interests which, in the evolving legal system, are deemed worthy of protection against interference by outside parties. Another marked feature in the history of liberalism, in Unger's view, is the growth of the state. In the initial stage of social organization, the real threat to an individual's rights was posed by fellow members of the society in question. But, Unger argues, in the liberal understanding of the genesis of modern social and political systems the rise of a political and legal authority transcends each individual's interests. Institutions of government serve as agencies to ensure that one individual cannot with impunity encroach on the bounded freedom of another. This is the rationale for the state.

Unger goes on to claim that the vital functions of the state in the liberal system create potential for bureaucratic elaboration and growth. Such growth in turn poses a new problem for the preservation of the liberal value of freedom. Rather than simply serving as a neutral arbiter for conflicts among individuals, the state can also use its power to interfere with the individual freedoms it was meant to preserve. On Unger's rendering, liberals are committed to the conservation of a zone of individual activity into which any state or governmental intrusion is illegitimate.[40] The moral or religious views of individual citizens, for example, are beyond the proper scope of state control. Liberal theory, as conceived by Unger, thus relies on the distinction between the public realm of legitimately state-regulated activities and the private realm in which individuals are free to pursue their own interests and advancement without the threat of state intervention.[41] This latter sphere has already been referred to above, in the language used by Karl Klare, as 'civil society.'[42] Analysis of the state/civil society dichotomy, especially as it has been used to structure judicial discourse in drawing boundaries around the permissible activities of government, has been a common theme in critical legal discussions of common law doctrine.[43] According to Unger, nineteenth-century versions of liberal ideology in England depended on the dichotomy of state and civil society. It underpinned the ideal of laissez-faire economic arrangements, in which merchants and commercial organizations pursued their goal of wealth maximization unhampered by governmental restrictions.[44] In the view of such critical legal writers as Unger and Gabel, the policy of laissez-faire, though not necessarily articulated as a description of present-day capitalism, was vital as a source of legitimacy for the later growth of monopoly capitalism and corporatism.[45]

Critical legal writers associate the liberal premises described above with another dichotomy important for modern jurisprudence. According to Mark Tushnet's critical legal version of the liberal ideal, the state is supposed to be neutral in any intervention into the everyday affairs of individuals. It would be inconsistent with the spirit of the original pact among naturally competitive individuals for the state to favour the interests of some members of society against those of others. For this reason, law must be separable from politics. While political processes arise out of the collision and compromise among fundamental wants and interests of different individuals, some of whom are inevitably stronger than the rest, law has a different genesis. The law is supposed to be impartial.[46] On Tushnet's formulation of liberalism, the mental faculty appropriate to the administration of laws is reason. By contrast, the faculty engaged in the practice of politics is will. Dispassionate reason is appropriate to courts, while passion, unprincipled desire, and self-interested trade-offs are the driving mechanisms behind the work of legislatures. This institutional difference, according to some critical legal authors, reflects the dichotomous nature of the human capacity for self-rule. As elaborated in the nineteenth century, the rational task of law is viewed as a matter of scientific understanding and procedure.[47] Officials responsible for tending the machinery of justice were thought to possess an élite capacity to understand and enforce the practical rules embodied particularly in the common law. Radical critics have viewed the supposed autonomy of legal reasoning as a crucial part of the ideology of modern legal education and legal practice.[48] By contrast with the development of the common law, which prizes continuity and predictability, the creation of statutes and regulations arose from a different process, in which the results are particularly tenuous and unstable. Legislative majorities, especially in the British parliamentary tradition, can change rapidly in response to new and shifting coalitions of power and interests. On a critical legal account, members of a liberal democratic society are not assumed to share a common view about what constitutes the best form of life. Any political arrangements enacted in a society at a given time can therefore be undone at the next opportunity for individuals to register their political preferences by voting.

The division between law and politics that critical legal theory attributes to political and legal liberalism is paralleled by a distinction made between politics and economics.[49] In its classical form, economics aspired to scientific status. This entailed a rejection of any attempt to formulate a theory consisting of normative economic assumptions. Economists were to conceive their professional role solely in terms of description. It was not within the ken of the economist to judge the relative worth of individuals' preferences;[50] rather, the economist was enjoined to concentrate on developing a schema for displaying what individuals in fact desired and for plotting the comparative intensity with which they desired it. Constructing an indifference curve to reflect the economic value was the limit of the classical economists' interest in values at all. As with law, this forbearance from applying judgments about the normative status of preferences is supposed to betoken an admirably scientific attitude.

Critical legal authors have tended to treat the distinctions made between law and politics and politics and economics as manifestations of liberalism's general partition of the normative from the factual. Here, the critical claim is that liberals are committed to a particular epistemology in which facts are different from values: the 'is' should not be confused with the 'ought.' From the perspective of critical legal authors such as Morton Horwitz or Mark Tushnet, who have discussed the ideal of the rule of law, liberals have had to embrace either positivism or some form of naturalism.[51] On a positivist understanding, knowledge (including legal knowledge) properly understood is a matter of being certain about what can be stated in the form of true propositions. Only on factual issues do individuals have any hope of reaching rational agreement. Positivists deny that a scheme of values can be devised that will attract the commitment of everyone in society. There can be no adequate general ordinal ranking of shared, society-wide norms. The pre-eminent legal form of this positivism is the theory associated with Austinian jurisprudence in the nineteenth century.[52] For critical legal writers, H.L.A. Hart's refinement of legal positivism in the twentieth century, while it discusses the place of values in selecting the primary rules of a legal system, still effects a radical separation of questions of law from questions of morality. According to the critical legal depiction of the positivist view, legal discourse is reduced to a factual level, in which the pivotal issue is whether there is an existing, authoritative rule that covers the dispute. In this type of liberal scheme, so thoroughly imbued with the distinction between facts and values, the rule of law itself has no moral content. That fundamental principle, which can be understood in several different ways, provides a broad basis for liberal conceptions of a legal system. For a positivist, the principle has several possible meanings. First, it could mean that law is a system of official rules that provide reasons for the practical resolution of disputes. The rule of law is supposed to guarantee that adjudication turns on articulable, defensible principles rather than pure arbitrariness. On this conception it is key that judges are unbiased and secure from the interference of other branches of government. Alternatively, the rule of law could be interpreted as providing a guarantee of generality: legal rules apply to everybody equally. It could also be understood as the principle that underlies the legal practice of appealing to precedents as authoritative statements of legal rules. According to yet another understanding of the principle the rule of law is supposed to emphasize the cardinal virtue of procedural fairness.[53] Critical legal writers have discerned, in the modern enthusiasm for the rule of law, a preference for interpreting the principle as a guarantee of formal justice.

The radical critics with whom we have been dealing do not assume that liberalism can be construed solely as a type of positivism. Another form of liberal political and legal theory claims that a legal system has an inescapably normative dimension. In other words, not all liberals are positivists. Some critiques of contemporary legal theory have acknowledged that Ronald Dworkin's account of legal adjudication, for example, shows that political and moral values are relevant to legal processes.

With these fundamental premises of the liberal outlook in mind, critical legal writers have raised a number of serious questions. From their perspective, it is a mistake to suppose that a person could have an identity without any knowledge of her own goals or values. Critical legal theorists have tended instead to view persons as already constituted selves who harbour conceptions of the good that owe something to the community to which they belong.[54] Second, these authors criticize liberal theorists for relying on a model of asocial individualism in explaining the rise of political societies. Where some liberal theorists view political community as the result of bargaining among radically self-interested, independent persons who create relationships with others only after entering society, critical legal authors have emphasized that a social matrix is necessary in forming its members' ideas of what is valuable in life. This understanding of the self is intersubjective. Once we recognize the problems underlying the liberal contractualist view of political obligation, we can conceive political bonds in a well-ordered society as arising from cooperation and a shared sense of the public good. Third, from a critical legal point of view, the best that liberal theorists can offer in describing a just society is to specify political and legal processes that are neutral among different goods. Some people might prefer a life devoted to, as its ultimate good, watching football or tending the garden. Others might prize a life in which the most valued activity is aerobic exercise, providing medical services to those who are poor and ill, or reading Homer in the original Greek. On another plane, some people are in favour of publicly funded health care, while others believe that many medical services should be available only on a profit-making basis. Politics provides one forum for the expression of, and selection among, competing interests favoured by different citizens. Critical legal writers generally regret the extent to which political liberalism denies any scope for enriched debate about which form of life is best. The decision is reserved as a matter of private moral choice, not public determination. From a critical legal perspective, this arrangement rules out in advance consideration of the extent to which principles of justice reflect communal aims. The ability of citizens to determine the political morality of their community is impoverished. In this way, it is argued, liberal political theory depreciates the public political life and experience of an active citizenry, for it directs each individual to find satisfaction in collective activities outside the political sphere – through church, family, club, or shared hobbies. From a critical legal perspective, the liberal conception of the limits on political deliberation weakens the democratic fabric of a society. It also undervalues the work of those citizens who devote their lives to ideological causes and who rate their own happiness by reference to whether their community has become more just as a result of their efforts.

Finally, another feature of liberalism disparaged by its radical critics is the sense in which the legal system is supposed to operate differently from politics. The various conceptions of the rule of law advanced by liberal theorists to justify the role of courts appeal to principles including reasoned resolution, independence of the judiciary, general application of the law, precedential authority, and procedural fairness. Whichever meaning is attached to the rule of law (and legal theorists, it should be stressed, disagree among themselves on a specific central meaning), critical legal writers have noted that the concept itself is subject to political controversy. According to Allan Hutchinson, for example, the rule of law is notorious for its 'political plasticity, its facility to accommodate itself to changing governmental situations and political forces.'[55] One of the hallmarks of critical legal writing is to deny that law and politics are different spheres of human discourse. Instead, law is viewed as one form of political activity, and legal institutions such as courts are characterized as a forum for practising politics in a different genre.

Critique of Liberal Institutions

In addition to challenging the hegemony and cogency of liberal ideas, critical legal authors have expressed disenchantment with liberal institutions. Although this topic is explored more extensively in Chapter 5, it should be briefly mentioned here that radical critics have repeatedly found fault with the policies and programs associated with modern liberal politics. For example, critical legal literature is full of doubts about the effectiveness of the civil rights movement in achieving social and racial justice in the United States. Critiques have been launched against the enactment and enforcement of laws to ensure racial equality and to end discrimination. The perceived failure of such laws is described not as the result of bad faith on the part of legislators, judges, or administrators of civil rights agencies. Those persons may be well-intentioned and conscientious individuals. It also does not matter, from the critical perspective, whether the U.S. Supreme Court has been predominantly liberal or conservative.[56] The real flaws lie in the way that both the problem and the remedial measures were conceived. Some critical legal writers have argued that, according to liberal ideology, racial discrimination is conceived primarily in terms of one individual denying the rights of another. This description makes discrimination appear as a discrete indignity practised at a personal level in an otherwise enlightened society devoted to an ideal of social justice.[57] Radical critics have faulted such an approach for failing to grasp the historical background to the problem of racial inequality in Western societies.[58] The social phenomenon of discrimination on grounds of race is not an odious, though exceptional, practice of a few bigots. Rather, from the critical legal point of view, it is the systematic victimization of an oppressed class by the dominant one. With its long history, the race problem is insoluble in one generation, not because of the prevalence of hard-hearted individuals, but because liberal institutional thinking reflects mistaken notions of equality. The error lies in conceiving equality as primarily a matter of opportunity.[59] From a critical legal angle, this conception manifests one of the central weaknesses of political liberalism. The liberal approach to solving a question of unfairness is to favour a formal measure of equal treatment. In the context of race relations this means that the member of the race traditionally discriminated against should be given an equal chance to pursue her goals. Critics have viewed this procedural guarantee not to be interfered with in the execution of one's life plan as the limit of liberal intervention.

Radical critics of liberal anti-discrimination doctrine and policy have trouble with such a purely formal conception of equality. They argue that it ignores the social and historical factors that affect how a person formulates ideas about which kind of life is worth pursuing. In other words, abstract liberal guarantees of equal protection do little to help the youth from a minority background whose family has suffered severe economic inequalities for generations. The guarantee of access to higher education will do nothing by itself to offset the circumstances of a member of a minority group who has been brought up in a situation where advanced education will never be financially possible. Nor will such a right help the young person for whom there are few models worth emulating in terms of academic success. The abstract civil right only protects a chance to pursue one's goals; it does not ensure that positive circumstances are created to help every person formulate such goals. Similar critiques have been offered of liberal approaches to gender inequality. Some critical legal writers have disputed whether past solutions, such as prohibitions on discrimination in various educational and employment settings, as well as affirmative action programs, actually address the root causes of such inequality.[60]

Critical legal writers have targeted several other institutions associated with political liberalism. These include welfarist economic policies, which use taxation measures and redistributive programs to reduce economic inequalities. Radical critics have claimed that these liberal policies treat inequality as flowing from market imperfections. Welfare schemes are typically instituted not to replace the market but to cushion its effects, particularly for those who are poorest.[61] Radical critics look upon these corrective policies as providing temporary assistance to disadvantaged individuals, with the hope that at some future time the recipients can be restored to the position of producers (and consumers) in a capitalist economy. According to these critics, the overall aim of such welfare and unemployment schemes is not to erase deep inequalities, but to provide temporary and often only token relief. In William Simon's assessment, even construing social security benefits as 'rights' or 'entitlements' indicates the extent to which liberal welfare principles favour a 'private law' and highly individualist model of recognizing human needs.[62]

Among the other liberal institutions identified by radical critics as problematic is representative democracy. Critical legal literature contains lengthy discussions of the manner in which both governmental and corporate bureaucracies have undermined democratic ideals in Western societies.[63] There is such an unequal distribution of wealth, knowledge, social status, education, and power that in actual political processes not all citizens participate equally in making decisions affecting community life. Representative institutions fail to be democratic when there is widespread voter alienation or when citizens are denied an equal chance to stand for office. On various critical legal accounts, Western liberal democracies are typically dominated by political élites who act to preserve their own vested interests. There is little scope for significant social transformation through the work of elected legislatures, for suggestions that would bring about massive redistribution of resources among all citizens are rarely raised. Within liberal theory there is a persistent fear of allowing majorities to decide questions of great social impact.[64]

The outline provided above reveals some of the main lines of attack brought by critical legal authors against liberalism. My focus has been on what the critique alleges are liberal theory's shaky foundations. In the remainder of this chapter, I assess the critical legal versions of political and legal liberalism. In the foreground of the discussion will be the issue of whether liberalism necessarily involves the assumptions credited to it by the radical critique. As it turns out, liberal theorists have actually been more resourceful than is implied in the portrait assembled by critical legal authors. Many of the claims made by critical legal authors about liberal principles have been repudiated by defenders of modern liberalism. At the very least, the principles in question have been sufficiently controverted among liberal writers that the critical legal account of what liberalism means might begin to appear suspect.

Irrelevance of the Metaphysical Dimension

Critical legal authors err in making the broad claim that liberal theorists rely on a certain picture of the metaphysical nature of individuals and society. While this description might plausibly be applied to Kant, who framed his moral system within a comprehensive theory of the person, contemporary liberals such as John Rawls have repeatedly argued that the point of constructing their accounts of the principles of justice is to offer a considered justification of political society and in particular to analyse how people should be treated. This kind of sustained project has not required invoking a comprehensive metaphysical or ontological framework. Especially in his more recent work, in which Rawls responds to the communitarian critiques of *A Theory of Justice*, the 'new' Rawls (as he has been dubbed by Stephen Mulhall and Adam Swift) has expressly denied any implications that his arguments are about the essential nature of the human self.[65] The description of the 'original position' in his political theory (within which individuals, in order to arrive at certain principles of justice, were assumed to have no knowledge of their particular talents, tastes, or position in society) was not intended to portray the self as antecedently individuated to the rise of human community, despite characterizations to the contrary found among the theory's radical critics.[66] It was not an attempt to describe a psychological or historical thesis about the formation of polities. By tapping into one liberal tradition (involving the hypothetical use of a social contract), Rawls was undertaking a thought experiment or constructing a model to help settle which principles could be rationally and publicly justified and therefore used as a standard for judging whether a particular society is justly ordered. Another way of putting this is to say that Rawls's conception of justice – at least as latterly presented, and arguably in its original form as well – is not based on the truth of certain ultimate philosophical premises, but rather on what members of a society can agree are the best institutional forms for ensuring that such basic values as liberty and equality are realized in the context of their particular society.

Another feature of Rawls's attempt to clarify his theory of justice is its emphasis on philosophical pluralism. He observes that metaphysics and epistemology, like religion and morals, involve deeply controversial convictions. Liberalism, which prizes toleration of such differences, so that in managing the state, no single alternative view should be favoured, also requires that the principle of toleration be extended to differences of view on fundamental metaphysical issues.[67] In the face of such intractable differences (which Rawls seems to assume are empirically evident), liberal theory is committed to reaching a practical rather than ontological or epistemological political conception of justice.

Therefore, it makes little sense to claim that arguments in liberal normative discussions about the importance of individual liberties or the autonomy of individual conscience must depend for their cogency on a theory of 'atomism,' or the ontological priority of a single person over the group. Unger's account of what he views as a 'pure' liberal position makes it appear that this form of metaphysical individualism is a fundamental postulate of liberalism. But liberals do not necessarily argue that a society can only be understood as an aggregation of individual parts.[68] Theorists such as Rawls have argued strenuously that it is a mistake to construe liberal attempts to delineate principles of justice as if all liberals were committed to a claim that the individual's interests and personality are somehow irreducible, metaphysically given and, in a liberal framework, unamenable to evaluation. Rather, liberal theorists are quite prepared to engage in rational discussion aimed at settling which goal a society should pursue. The discussion would not be fruitless or interminable. Nor would it presume, as a matter of either logic or experience, that there is no possibility of consensus on basic ideas or principles. In part as a response to such possible misreadings, Rawls has emphasized the importance to his scheme of an 'overlapping consensus' that provides some 'shared fund' of political ideals.[69] Social goals are more than a convergence of individual or group preferences and more than the result of political bargaining. According to Rawls, modern liberals have rejected this latter view, which he calls part of 'the Hobbesian strand of liberalism.'[70] The political tradition on which Rawls draws, including the variety of political motivations, is more textured than that which Hobbes relied on in the design of his idea of the state (which, of course, turned out to be more absolutist than liberal).

Political liberalism does not interpret individualism as a theory of human nature or a theory about the goals of human existence.[71] Rather, liberals emphasize the importance of requiring the government to treat each citizen as an individual worthy of respect. This respect is owed simply because the individual is a person, and not, for example, by virtue of any status or privilege into which that person may be born. This is a political principle, germane to liberal theories of equality, and neither a metaphysical nor a psychological point about the solitary nature of egoistic individuals who are prone to loneliness and anomie. Critical legal writers thus err when they credit liberalism with a belief in the radical moral and cognitive independence of each person. There is a significant difference between arguing that the state has no business imposing a particular set of values on its citizens and arguing that individual citizens are moral monads, each oblivious to the views of fellow citizens. Political liberals can adhere to the former belief without committing themselves to the latter. Practical questions of how a democratic society should be governed so as to guarantee equal respect for all its citizens do not depend for their resolution on the idea that all citizens should be treated equally indifferently. On a liberal scheme of justice, governments can justifiably be concerned about the welfare of individual citizens, as well as that of groups or classes that may be especially vulnerable to unequal treatment.

One major liberal motif, namely, the requirement to place limits on the state's power (for example, through granting constitutional rights) to intervene in a citizen's pursuit of her own conception of the best form of life, is not based on the virtues of unfettered individualism. Political liberalism arose in reaction to other political theories, such as feudalism, that had a different underlying morality. When liberal theories focus on individual differences and defend the view that a government should not impose particular values on citizens, the arguments used in support of this proposition are usually directed against earlier political theories that ascribed stations and attendant duties or particular values to individual citizens. Some versions of liberalism were generated in reaction to the claim that a hierarchy of values determines which is the best life to lead. Political liberals generally argue against the view that, at least for the purpose of making government policy, a particular conception of the good life should be exalted above others. The liberal virtues of pluralism and tolerance reflect normative principles about social order, not rampant metaphysical individualism.[72]

Liberalism has evolved to an important degree in reaction to its rival theories and in relation to the history and variety of political societies,[73] in reaction to, among others, the dangers and excesses of authoritarian governments, in which basic democratic liberties, such as the opportunity to vote or the freedom to criticize the government, were denied. Another inspiration for political liberals has been the evils that arise out of religious persecution or struggles over ethnic or linguistic differences in divided societies.[74] Such problems are not confined to the remote past but are a source of contemporary strife, as the violence in places such Bosnia or Kosovo demonstrates.[75] Liberal political theorists have also sensed the dangers of civil war and problems associated with both political succession and, again with contemporary relevance, political secession.[76] Other liberal concerns have been government measures that amount to arbitrary confiscation of property, oppressive criminal procedures, and cruel forms of punishment. From time to time modern political liberals have also faced the issue of when citizens can justifiably engage in civil disobedience directed against their government.[77]

In view of these reminders about the context in which liberal theorists write, it is fair to say that some critical legal accounts of liberal democratic principles offer a skewed version of the underpinnings of political liberalism. They try to isolate liberalism by separating key ideas from the historical context in which those ideas were originally formulated. The danger is that liberal conceptions of justice, as they are presented by critics, can become abstract and stylized. They are no longer accurate, either historically or in terms of the principles that animate the work of contemporary liberal theorists.

Different liberal theorists are engaged in exploring the normative background to concrete social issues. The process of close philosophical examination is not carried on as if the job could be accomplished simply by making relatively uncontroversial deductions from metaphysical premises. The nub of the mistake here is to assume that, because liberal theorists appeal to abstract principles, this appeal necessarily entangles them in metaphysical postulates that might either accurately reflect or detach them from present realities. Liberal theorizing can be intensely practical, in the sense that the theorist tries to illuminate and resolve issues liable to cause sharp fractures in her society. The task here is not to arrive at the most admirable conception of human nature, nor to decide which account of political society is true. In the case of Rawls, his explication and defence of a liberal theory of justice is intended to help citizens assess the arrangement of their society's social, economic, and political institutions. His aim is to help citizens agree on a 'regulative ideal,' at least in relation to the political sphere of life. Rawls explicitly refrains from arguing that the virtues associated with the political conception of justice (such as autonomy) should also be ideals in other areas of life.[78] He offers a political theory, and not what he calls a 'comprehensive moral ideal' that ought to govern the personal or religious sides of a citizen's life. Critics, such as early critical legal enthusiasts, who treat liberalism as if the ideals that inform liberal political doctrine were identical with the ideals of private morality miss one of the key messages of contemporary liberal theory.

There is scope for 'perfectionist' arguments to be advanced within debates over which liberal conceptions of justice are defensible. Tension exists within liberal theory on this issue, owing to debates over whether, as some liberal theorists have argued, the state should be permitted to make laws recognizing that some ways of life are better than others. Anti-perfectionists, such as Rawls, contend that an individual should be free to choose her way of life, even though it proves to be wasteful. This again involves philosophical controversy that has political and practical, rather than metaphysical, depths. Some liberals (and non-liberals) have claimed that within a particular society resources should be distributed on the basis that some ways of life are better than others. Through appropriate incentives or subsidies the state, it is argued, should encourage lives that pursue forms of excellence or perfection, while less worthy lives should be penalized. This perspective appears to contrast with the strands of liberalism invoked by critical legal authors, and also with, for example, Rawls's understanding of liberal traditions. One non-liberal locus for perfectionist views can be found in Marx's theory of alienation, where he argues that justice requires the state to create conditions under which all individuals can realize their distinctively human potential.[79] Not all Marxists are perfectionists, in the sense that they are willing to leave the state to prescribe which forms of life are valuable.[80] Nor have all liberals been anti-perfectionist. Rawls's rejection of perfectionist standards has been challenged from within liberal political philosophy on the ground that, even though a society embraces moral pluralism, political action can be justified that would punish or eradicate 'worthless and demeaning' conceptions of the good.[81] Such arguments have been based on an elaboration of what certain theorists, such as Joseph Raz or William Galston, perceive as the true meaning of liberal commitment to the even-handedness or neutrality of governments.[82] According to their attempt to revise liberal theory, this commitment does not entail that the state must exclude all moral ideals from politics. Raz, for example, thinks it clear that some forms of life (say, a life of medical research) are better than others (such as a life of gambling) and that there are no valid grounds for excluding such judgments from being used by the state to decide which rights or duties should be identified and enforced. Raz concedes that the perfectionism of his theory, along with its rejection of moral individualism, makes it appear similar to a communitarian perspective.[83] His continuing emphasis, however, on an autonomous conception of personal well-being and on social pluralism align his theory with political liberalism.

Why have critical legal writers, especially in the early phases of the movement's history, been inclined to analyse liberalism as a series of complex metaphysical commitments? First, the appeal to a vaunted metaphysical level is simply part of a desire on the part of critical legal authors to argue that deep structures or social visions underlie legal and political understanding. In this context, the desire of law's radical critics has been to explore the political and epistemological substructure of liberalism as if, at the deepest level, all human disciplines shared the same assumptions. This ambition makes sense if one is persuaded that beneath the superficial variety or diversity of many forms of knowledge, common elements can be exposed. Part of the radical critique involves the removal of barriers between, for example, law and politics; demonstrating that highly contestable political doctrines underpin legal rules thus becomes a valuable exercise.

Second, even without necessarily treating their methods as involving metaphysical analysis, one can discern a tendency among early critical legal writers to understand ideological differences as a matter of competing thought structures, the elements of which lie below the surface. On this view, generic liberalism can be illuminatingly revealed through a systematic exposure to types, patterns, structures, visions, or ways of thinking. As much critical legal work attempts to show, these often occur in dichotomous form, as a pair of concepts that appear to be opposed to each other. A good example is Kennedy's contrast of individualism with altruism, which he labels the ultimate contradiction. One critical legal tack has been to claim that such concepts, upon a fresh, radical rereading, may turn out to be non-antagonistic, even complementary. At any rate, they may not be natural and inevitable features of human cognition and valuation.[84] They could be revisable. From a critical perspective, each of the pairs can be interpreted as a shorthand or disguised form of political rhetoric that tends to obscure which values are really at stake.[85]

Even if we agree that this kind of unpacking of the normative content of legal doctrine is useful, it does not have to force the inquiry to a level of ontological dispute. It would make as much sense to treat it as a question of rhetoric or persuasion. For example, we could understand Duncan Kennedy's account as not so much about metaphysics as it is about entrenched attitudes and the possibilities of using law as a vehicle for persuasion, in which the goal would be to change dominant attitudes. Like Robert Gordon, Kennedy – especially in the second half of the 1970s – was inclined to frame his critique in structuralist terms.[86] Coincidentally or not, structural models of explanation in the human sciences (focusing on myths, musical or literary works, and cyclic social patterns) briefly flourished around the same time in both European and American universities. One of the attractions of a structuralist understanding of the legal system may have been the belief that it would help bring to the surface, to full self-consciousness, the underlying premises of the system of which even participants in that system, such as judges, lawyers, or legal academics, were unaware.[87] The possibility of uncovering heretofore hidden links among the disciplines presented an alluring vision: a radical critique of the legal system would pay off in increased comprehension of the normative underpinnings of legal theory. It should also be noted that the structuralist orientation of critical legal writers did not survive the subsequent pronounced swing towards sweeping doubts about any attempt to conceive legal doctrine as explicable by reference to recurrent patterns that create the image of an inherent logic.[88] In Kennedy's case, his ambition to unearth the ultimate elements of legal thinking gave way to other forms of analysis, the basis of which included first phenomenology and then law understood as a system of signs.[89]

Another possible reason for critical legal writers to attribute metaphysical foundations to liberalism lies in the sources they have quarried for liberal ideas. Philosophers such as Hobbes drew connections between political philosophy and systematic metaphysics. For instance, Hobbes adopted a reductionist method of analysis and applied it both to issues of political authority and sovereignty and to matters of language, religion, and ultimate essences.[90] Hobbes's contributions to deductive methods in analysis, as well as Locke's attempts to relate an empiricist epistemology to his political philosophy, could make it seem that liberal theories must presuppose an underlying metaphysical system.[91] But these are just contingent features of their philosophizing. Liberals do not have to commit themselves to any particular type of metaphysics, such as realism, idealism, monism, or phenomenalism. Nor do they have to adopt any particular psychological theory. The only kind of analysis for which this would make a difference would be one which seeks to find a unitary pattern that tries, in the language of Isaiah Berlin, to 'escape or "transcend" categories – or ways of thinking – which split and isolate and "kill" the living reality.'[92] Though Berlin views this as a natural human desire, it contains the danger, which he associates with illiberal political philosophies, that history or political events are perceived as the result of structural, impersonal forces, removing human agency and responsibility as factors in the explanation.

The Meaning of Subjectivism and Autonomy

There are numerous problems with the critical legal allegation that liberal theorists believe in an extreme form of human subjectivity that contradicts our self-understanding. Part of the attack is aimed at the view, which critical legal writers think is distinctively liberal, that a person can be individuated without any reference to the attachments that he or she may have to ends and values, or to the community in which that person has been nurtured. From the radical perspective, this conception of the person denies the extent to which his or her attachments constitute the individual person. Several ways in which contemporary liberal theorists might defend themselves against this charge have already been covered. But the radical critique also faults liberal theorists for promoting the idea that the state should be neutral on the issue of whether citizens' lives go well. A further use of the concept of subjectivity by critical legal writers has been made in the context of whether morals are objective or subjective. According to Unger, liberals adhere to 'absolute moral skepticism.'[93] Each of these two criticisms will be discussed in turn.

The first allegation is that liberalism is blind to the importance of an individual's non-political interests or goods. That is, while Rawls for example grants that each citizen is entitled to what he calls the 'liberties of equal citizenship,' in doing so he draws a boundary around those concerns that can justifiably motivate state intervention. A government would breach the principle of equal concern for its citizens if it implemented a scheme that favoured a particular conception of the good. A cardinal feature of Rawls's theory is that the individual must be free to formulate and to change her beliefs about which things are valuable.

The only legitimate ground for a government to restrict a basic liberty (such as the right to vote or freedom of conscience) would be to secure a more extensive system of basic liberties for everyone.[94] So, for example, in the face of moral or religious pluralism, where reasonable disagreement is widespread, the state should not dictate a hierarchy of values in order to ensure that all its citizens pursue satisfying lives.

It might seem to follow that, according to strict liberal logic, the state could justifiably be indifferent to whether citizens' needs outside the political realm were satisfied or not. Critical legal authors like Allan Hutchinson have construed the idea of state neutrality as authorizing only a 'minimal' state, or one in which the government makes few laws and generally leaves the distribution of wealth and resources to be determined by market operations.[95] This, however, is not the necessary result of liberal neutrality. Against Hutchinson's claim it is plausible to argue that a state could enact a progressive taxation regime that favours the least well-off individuals. As long as the scheme does not 'presuppose the superiority of some views of human flourishing over others held in society,' it will not violate the principle of liberal neutrality.[96] A government may pursue goals in line with its policies and intervene in the marketplace, provided it observes the constraint of neutrality.[97] Among the goals that may animate a government is the overall economic welfare of its citizens. This concern justifies the establishment of unemployment insurance plans or social benefits for the poor, with the accompanying bureaucratic agencies needed to administer such schemes. A government could, without violating the political ideal of neutrality, permit the deductibility of contributions to retirement savings plans, because this creates an incentive for citizens to put money aside during their working lives to cover expenses during their retirement. Governments that exhibit concern about whether all their citizens are provided with adequate levels of literacy, health care, unemployment benefits, and old age security are not transgressing the principle of political neutrality. On Rawls's interpretation of liberal justice, such concern is consistent with a state's role in promoting a community in which citizens are free to make choices about which form of life is best for them. Those particular ideals most worth pursuing remain an object of permanent dispute.

It can also be argued that liberal neutrality prizes virtues on the part of individual citizens that make a liberal democracy work best. Rawls has enumerated several of these, including 'civility and tolerance, reasonableness and the sense of fairness.'[98] These virtues are compatible with political liberalism because they are peculiarly appropriate to a democratic culture. Their presence among citizens helps ensure that debates within a political forum about which goals the government should pursue are not skewed because one group manages to impose its view of the supposed intrinsic superiority of a conception of the good life on citizens who harbour different ideals. Using political forums to compare the merits of different forms of life is justifiable in a liberal society: debates in Parliament or Congress can usefully examine controversial conceptions of the human good. Proponents of vegetarianism can try to convince others of the inferiority of their idea of the good life as including the consumption of red meat. But parliamentary discussions could also revolve around the central liberal complaint that a government is acting unjustly when it decides to force everyone to eat broccoli with each evening meal.

The critical legal accounts surveyed earlier in this chapter attribute to liberal theories the assumption that individual desires, passions, or interests do not bear scrutiny. Liberals are supposed to view them as shaped without reference to social conditioning; such motivations are characterized as incorrigible preferences that cannot be rationally evaluated or changed through an application of understanding. Hume's argument that 'reason is the slave of the passions' is treated as part of the stock liberal portrait of the self.[99] This view has been disputed by some historians of liberal political theory, who cite examples of how liberal thinkers such as Tocqueville and Adam Smith comprehended the ways in which understanding or reason shapes desire.[100] Other liberal theorists acknowledge that social conditioning as well as formal education play a role in the development of individual personalities, including the cultivation of tastes, values, and opinions.

With respect to the other meaning of subjectivism suggested at the outset of this section of our discussion, it should be noted that when liberal theorists write with an emphasis on 'subjective' values, this emphasis does not necessarily indicate absolute scepticism. Their so-called subjectivism can arise in any of several contexts, to which a careful analysis should be attuned. In some cases, for example, a liberal insistence on subjectivity is a response to (and criticism of) claims made on behalf of 'objective' values, that is, political or legal norms imposed by reference to some authoritative source, such as the church, which might have tried to coerce individuals into accepting certain ways of life and to punish non-believers for failure to adhere to a particular moral code. Similarly, efforts by totalitarian governments to prescribe an official ideology for an entire population to follow, with punishment for any dissent, have prompted liberal objections. But criticism of such practices is possible without having to argue in favour of utter scepticism. A liberal can hold political beliefs, which include tolerance and respect for freedom of thought, without believing that all values are continually 'up for grabs.' She can logically think that her conception of the good is better than conceptions held by her neighbours, without ceasing to be a liberal on that account. Political liberalism would not authorize her, of course, to use her position as mayor of a city to exercise her discretion and order the police to detain her neighbours for holding what, to her mind, are errant beliefs.

It is a mistake then to think that, because moral pluralism is taken as a striking feature of modern constitutional democracies, all liberal moralists have therefore adopted radical or absolute moral scepticism.[101] It is possible for a theorist to argue that morals could be objectively grounded, not because of some revealed truth, inspired authority, or foundationalist epistemology, but on the basis of what Charles Larmore calls 'contextual justification.'[102] Moreover, even if a liberal conceded that morality could be objective, this would not mean that the state should abandon its neutral stance in relation to differing conceptions of the good life. In areas of social life outside the political realm, individuals could continue to conduct themselves according to controversial ideas about what things are valuable. They may hold dear their attachments to friends, family, religion, or pastimes. Still, the main virtue of the state according to political liberalism would be neutrality, not scepticism.

If critical legal writers were correct about the scepticism underlying legal and political liberalism, it is difficult to see how liberals could justify the imposition of prohibitions on certain kinds of conduct. The limits suggested here include not just criminal sanctions against murder or assault, but other forms of legal duties or rights identified by legislatures and courts. How can such laws be reconciled with a robust scepticism about whether certain values can be rationally grounded in a liberal society? One critical legal tack is simply to explain these limits as the result of a 'convergence of individual preferences.'[103] An alternative explanation – that these kinds of legal limits are the outgrowth of shared values about the evils of taking human life or causing injury to another through negligence – does not fit at all with the portrait of liberal theory offered by the radical critique.

Another problem with the critique offered of the allegedly normative poverty of liberalism involves a failure to grasp the importance of egalitarian ideals to liberal political theories (one of the crucial ideological characteristics that allows us to distinguish liberals from conservatives). The radical version of subjectivity does not accord with efforts by liberals to preserve and promote political and legal forms of equality, regardless of the preferences of individuals. Equality is at least one moral belief that liberals can plausibly share, even if they differ over the exact contours of the policies required by a principle of equality in specific social circumstances. For liberals such as Ronald Dworkin, a certain conception of equality forms the 'nerve of liberalism.'[104] So, for instance, it would be peculiar or perverse for someone to claim to be a liberal if she did not believe that government bears a responsibility to reduce inequalities of wealth through welfare or taxation measures. Similarly, it would seem strange for a professed liberal to object when the state proposes to intervene in the economy to correct market imperfections or to provide necessary services to the public that otherwise would not be available. As a third example, it would be paradoxical for a liberal to oppose legislation designed to combat racial discrimination. But Dworkin's account of the importance of equality extends beyond convictions individual citizens may hold from time to time and over which they may vehemently disagree, in terms of how a conception best satisfies the liberal political ideal of equality. On his account, the principle that a government must treat all its citizens with equal concern and respect best captures what Dworkin calls the 'constitutive morality' reflected in modern democracies.[105] Rawls, too, both in A Theory of Justice and in his later work, places a pronounced emphasis on equality of citizens. He elaborates his two principles of justice by noting that they contain several egalitarian elements, including the so-called difference principle, which declares that any social or economic inequalities attached to offices and positions should be adjusted so that they benefit the least advantaged members of society.[106] Both Dworkin's and Rawls's deployment of the concept of equality reveals their awareness that, for individuals to have a decent chance to form their own ideals of a good life, material prerequisites might legitimately require state action.

Other liberal theorists have argued for more than just the redistribution of economic goods. Another egalitarian concern has been to ensure that citizens have a fair chance to participate in political life, thus meeting the complaint of communitarian critics that while liberal communities might follow Rawls's principles of justice, they could still be composed of a remarkably passive citizenry. For Amy Gutmann, for example, participatory forms of equality are broadly conceived.[107] Her argument is aimed at defining the conditions, including access to political information, necessary for citizens freely and rationally to employ their democratic procedures.[108] Such emphases on distributive equality are an advance on earlier liberal theories that simply proposed, as a formal goal, that governments ought to provide equal opportunities for citizens but were not empowered to use the welfare, taxation, education, or electoral systems to equalize background conditions. Claims by radical critics that a normative theory is flawed because it fails to pay sufficient attention to the needs or interests of those citizens who are poor may be fair comment. It would be wrong, however, to argue that political liberalism, because it holds that values are radically subjective, cannot entertain debates about how citizens should be treated in terms of their material needs. On this last issue, rather than demurring on the ground that the issue in question is properly a matter of individual conscience, contemporary liberals have been willing to engage in healthily contentious dialogue.

The gist of this chapter has been that many of the charges levelled against liberalism by critical legal writers have missed the mark. Contemporary liberals have dissociated themselves from many of the assumptions identified by radical critics as integral to legal liberalism. These include conceptions of individualism, self-interested motivation, radical subjectivity, and epistemological and moral scepticism. By substituting alternative premises for a universalistic theory of human nature and interpersonal association, critical legal writers have in the past tried to lay the foundations for a fresh communitarian reconstruction of law and society. The details of this vision are explored in Chapter 5. The lesson of the present chapter is that the critique offered by critical legal authors has failed to unravel the normative background of liberal conceptions of justice.

3

A Simple Matter of Conviction: Legal Consciousness and Critical Theory

All our civilization is like that, it has developed in the midst of internecine moral strife; breaking out from the schools and monasteries, it did not emerge into life, but sauntered through it, like Faust, merely to take a look at it, to reflect upon it, and then to withdraw from the rude mob into *salons*, academies and books.

Alexander Herzen, *From the Other Shore*
(trans. Constance Garnett)

In Chapter 2 we became familiar with those normative ideas which, according to critical legal writers, have been insinuated into and dominate legal doctrine. From this critical perspective, liberalism exerts a tenacious grip on modern thinking about the concept of law; legal institutions; and the respective roles of citizens, lawyers, judges, and legislators. Law is supposed to be shot through with liberal presuppositions and values which pervade the field to such an extent that a participant in the legal process may not even detect their presence or realize their power. These normative assumptions have been the focal point of critical legal inquiries into the interrelationship of law and politics. One of the overarching purposes of early critical legal writing was emancipatory: after demonstrating the centrality of liberal ideas, radical critics attempted to show the value of adopting an alternative conceptual scheme. Rephrased in political terms, the goal was to expose the ideological content of law. Releasing political agents from a mental straitjacket, so that they might finally realize that their real interests are not served by current forms of law, is the task of ideological critique. On the critical legal view, once exposed to the liberal underpinnings of the law, lawyers and citizens alike will in their newfound enlightenment acknowledge that legal doctrines and institutions should be radically overhauled.

Lawyers as a profession typically pride themselves on their training as acute critical thinkers. They confidently approach complex factual and theoretical problems with highly developed logical and persuasive skills. Critical legal writers, however, have viewed their function as critical theorists differently.[1] The type of critique these radical critics offer is, to their minds, without precedent in legal theorizing. For instance, as Karl Klare has pointed out, when critical legal authors handle legal doctrine, they reject traditional approaches. They find it 'sterile' simply to ask, in regard to a specific case, whether the court reached the result because of certain policy factors, such as the need to protect the parties' expectations or the need to encourage the productive development of resources.[2] In conventional legal analysis, such policies are treated as relatively stable and unchallengeable: they foreclose analysis rather than expose legal outcomes to searching examination. The radical critic finds it more powerful and illuminating to examine the extent to which both lawyerly arguments and judicial reasoning are predicated on politically controversial normative values. Rather than straining the case through an apparently neutral filter of a few policies the law might favour, depending in part on the factual circumstances, the radical critique questions whether judicial reasoning and the outcome of a case contribute to building a free, egalitarian, and genuinely democratic society.

In attempting this kind of emancipatory project, critical legal theory is reminiscent of the ideology critique of European critical theory, particularly as practised by members and heirs of the Frankfurt School. No adequate clarification of the relationship between critical legal studies and other radical traditions in modern social or political thought has yet appeared,[3] although some observers of critical legal work think that its roots can be traced to Hegel, practitioners of Marxist analysis, and critical theorists such as Horkheimer, Adorno, and Habermas.[4] Nor has the precise nature of such connections adequately been spelled out by critical legal authors themselves. Critical legal writing doubtless owes something to the Hegelian idea of the dialectic, or to Marxist critiques of bourgeois legal practices, if only as sources of inspiration rather than models strictly to be followed.[5] Whether critical legal thinking simply restages some of Hegel's or Marx's key ideas or philosophical methods remains to be explored in depth.[6]

This chapter provides a conceptual scrutiny of the idea of legal consciousness as employed in early critical legal writing and investigates radical claims about how legal consciousness is created, sustained, and altered. In tracing the liberal contours of modern legal thought, and subjecting that tradition to ideological analysis, critical legal writers have often framed their task as identifying and describing the 'consciousness' that shapes law and legally influenced institutions.[7] They have also tried to imagine the conditions under which such consciousness might change. These critics have treated the development of laws through interpretation and application by the courts as largely determined by the worldview or mind-set of the participants in the legal process. Various critical legal explications of the importance of consciousness as a background condition of legal reasoning and legal scholarship have both retrospective and prospective dimensions. The history of common law adjudication has been broken up by radical critics into approximate periods depending on which particular types of consciousness were paramount. From a forward-looking perspective, once citizens recognize the elements that mark their current reigning consciousness, they are presented with a choice between perpetuating that consciousness or, more agreeably from a radical point of view, striking out in a new direction defined by considerations of post-liberal justice. Social transformation depends on loosening the grip of legal ideology.

The notion of legal consciousness does not necessarily exist only at the level of, say, what individual judges might describe as going on in their minds once they have donned their robes and ascended the courtroom bench. Even if such privileged access were interesting, critical legal analysis does not depend on some (allegedly) liberal conception of the untrammeled autonomy of each judge's conscious processes and individual experiences.[8] The critical analysis is focused instead on the 'conceptual scheme' (to use Quine's expression) widely shared among participants in legal processes.[9] Thus, critical legal writers claim more adventurously to have discerned striking similarities among the thinking of judges and lawyers separated by different jurisdictions and working within different doctrinal spheres. They are fascinated to find significant structural points of similarity between, for example, the reasoning behind the disposition of a constitutional claim and that behind a family court adjudication.

A number of questions arise from this approach. What are the origins and scope of a legal consciousness? What sorts of beliefs and assumptions does it encompass? In so far as it is related to the concept of ideology, as that term is used by political theorists to describe belief structures or political discourse, is legal consciousness something that can be true or false? Is the force of such a consciousness confined to those persons most immediately involved in processes of law, or is it more widespread? These questions are addressed below.

One apparent advantage of the concept of legal consciousness is that it avoids many of the problems associated with vulgar Marxist conceptions of the relationship between the law and other institutions, in particular economic arrangements which, it may be argued, determine the content of the law in a particular society. On this economistic view, law is merely epiphenomenal. Early critical legal notions of a shared consciousness were apparently meant to remedy the defects in other leftist accounts that try to explain the relationship between legal structures and the economic and social features of a society. The conception of a shared consciousness also is bound up in claims made by critical legal writers about the level of popular delusion caused or perpetuated by legal ideas.[10] The discussion below assesses some of these claims, which are often expressed in forbiddingly technical terms. On the radical view law represents a mystification of true social relations. Second, a passive citizenry is kept quiescent by processes of legal hegemony and reification. Third, law contributes to the legitimation of objectionable economic and political forms of domination. The final section of this chapter analyses problems that arise out of the political conception of the domination and reproduction of a single form of consciousness. I will argue that the logic of the critical legal explanation is seriously flawed and susceptible to criticism from several angles. The critical legal account of the reproduction of social life is unfortunately equivocal about whose consciousness is in issue. It is also marred by archaic Marxist notions about each agent's 'objective' interests. In addition, critical legal writers have failed to agree on whether forms of consciousness can be judged as true or false. While some radical critics have committed themselves to an epistemological relativism, this has not stopped them from claiming, or at least appearing to hold, that liberal legal ideology is delusive and misrepresents social reality. The discussion at the end of this chapter also questions whether it is a necessary outcome of all reflective activity that each member of liberal democratic societies will reject the beliefs which, according to critical legal writers, form the legal foundations of those societies. The radical critics' confidence in this regard flows from their conviction that any engagement with critical theory guarantees political enlightenment and inspiration. But the radical perspective only makes sense because those critics exaggerate the presence of coercion in contemporary democracies. The most telling

criticism of all is that early critical legal writing treated legal consciousness as a monolith, without due regard for relevant social divisions. As
the expository part of this chapter shows, the form of legal consciousness
used by critical legal writing as an explanatory device has been attributed
broadly. The portrait involves a ruling class that uses various mechanisms
to keep in check a subjugated class. This perspective ignores the distinctive interests of those members of a society who, because of their gender,
race, language, or sexuality might differ from the class-based norm
presupposed by early critical legal studies.

Meaning and Scope of Legal Consciousness

Parallels to the critical legal use of the notion of consciousness as an
explanatory vehicle are found in other movements in twentieth-century
intellectual history that try to explain the hidden foundations underlying human practices and institutions. For example, the doctrines of
Freudian psychoanalysis emphasize the role of psychic structures, especially the unconscious, in determining individual and group behaviour.[11] In hermeneutics, which stresses the interpreter's embeddedness
in history and tradition, one of the goals is to make transparent the
'cultural unconscious.'[12] In the political context, Frankfurt School critical theory was concerned from the outset with accounting for the
disparity between the principles on which Western bourgeois societies
were supposed to be grounded and the actual economic and cultural
conditions found in those societies. Critics such as Max Horkheimer
sought an explanation that gave due weight to the presence of intellectual forces in maintaining entrenched systems of power.[13] Purely coercive force is not necessary to sustain ruling groups in power: most
members of Western capitalist societies are simply not inclined to
combine their influence and secure changes that would break down
hierarchies of power and wealth. Like European critical theorists before them, critical legal writers have tried to illuminate the causes of
such passivity, to explain the deference to authority paid by even the
most disadvantaged classes in a society. Explaining the passive behaviour of the disadvantaged is one of the major issues addressed by
critical legal writing on consciousness.[14]

Karl Klare has provided a comprehensive definition of the phenomenon of legal consciousness that illustrates the multifaceted nature of
the concept. Although it has been adopted by other critical legal writers,
Klare's definition does not, as we shall see, exhaust the possible mean-

ings attached to the concept of consciousness. Klare elaborates as follows:

> By 'legal consciousness' I mean the vision of law and the world characteristic of the legal profession (or of a particular elite or other subgroup within it) at a given moment in history. 'Legal consciousness' imports not only explicit theorizing and discourse about law, but also conscious and unconscious assumptions and values pertaining to law and legal institutions as well as those pertaining to politics and social life generally, to history and to the nature of justice. Legal consciousness includes the characteristic style or mode of reasoning of a group or epoch, the nature of the intellectual operations recognized as appropriate legal argument, the nature of the connection sought to be established between legal authority and legitimate adjudicatory outcomes, the manner in which legal problems are defined, and the types of evidence deemed relevant to legal inquiry. In sum, 'legal consciousness' refers to the constellation of assumptions underlying law and the structures and patterns of thought about law. It is assumed that legal historians can reconstruct the contours of the legal consciousness of a period. Likewise it is assumed that structures and styles of legal thought, by establishing the terrain upon which legal questions are posed, to some extent establish limits on the ways in which they are answered.[15]

Along with the formulations of Duncan Kennedy, this definition has exerted a vast influence on the subsequent course of critical legal writing.[16] Kennedy's description of legal consciousness substantially matches that provided by Klare, perhaps placing an even greater emphasis on the types of structural constraints liable to be uncovered by examining any historically situated sample of legal discourse.[17] According to Kennedy, legal consciousness is: '... the particular form of consciousness that characterizes the legal profession as a social group, at a particular moment. The main peculiarity of this consciousness is that it contains a vast number of legal rules, arguments, and theories, a great deal of information about the institutional workings of the legal process, and the constellation of ideals and goals current in the profession at a given moment.'[18]

In Kennedy's articulation of the concept of consciousness the fundamental premises of a legal system are so basic that participants within the system 'rarely if ever bring them consciously to mind.'[19] They remain largely unstated and unchallenged assumptions around which lawyers' arguments or judicial reasoning are organized. As an example of a particular type of legal consciousness Kennedy describes the rise, the flourishing, and the decay of what he calls 'Classical legal consciousness' in the United States between approximately 1850 and 1940. Among the premises of this particular example of consciousness he lists the following as the most important. First, when classical legal thought was in the ascendant, it seemed natural to lawyers and judges to analyse disputes as essentially involving 'the concept of a power absolute within its judicially delineated sphere.'[20] A federalism issue, in which a court is required to consider the boundaries between federal jurisdiction and that of state governments, could be neatly subsumed under this description. Similarly, it could be applied to disputes between private individuals (pitted against each other in a property or contract case), between individual citizens and the state, and between the legislature and the judiciary. On Kennedy's reconstruction of the growth of U.S. law between the mid-nineteenth century and the outbreak of the Second World War, virtually all cases could be understood by reference to this type of legal consciousness.

By emphasizing the integration of these kinds of cases under a general type of consciousness, Kennedy purports to describe 'the body of ideas through which lawyers experience legal issues.'[21] His second defining characteristic of classical legal thought is that, compared to the period before it, the classical period, at its zenith, offered lawyers the sense of 'compulsion by which an abstraction dictates, objectively, apolitically, in a non-discretionary fashion, a particular result.'[22] According to Kennedy, with the gradual decline of the classical period during the first half of the twentieth century, this sense of compulsion was lost.

Both Klare and Kennedy focus on the legal profession as the group in which this consciousness is created and operates. Thus, the evolution of forms of consciousness appears to be primarily a matter of shifts and reversals, largely unnoticed at the time, in the understanding, training, and performance of such agents as lawyers, judges, and treatise writers. This view of consciousness would confine the scope of the notion to professional communities whose work is generally beyond the comprehension of the laity.

To critical legal writers, this account of professional legal consciousness is promising in so far as it parallels explanations of change and resistance to change in the history of scientific disciplines. It could illuminate how certain élite conceptions of justice and of the very notion of legality have managed to hold the field against alternative conceptions based on different political or economic premises. Also, from a critical perspective, such an account would demonstrate the conservative nature of what passes for legal scholarship. Like Thomas Kuhn's description of scientific practitioners as working within the confines of 'normal science,' the ordinary legal commentator or practitioner could be pictured as a handmaid in a system designed to maintain intellectual domination.[23] The analogy between 'mainstream' legal writing and the role of orthodoxy in science should not be pressed too far, but the rise of critical legal theories about historicizing legal consciousness coincided with more notorious controversies over the relativity and rationality of research procedures in the natural and social sciences.[24] By developing a series of models or patterns of legal reasoning (which, as noted above, may be found in various types of sources) the inquirer into a specifically legal consciousness would be able to propose significant generalizations about how doctrinal and theoretical change occurs through subsequent generations in the profession. The exposure of the legal élite's political, economic, and philosophical views would prove to some extent the distinctiveness of such views in a given period. They might have been so ingrained that the élites of a particular period would not easily have articulated them. Nevertheless, the views in question may be isolated against the different assumptions made by lawyers, judges, and commentators who preceded or succeeded that period. The critic can then periodicize the course of legal history, using rough sets of dates in a manner that reveals dominant thought patterns. Interestingly, on this issue of constructing a genealogy of a discipline, and in discussing what he calls 'stylistic paradigms' in the work of analytic philosophers in the twentieth century, Richard Rorty has claimed that, rather than comparing themselves to scientists, philosophers might more tellingly see themselves as quasi-lawyers.[25]

The analytical procedure described above implies that legal thinking will continue to evolve as different sets of beliefs, assumptions, and forms of argument gain ascendancy. It would also shed new light on such issues as judicial activism, efforts to erect a legal science, and the role of discretion in judging.[26] As Kennedy thinks his early work illustrates, the kind of historical appraisal achieved by bringing to the surface the deep political and philosophical commitments of legal élites is designed to avoid the failings of traditional legal historiography. According to Robert Gordon, one of the strengths of critical legal history is that it eschews describing legal achievements as necessary or inevitable steps leading to the triumph of the current, and thus presumptively most rational, form of legal thought. This is the fallacy of a Whig interpretation of legal history, which distorts events in the interest of glorifying political victors.[27] Analysing standard legal materials for their philosophical and political content also amounts to a form of political interpretation. According to Gordon, critical legal history is politically sensitive and does not, as earlier legal historiography did, pretend to be free from the taint of politics.[28]

Critical legal conceptions of consciousness have not only been used to revise standard accounts of history, they have been applied as well to contemporary legal doctrine and legal theory. One of the boldest expressions of the revolutionary potential of the leftist legal critique has been made by Roberto Unger. His critique of liberalism and its associated legal theories in the 1980s places significant emphasis on the human tendency to adopt constraining routines, in terms of both institutions and imagination. In his words,

> None of the social and mental forms within which we habitually move nor all the ones that have ever been produced in history describe or determine exhaustively our capabilities of human connection. None escapes the quality of being partial and provisional. But these mental and social worlds nevertheless differ in the severity as well as the character and content of their constraining quality. The search for the less conditional and confining forms of social life is the quest for a social world that can do better justice to a being whose most remarkable quality is precisely the power to overcome and revise, with time, every social or mental structure in which he moves.[29]

Unger does not use the term 'consciousness' to signify the congeries of beliefs, attitudes, assumptions, or habits of mind that, he argues, can be changed through voluntary action. Rather, in his terminology, the important constraints that operate at both institutional and imaginative levels are frameworks, structures, or contexts.[30] In particular, he refers repeatedly to 'formative contexts' that serve as instruments for reproducing societies and resisting disturbances. In Unger's scheme, formative contexts have such an overwhelming influence over social life that they appear to make individuals 'mere puppets of these frameworks or of the forces that generate and sustain them.'[31] Formative contexts include institutional arrangements (such as legal or economic systems), non-institutionalized social practices (reflected in moral and social ideals), and what Unger calls 'imaginative assumptions about the possible and desirable forms of human association.'[32] One way of looking at these contexts is to see them as pre-existing scripts that provide a 'background plan of social division and hierarchy.'[33] By freeing themselves from having to adopt these scripts, individuals can refashion their relationships, whether they pertain to work situations (with attendant hierarchies of superiors and subordinates) or intimate connections (for example, between men and women).

The type of cultural-revolutionary politics Unger has in mind would undermine any attempt to separate legal analysis from ideological conflict. To his way of thinking, modern legal theories essentially depend on some form of resignation to the established social order. They accept the limits that surround substantive legal doctrine. Legal consciousness is another formative context, one that exalts the monopolization of certain forms of authority or power 'in the name of expert knowledge.'[34] Instituting a program of what he calls 'revolutionary reform' would change these assumptions. Legal argument would be treated as part of a continuum that includes ideological discourse. Current liberal ideals (such as rights to liberty or equality) would be radicalized; existing institutions (such as markets or democracy) would be reconstructed; and, finally, Unger envisions the possibility of changing, through a 'personalist' conceptual revolution, the 'direct practical and passionate relations among individuals.'[35] Formative contexts thus govern the lives of everyone in a particular society. On Unger's scheme, insight into the possibilities of change are vouchsafed to those who understand most clearly how legal doctrine relies tacitly, if not explicitly, on some vision of the forms of human association. This is why the one group that may be expected to escape these 'delusive conceptual necessities' and to propose alternative forms of political arrangements is made up of legal scholars.[36] Legal scholars are the counter-élite who, through their knowledge of the nuances of established legal doctrine, can anticipate and articulate the legal framework for a more progressive society. Unger's use of formative contexts attributes to members of the legal profession and to law teachers an extraordinary role as political visionaries. Unger pays lawyers a high compliment. A society desiring to transform itself in a host of dimensions – including transformation of its moral, political, economic, and military systems – would be well-advised, at least at the outset, to consult its lawyers, for they are the most likely agents for revolutionary change. This is not because they can achieve an Archimedean point outside the system they are asked to reshape. Rather, according to Unger, lawyers can work from the inside and, using the institutional haven of their law schools, or their positions in privileged firms, they can help change the terms of collective life.[37] Changes of legal consciousness in this scenario would have wide-ranging effects.

It should be noted, however, that legal consciousness is not uniformly interpreted in critical legal literature as a matter of professional ideology. Other critiques expand the scope of consciousness to cover a widespread, popular understanding of the forms, justifications, and content of law.[38] For example, in the case of harsh criminal provisions regarding property that were instituted and applied in eighteenth-century England, an ideological analysis of those laws will attend closely to the response they engendered in the people who lived under the shadow of such extreme measures.[39] Legal consciousness is thus not solely a phenomenon in which a legal élite would be interested. Grasping and rationalizing the connection between the authority of legal adjudicators, enforcers, and possible intervenors and the outcomes of legal procedures can be an intensely immediate experience to the subordinated classes as well. Reconstructing an adequate picture of an era's distinctive legal consciousness would presuppose, then, a broader investigation into social practices and the creation of expectations than strictly doctrinal materials would disclose. In the words of David Trubek, who appears to subscribe to this expanded view of what the term signifies, 'legal consciousness includes all the ideas about the nature, function, and operation of law held by anyone in society at a given time.'[40]

On this approach the phenomenon of legal consciousness operates on a mass scale. Consciousness in this context means how 'ordinary people understand and make sense of the law.'[41] The example cited above from Douglas Hay's essay 'Property, Authority and the Criminal Law' illustrates the kind of inquiry this conception of legal consciousness would involve.[42] Here it is not sufficient merely to infer what the members of the legal élite took for granted in establishing and administering a regime of laws; a full explanation of the habits of mind that explain social behaviour would require in addition an extensive survey and analysis of the popular understanding of legal structures. A doctrine such as freedom of contract, which is supposed to have been the main principle underlying the formulation of commercial and constitutional laws during the latter half of the nineteenth century throughout the common law world, was not only a feature of lawyers' thinking. Somehow the ideology of the market, of individual freedom to enter into agreements to exchange labour for wages, and of the limited capacity of the state to make laws regulating such bargains penetrated deeply into the consciousness of workers themselves. Only this could account for the relative docility of the disadvantaged classes, who must have believed there was something natural about the state of affairs in which a government was denied the capacity to prevent certain wage bargains on the grounds of constitutional overreaching. Kennedy's account, which stresses how U.S. Supreme Court judges, for example, were in thrall to professionally inculcated conceptions of the root principles of contract law and laissez-faire political theory, still fails to explain why the labouring masses acquiesced in judicial decisions that went directly and obviously against their interests. Doctrinal scrutiny reveals only the élite's preconceptions and perceptions. It does not show the link between those elements of consciousness and the behaviour of non-élites in the face of the law as it was developed and enforced. The latter sort of inquiry would call for types of evidence far removed from case reports and treatises.

The emphasis on describing and making sense of popular legal consciousness seems to have encouraged a few critical legal writers. Supplementing the critique of doctrine and élite legal institutions are thoughtful investigations of historical and contemporary situations in which people are subjected to legal constraints. These include the workplace, the legal aid clinic, the corporate board room, community organizations, and huge bureaucratic settings such as systems for the delivery of health care and social security benefits.[43] The message behind such attempts to capture what is extraordinary about the ordinary is that a 'local' critique of social behaviour may ultimately be more revealing than showing how legal doctrine is marked by traces of grand social theory.[44] Establishing claims about the pervasiveness of liberal legal categories of thought depends on adducing some evidence that the mass of people really do conceive issues in those terms: that is, 'some convincing link between the structural analysis of doctrine and the actual subjective consciousness of political actors other than lawyers and judges' must be demonstrated.[45]

There would appear to be a significant split within critical legal ranks on the question of whose consciousness is to be cited to exemplify an era's legal understanding. This issue is crucial, for its resolution will determine, first, what sort of evidence is pursued and, second, what kind of methodological approach is followed in criticizing existing institutions. The two distinctive positions, which are here called the professional and the popular views, can be outlined as follows. The professional or élitist view of the role of a shaping consciousness that lends unity and justification to legal structures would direct the radical critic to the kinds of materials found in law school classrooms. The data to be scrutinized for its subtle indications of the assumptions, beliefs, and background social and political biases would include judicial opinions, counsel's arguments in briefs or pleadings, and the compilations and rationalization of doctrine contained in scholarly treatises and works of legal history.[46] Theoretical writings would obviously provide direct testimony of the conceptions predominating in a given period, though the critic would have to exercise caution. Contemporaneous theoretical statements are not necessarily an adequate summary of the primary motivations of legal behaviour in that period. A further valuable source of information would be the occasional literature resulting from lawyers or judges reflecting on their jobs: for example, when a leader of the profession speaks publicly about the role of lawyers and courts in ensuring social order and commercial prosperity. From the perspective of critical legal writers, such literature could be valuable source material for the reproduction of professional ideals and, thus, professional ideologies.[47]

It is difficult to reconcile the professional view of legal consciousness with the popular view. As we shall see in Chapter 5, critical legal writing is marked by strong claims for the sufficiency of dealing critically with legal doctrine in its élite form alone. Added to these claims is a deep aversion to empirical studies as a part of critical practice. Some critical legal writers have distinguished themselves from legal realists by noting that the realist project foundered once it turned to gathering evidence about the operation of the law.[48] Sociological explanations tend to be positivistic in so far as they aim at reproducing existing social relations. Nor have critical legal writers been readily impressed by claims that a scientific method can be used to gather and interpret data. The allegedly scientific status of some forms of legal scholarship is seen as part of the problem, and not any kind of solution that will throw light on why people lack the urge to re-order the political priorities that determine the form of their law.[49] In this respect, critical legal writers echo critical theorists who deny that their social investigations are analogous to empirical sciences aimed at acquiring objective knowledge. Such 'scientism,' with its emphasis on objectivity, leaves out of the account any scope for critical reflection on the formation of social frameworks in which individuals operate.[50]

In an apparent attempt to relax the tension between the theoretical and the empirical approaches, David Trubek has asserted that the empirical study of 'practice at the field level and the micropolitics of legal consciousness would be quite consistent with the Critical Studies tradition.'[51] Merely undertaking such studies would not of course amount to a guarantee that the elements of mass, everyday consciousness would match the elements of élite legal consciousness. At best, critical legal analysis can only hypothesize that such a connection exists. It is doubtful whether this type of study fits very well with the original conception of a critique of doctrine.[52] One of the most appealing aspects of the original critical project was the notion that legal doctrine contained within itself the entire ideological content of liberalism. There was an implicit faith in the intellectual influence of the legal élite. The way problems as well as remedies were shaped in the law was the dominant form of consciousness. This result could simply be predicated on the closed nature of the profession, with its uniform education, self-governing status, self-imposed isolation from other occupations and disciplines, and structures of authority and argumentation. The idea that a limited number of paradigms gripped the imagination of lawyers and judges made a kind of sense in the context of a close community. By expanding the idea of legal consciousness to encompass everyone who lives under a regime of law in Western societies, one of the original charms of the theory of consciousness begins to fade. As critical legal writers interested in this topic themselves confess, modern empirical studies so far indicate that, in Trubek's words, 'relations between elite doctrine and social behavior cannot be assumed a priori.'[53] That is, it has not been conclusively shown that mass behaviour invariably correlates with the legal rules propounded to regulate such behaviour. The most elaborate examples of such justified scepticism are Stewart Macaulay's studies into the influence of contract law doctrine on the business policies of firms.[54] The division between those critical legal writers who are content with dealing imaginatively with doctrine and those who would expand the focus of analysis to include studies on how conceptions of law are actually formed and influence behaviour is not explained away by saying that both inhere in the critical legal tradition and that they are simply alternative means to accomplish the same analytical project. In fact, the two approaches represent radically different visions of what the critique must take as its data, and more importantly, of how intellectual enlightenment is a necessary and sufficient condition for effecting social change. We will find echoes of this contest when, in Chapter 5, questions arise over the scope for political action alongside practising critique, and whether the two activities can really be conflated.

The Contents of Legal Consciousness

The idea of a legal consciousness has so far been discussed in the abstract. It would be worthwhile to consider some examples that show how swings and fortunes in legal thinking may be reduced to a few graspable elements. Duncan Kennedy's influential description of one form of legal consciousness will serve our purpose here. As described above, in differentiating periods of American legal thought, relevant to all areas of law, Kennedy formulated the concept of a classical period that flourished roughly between 1850 and 1940. Dominating judicial thinking in that period was the notion that '... the legal system consisted of a set of institutions, each of which had the traits of a legal actor. Each institution had been delegated by the sovereign people a power to carry out its will, which was absolute within but void outside its sphere. The justification of this judicial role was the existence of a peculiar legal technique rendering the task of policing the boundaries of spheres an objective, quasi-scientific one.'[55]

Unfortunately, Kennedy does not elaborate on how this fundamental premise differs from the premises underlying the form of consciousness that preceded the classical period. For example, are not the decisions of the Marshall Court in the United States on constitutional issues also construable under this model? The most help we are given on this point is the assurance that, first, in pre-classical judicial decision making there was no 'assimilation of a great deal of law to a single subsystem dominated by the concept of a power absolute within its judicially delineated sphere,' and, second, that there would formerly have been no 'claim that very abstract properties were nonetheless operative.'[56] Kennedy's description appears to add up to the claim that between 1850 and 1900, at least, judges and lawyers believed more strongly than they have since that doctrinal rules can and ought to dictate the results of cases: that is, in Kennedy's terminology, during the period in question there was an increase in the 'felt operativeness of constitutional and doctrinal principles.'[57] The background to any dispute could be pictured as a struggle in the judicial mind between freedom ('conceived as arbitrary and irrational, yet creative and dynamic') and restraint ('conceived in similar stark terms, as rigid, principled in an absolutist way, yet necessary as the antidote to freedom').[58] Judges and lawyers of that era did not, of course, inexorably reduce the issues to this pair of alternatives. Such reduction is Kennedy's own interpretation which, he claims, best explains the patterns or forms of reasoning in which those judges and lawyers were engaged. Although it seems more plausible to think of these patterns as impersonal structures that are illuminating when looking at legal materials in retrospect, there is some evidence that, on Kennedy's use of 'legal consciousness,' he actually viewed judges and lawyers as having such a consciousness individually.[59] These theoretical claims raise a number of issues. Among them is the relative degree of rule-based or formalistic thinking that marks different historical periods. A second issue is the explanatory value of representing forms of consciousness through contradictory pairs which, it is claimed, dominate judicial discourse.

Kennedy argues that formalistic modes of reasoning distinguished the legal process in the nineteenth century in a manner not seen since. The adoption of such a judicial style was not just a reflex of non-legal forces. Kennedy is clear that legal consciousness changed 'autonomously' and not necessarily under pressure from economic causes or political factors.[60] This leaves open the question of whether such consciousness might have changed as the result of jurisprudential influences originating outside the U.S. legal system: for example, the importation of theory from continental Europe.[61] Kennedy does not impute such causative links. Instead, the dynamics of change appear to have involved interactions among the ideas within legal consciousness, which seem to have had an impulsive force of their own. The real question on this issue then becomes whether Kennedy's tracing of similar techniques of reasoning (or images, analogies, and metaphors) amounts to an explanation at all. It seems only that in their conception of law judges and lawyers were once not so captivated by the idea of an exhaustive set of applicable and determinative rules, in the late eighteenth century that idea predominated, but recently the legal profession has shown less faith in the adequacy of this conception (though lip service continues to be paid to it). It is difficult to see how this history satisfies the appeal to a 'form of legal consciousness' which, as Klare's definition above illustrates, is supposed to denote a strong connection between legal principles, institutional constraints, political theory, and economic assumptions. If in the end unpacking legal doctrine amounts simply to an analysis of how judicial thinking involves setting boundaries and following rules, then the results of the critique hardly live up to the promise it appeared to hold out.

By arranging the analysis in this way, Kennedy only invites further questions. First, why was boundary analysis brought to a higher pitch in the period he isolates and, second, why is the situation different today? Neither of these queries is addressed. The critical treatment therefore lacks a necessary genetic dimension. Moreover, the only description Kennedy provides of post-classical legal consciousness is that it is simultaneously marked by the disintegration of formalism (though the ambitions of formalist theory, if not its practices, survive) and by some sort of nostalgic longing after the formalist ideal, so that formalism retains its grip on law teachers, treatise writers, and those responsible for the apologetics of ceremonial speeches, even to this day. On a broad definition of formalism, such as that adopted by Neil Duxbury, who conceives it as 'the endeavour to treat particular fields of knowledge as if governed by interrelated, fundamental and logically demonstrable principles of science,' it may make sense to think of formalist models lingering into the twentieth century, despite the vaunted 'revolt against formalism' that legal realism was supposed to represent.[62] But Kennedy understands by 'formalism' something narrower. Such a theory arises out of what Kennedy views as a discrepancy between a legislature making general legal rules and a judge applying them in particular cases. On Kennedy's scheme of adjudication, the judge cannot stay within the boundaries of legal formality (what the enacted rules provide), but is always tempted to take up the 'obviously dangerous job of substantively rational arbiter of disputes about a constantly changing pattern of distributive justice and injustice.'[63] Kennedy offers a normative critique of the possibility of a judge reaching a decision grounded strictly on a strong concept of determinacy. It may sensibly be queried whether many theorists in the twentieth century in fact hankered after this formalist standard, as conceived by Kennedy. At best, formalism on his account is framed as an ideal type for the sake of analytical clarity. In any event, contemporary legal theorists have abandoned the quest for formalist models in Kennedy's terms, and instead concentrated on the link between law and morality, which Kennedy's version of formalism had sought to sever.

A further problem is the reduction of a form of legal consciousness to its ultimate elements, a reduction achieved by the use of contradictory pairs in setting the terms of legal debate. Kennedy uses, as we have seen, the example of freedom and restraint, with a gloss on each to show the peculiarly judicial connotations of each of those terms.[64] Elsewhere, he has invoked the allegedly polar concepts of individualism and altruism.[65] Other examples of dichotomous analysis rely on such pairs as individualism/collectivism,[66] public/private,[67] self/other,[68] freedom/security,[69] and form/substance.[70] Any one of these pairs on its own means very little in terms of giving direction to decision making. Although it is sometimes claimed in critical legal writing that polar concepts in their most elemental form set the limits to the possible reasoning, the claim is somewhat misleading. For one thing, the concepts would first have to be interpreted. A legal consciousness, so far as it includes such concepts, must make something of each half of the dichotomy. Kennedy's illustration purporting to spell out the meaning of freedom for his nineteenth-century classical judge demonstrates that a concept, in order to be used as a premise in legal reasoning, must be transformed into a statement of principle. What is done with these concepts afterwards is an essential step in creating a politically charged vision of the social world.

According to Jay Feinman, attempting to 'balance' the interests represented by, for example, freedom and security, is a common liberal technique. In a legal decision, a judge might assert how one adjudicative result would favour a principle of maximum protection of individual freedom. A different result might favour the importance of keeping to a minimum the opportunities for one person's actions to interfere with the personal or proprietary interests of another. The technique by which a judge might go on to claim that a 'balancing' or subtle adjustment of these interests represents the best rationale for a solution to the dispute is anathema from a critical legal point of view.[71] Nor does the imagery of a unification of the dichotomous pair have any great appeal. Such a unification smacks of 'mysticism' and offends what, according to Mark Kelman, is 'most distinctive' about critical legal studies, namely, 'its resolute refusal to see a synthesis in every set of contradictions.'[72]

Another legal liberal strategy criticized in the critical legal literature is the denial of one part of the dichotomy. This reasoning technique means that a false image of the subject is being propagated. The depreciated concept or, as we should say, the rejected principle, is thereby suppressed and excluded from the contemporary legal consciousness: that is, it becomes unavailable as a legal argument in other cases. The dynamics of such suppression whereby, to borrow Derrida's language, the suppressed alternative becomes a 'dangerous supplement,' sets the stage for the 'redeeming' or 'retrieving' aspect of the critical legal project.[73] The point is not somehow to reconcile the concepts that form the foundations of our world-view, but to bring each of them fully into the legal forum. In Kennedy's depiction, '... the experience of unresolvable conflict among our *own* values and ways of understanding the world is here to stay... [But] there is order and meaning to be discovered even within the sense of contradiction.'[74]

The source of these contradictions is not clearly specified in critical legal accounts. The possibilities seem to be twofold: the first explanation is psychological and the second, which is vastly more emphasized in critical legal literature, is historical. A leading example of the psychological explanation has been offered by Peter Gabel.[75] Gabel traces the development of a dominant consciousness to an apparently universal childhood experience, where offspring learn from their parents to fashion what he calls a 'false self.'[76] Invoking a perspective that leans heavily on French existentialism, Gabel argues that the loss of a true self creates the conditions (and in particular the need for belief in authority) in which law provides 'magical credibility.'[77] Legal consciousness is thus a form of alienation that afflicts individuals in so far as they refuse to recognize the contingent character of such legal phenomena as rights or the state.

The historical explanation relies in particular on the history of liberal thought. The dichotomies seem very close in appearance and tenor to the 'antinomies' of liberal theory as they have been characterized by Roberto Unger.[78] The form of the antinomy involves a pair of propositions that together form a paradox. The two propositions cannot simultaneously be true, and yet we would want to adhere to both as principles of our knowledge and conduct. The antinomy of reason and desire, for example, would have us agree that our ethical conduct is based on two contrasting grounds. On the one hand, we use as our standard of moral judgment the satisfaction of desire. For Unger, this would be exemplified in the ethical systems advanced by Hobbes or the utilitarians, and in particular by Bentham. Yet, on the other hand, a morality of reason, with a standard that looks beyond the satisfaction of our appetites, also appeals to us. The morality of reason is embodied in systems that promote general rules or injunctions aimed at controlling desire, such as Kantian ethics.[79] At any rate, Unger uses the form of the antinomy to illustrate the conceptual difficulties posed by liberal thought. His criticism of the 'deep structure' of Western thinking in modern times is intended ultimately to result in a transformed sense of alternative, but so far unrealized, types of personality, politics, and community. The antinomial conceptions were dead ends in which liberal thinking has unfortunately trapped us. As this entrapment is a historical condition, however, it is still possible for us to refashion both our theory and institutions. We can escape from the conceptual categories that currently dominate our ideas of how to choose the good life for ourselves and for the groups to which we belong.

This historical understanding of basic contradictions is stated rather differently by Kennedy and those influenced by his postulate of 'the fundamental contradiction.'[80] That idea can be summarized as the awareness that 'relations with others are both necessary to and incompatible with our freedom.'[81] Operating under this paradoxical belief, we engage in disputes that invariably require a decision that favours one side of the contradiction. Within the framework of our current practices and institutions we cannot escape such choices, nor can we reconcile, balance, trade them off, or reinterpret them as something more basic. Again, Kennedy follows a severely reductionist path. In his earlier work, he would reconstruct the entire history of legal thought as a variation on the theme of the fundamental contradiction. This reconstruction consists of charting the development of liberal legal modes of thinking as they are manifested in each doctrinal area.[82] Every dispute imaginable within the then existing system of legal adjudication can be portrayed as a configuration of an ultimate paradox. The following aspect of Kennedy's account forms an important part of the background of critical legal studies. He claims that 'The task of criticism is to demystify our thinking by confronting us with the fact that the contradiction is a historical artifact. It is no more immortal than is the society that created and sustains it.'[83]

In assessing Kennedy's use of the notion of contradiction (at both intermediate and fundamental levels within legal doctrine), we might ask first whether there are any contradictions here at all. For example, while Kennedy's assertion that 'relations with others are both necessary to and incompatible with our freedom' might sound like a paradox, on examination, it may not turn out to be so. It is difficult to think of any legal theorists who have actually argued that the point of law is to preserve a naturally unlimited amount of individual freedom, with no concession made for why citizens' activities may on occasion legitimately be restricted. Conversely, the view that legal constraints, no matter what their purpose, will invariably 'be incompatible with our freedom' would be so exaggerated that it is not surprising that no particular theorist would adopt it. For example, the imposition of rules of the road, setting out which side motorists must drive on and what should guide their practical choices at intersections and train crossings, while they may deny me the freedom to drive capriciously, certainly benefits everyone who lives in the society. It is rational for me to observe such limits on my individual freedom, so that I am able to enjoy more freedom than if nobody were willing to abide by those limits.[84] Perhaps a better way to construe any perceived tension between the desire for individual freedom and the need for legal limitation is to view it as a matter of conflicting or competing values, rather than a structural contradiction.[85]

Secondly, Kennedy's thesis about the historical origins of such contradictions is bound to cause as much mystification as it was supposed to dissolve. If an alleged contradiction is purely logical, then in the absence of some powerful account of the historical foundations of logic (which Kennedy has not offered), the contradiction cannot be altered simply by members of a society resolving to change it. The contradictions Kennedy has in mind are not logical contradictions, analogous to the claim that I am at one and the same time both married and a bachelor. It would seem to make more sense to interpret Kennedy as committed to a strong thesis about the social construction of the categories of human thinking. Contradictory pairs would then be viewed as the product of a society's unique historical development. But even this thesis would be insufficient to ground what Kennedy is primarily interested in establishing, namely, that judicial reasoning, although (on a formalistic model) it purports to resolve disputes objectively, is really based on arbitrary choice.[86] The historicist model of understanding contradictions does not yield the implication that all legal reasoning is a matter of arbitrariness or irrationality. Even if Kennedy's vaunted 'fundamental contradiction' were indeed a contradiction (which is denied above), and even conceding such contradictions were culturally specific (which is assumed, rather than proven, in Kennedy's account), it is not the case that reference to one of the limbs of the contradiction, in the process of resolving a particular dispute, would therefore constitute an arbitrary choice.

To illustrate the gap in Kennedy's chain of reasoning, take the example of a judge faced with a claim in the law of nuisance, and therefore with choosing between competing principles, each of which has some authority in the existing common law.[87] Let us assume that one principle is the freedom of an individual property owner to use her land as she wishes, while the other is the right of her neighbour to enjoy his property free from any nuisance originating in the adjacent property. By nuisance (to give a loose definition here) is meant anything created by one property owner that has harmful effects on a neighbour's property.[88] Right at the start, it may be difficult to agree with Kennedy that in such a situation there are equally compelling conflicting values when it comes to suggesting a resolution to the legal dispute. But, assuming that the principles were of equal weight, when a court arrives at a decision that finally settles the dispute, for example by choosing the principle that a property owner should be protected against nuisances created by any neighbours, this decision does not represent an arbitrary choice. The process of reaching the result would not necessarily be dictated by a choice procedure that guarantees the correct result every time, but then this may not be the relevant standard by which to judge whether an exercise of practical reasoning is rational or not. What rationality would require, according to the ideal standard Kennedy seems to have in mind, is a choice that a judge would feel compelled to make. The sense of compulsion involved here would approximate the compulsion we might claim to feel when we derive a conclusion from a demonstrative syllogism. Kennedy's account appears to rely on an analogous type of stringent imperative, so that any other standard would result in an arbitrary choice. My example suggests that Kennedy's standard is misplaced in the context of legal reasoning. To avoid the charge of arbitrariness when more than one principle is available, a court simply has to provide reasons for its decision that are neither irrelevant nor utterly beyond the pale. To continue with our hypothetical example, the judge might decide in favour of the plaintiff complaining about his neighbour's stack of leaking oil drums because it is best overall for property owners to refrain from keeping materials or substances on their premises which, if allowed to escape, would interfere with the use or enjoyment of the adjacent property owned by someone else.[89] By contrast, if the court based its decision on the difference in height of the two respective parties and upheld the plaintiff property owner's action merely because he was taller than the defendant, that decision would be purely arbitrary. The grounds for resolving the dispute would be unreasonable. Kennedy's deployment of the scheme of fundamental contradictions would assimilate the latter kind of decision making to the former and label both an exercise in arbitrary reasoning.[90]

The final question to be dealt with in this part of the chapter is the following: does it make sense to see any truth-value in forms of consciousness? Claiming a truth-value for a form of legal consciousness assumes that there is a standard of truth that is both articulable and applicable. In general, critical legal literature is ambiguous about whether claims that purport to match the contents of a consciousness against some social reality can justifiably be made. Vital to the historicist outlook of critical legal studies is the denial of a 'reality' of which consciousness can be more or less perfectly aware. The whole thrust of Kennedy's work on the fundamental contradiction is that nothing exists beyond socially constructed systems of meaning and interpretation. The task set by critical legal studies is to create maps of 'interlocking systems of belief' for the purpose of demonstrating that law is not an autonomous discipline existing apart from other normative structures.[91] In the words of an ethnographer whose work has influenced this strand of critical legal theory, it is through 'the construction of ideologies, schematic images of social order, that man makes himself for better or worse a political animal.'[92] Historicist critical legal writers are suspicious of any attempt to formulate an epistemology based on a realist theory of truth. At its extreme this criticism tends to subvert the very possibility of an epistemological enterprise at all.[93] At best we have a series of discourses or forms of consciousness that can be justified solely on pragmatic grounds. The progress of intellectual insight will occur in the form of a general 'conversation' in which participants will weigh up one another's right to believe and to make justified assertions. There will be no room for recourse to what 'really' exists in order to establish indubitable epistemological claims.

However, there is a competing view within the critical legal movement. Critical legal studies owed its rise in part to dissatisfaction with the failure of liberal legal theory to describe the class-based discrepancies in the way people live in industrial societies.[94] The concept of an immanent critique depends on the critic being able to point out the obvious contradictions between, for example, the promises of equality contained in liberal normative theory and the failure of law to do anything towards the substantial removal of existing bars to such ideals. On this view the form of legal consciousness currently operating has continued to be unaware of the social conditions that would undermine the beliefs, assumptions, and values that compose it. Such consciousness is blatantly false.

It is ironic that both orientations – that which is fearful of the possibility of freezing a 'real' situation by trying to describe it outside the ceaseless flow of history and that which seems to depend on an appeal to the immediate grasp of how consciousness differs from our material conditions – can be found at the centre of early critical legal assumptions about the creation of meaning, the possibility of communication, and the fleeting nature of our categories. On one side, legal consciousness is all there is to 'reality.' On the other, liberal legal consciousness is completely out of touch with reality. Critical legal writers are not alone in facing a serious problem of incoherence. It has afflicted recent controversies in Marxist theories of ideology,[95] and, according to Raymond Geuss, European critical theory is bedeviled by it as well.[96]

Critique of the Theory of Legal Consciousness

One of the central tenets of any critical theory is that it can be used to help members of a society achieve self-knowledge. The point of the theory is not merely to predict that those people will be able to understand themselves. Rather, constructing a critique of legal and political relations will in some logical sense be compelling: it will demand that agents adopt the critical theory and work to transform their society.[97] The job of the critical theorist is to help agents understand, first, what interests it is rational for them to have and, second, how those interests are being denied in their current social milieu. This reflective stage of the critique calls for law's critics to demonstrate that legal concepts and institutions work to 'mystify' what is really happening in a particular society. Ridding the law of its capacity for mystification, for entrenching delusions among the legal élite and all who come in contact with the law, assumes that there is a standard of truth that can be articulated and applied. As argued above, this standard will not resemble that required by a realist epistemology. The mystification to be shed has been described this way: 'Inequalities in access to power are successfully hidden within structures of liberal democracy, constitutionalism, and the rule of law. Inequalities in access to satisfaction of needs are successfully hidden within a flood of consumer products, the availability of stock ownership, welfare supports and other governmental redistributive schemes, and belief in the freedom of opportunity. Class lines are blurred, and struggle is defused or deflected, as most people are unable fully to sense their own objective interests resulting from their objective economic situation.'[98] This description recalls the discussion provided above of the ways in which forms of legal consciousness can be false. The mystification function of law depends on convincing the subordinated classes, through a system of images of legal rights and protections, that it is not worth the struggle to change their situation. The major problem with the imagery of mystification itself is that it assumes people have a set of 'objective' interests that depend on their 'objective economic situation' (determined, as with orthodox Marxism, by membership in a particular economic class). This assumption is difficult to reconcile with the theory of legal consciousness. 'Objective' situations cannot, in these theories, be invoked to prove the falsity of assumptions or beliefs. How an individual chooses to live and the effect of law on his or her choices is largely a question of ideas. The standard of truth to be applied would be a matter of testing how those ideas cohere with other suppositions and inferences that will, for the most part, be derived from social conditioning and intersubjective agreement. With this sort of explanation before us, it begins to seem odd that demystification can be achieved by an individual breaking free of ideological constraints. Without an external standard of truth, or some other justifiable means to verify an idea, the agent is left precisely in the mystified position. Consequently, even if the critical legal theory of consciousness is sustainable, the agent is still no better off than before: there is no standard available by which she can tell whether she has escaped a possibly delusional state.[99]

A second problem with the critique invoking legal consciousness is that, in one version at least, it attributes a dominant ideology to all members of a society, regardless of class. From its inception, critical legal writing held out the promise of universal emancipation. By undermining the unreflective categories and certainties of legal consciousness, critical legal insights were supposed to become available to everyone, regardless of the particular social circumstances of their lives. This universalizing tendency goes against the grain of other movements dedicated to a progressive social change, such as feminism, which have encountered problems with models of justice based on assimilationist or essentialist criteria.[100] One of the blind spots of early critical legal writing was its general failure to comprehend that distinctive social classes, or other groups based on gender or race, adopt ideologies that differ from the dominant consciousness. Critical legal writers tended erroneously to treat as axiomatic the idea that a particular legal consciousness frames the thinking of all types of agents, who also share the same interests. Against this, feminist writers have pointed out that not only do the interests and aspirations of bourgeois men differ from those of poor men and women, but they differ as well from the interests and aspirations of bourgeois women. Feminists have justifiably criticized attempts to base a social or legal theory on allegedly universal conditions that pertain to all individuals in a society.[101] The idea that peculiar forms of consciousness might arise in respect of other salient social divisions should also have been taken into account. In their overriding concern to explain, using a single model, the dynamics of social injustice, early critical legal writers tended to follow their more traditional peers in constructing theories that ignored how characteristics of gender or race might lead to a different consciousness of inequality and lack of power. Just as orthodox Marxist analysis was an attempt by bourgeois men to analyse society from the perspective of the industrial proletariat, early critical legal writers tried to represent the problems of all subordinated individuals in a society as roughly comparable and equally capable of amelioration once critical theory had made inroads.[102] This approach flies in the face of social and political theories that advance competing claims based on conceiving identity and agency in terms of such social divisions as gender, race, or sexual orientation. A single legal consciousness, defined by early critical legal writing as a mechanism to explain the predominance of liberal ways of thinking about legal and political institutions, fails to grasp the way women, for example, look at legal practices differently from men. Women in a particular society have a different understanding of marriage, divorce, childrearing and custody, work inside and outside the home, career, property, participation in public life, physical and psychological security, sexual harassment, representations of women in the media and in art, and freedom to make decisions about matters of intimate concern. A feminist consciousness on each of these dimensions will be woman-centred rather than gender-neutral. Of course, there are differences of view over whether a single version of feminist consciousness adequately captures the multitude of ways that women think about their social life and whether the law contains biases that exclude such thinking.[103] One of the striking features of feminist analysis is the extent to which concepts of consciousness and legal ideology continue to be employed.[104]

From the perspective not only of feminists, but also of those authors who focus on the formative experiences of racial discrimination, the early critical legal account of dominant consciousness is deeply troubling. As pointed out at the beginning of this chapter, the radical critique originally emphasized legal consciousness as a device for explaining the lack of resistance among the subordinated classes to established social and political structures. The imagery of a dominant liberal ideology made it appear as if minority groups had somehow consented to the political practices and institutions that denied them equal treatment. This account will invite objections from minority writers who claim that, rather than a single belief system, there are contrasting forms of consciousness in respect of laws that create or maintain discriminatory effects.[105] The belief system of the élite political groups responsible for making the laws may be quite different from those of the minority groups which have suffered the resulting discrimination. From the point of view of legally disadvantaged minorities, liberal ideology may not be irredeemably flawed, for it has at least provided some scope for the promotion and enlargement of minority individuals' civil liberties.[106]

General theories that universalize political or moral subjects, so that differences among individuals are bracketed for the sake of discovering what is supposed to be in the common good, have become notoriously problematic. One of the central themes of post-structuralist thinking, and one which finds echoes in the work of post-Marxist theorists, is that universal discourses are obsolete.[107] At best, the early critical legal emphasis on forms of legal consciousness offers one of a number of alternative explanatory factors that might be used to explain legal phenomena.

The limits entailed by this recognition are significant. Critical legal accounts would have to abandon the project of analysing legal formations by reference to a single form of consciousness that affects all individuals homogeneously. Radical critics would no longer be entitled to their confidence that an agent's reflective self-understanding would automatically drive her to press for substantial social change. Such confidence would disappear in so far as it reflects a sense that history is the unfolding of a unilinear process with an internal logic of causality and determinism.[108]

One of the primary beliefs inherent in any critical theory is that the ideological world-picture that grips members of a society somehow manages to legitimize oppressive conditions (often called, in the critical legal vernacular, conditions of hierarchy and domination).[109] Here, it is commonly argued that all forms of coercion are illegitimate. The notion of legitimacy used in this context is laden with morally radical connotations. When radical critics suggest that typical patterns of legal reasoning, the rules declared by judges, or the constraints imposed by established legal procedures are all coercive, these practices become part of the ideological scheme that runs counter to the agents' true interests. Moreover, the critique is aimed at showing those agents that such coercion is, in a mysterious sense that we shall examine shortly, self-imposed.

One of the principal problems with this perspective is that it assumes, on behalf of the agents it seeks to liberate, that the ideas or beliefs characterized as false or delusional will upon reflection be unacceptable to those agents. In other words, they could only have adopted such a legal consciousness under coercive conditions. Ordinarily, we would tend to think of such coercion as taking the form of bans on freedom of discussion or criticism. A critical theory would thus have especial relevance to a society in which any opportunities to exchange political views were tightly controlled, either by prohibitions or restrictions. It is a striking feature of early critical legal accounts that they treat all forms of modern governments as equally engaged in exercising and maintaining power through coercion. Because coercion is treated as virtually synonymous with law, these radical critics believe the emancipatory potential of their theory can be fulfilled by reference to any kind of legal regime. Thus, by conceiving of Western democracies as invariably coercive, in the sense that (to use Wythe Holt's terms) 'structures of liberal democracy, constitutionalism, and the rule of law' all contribute to a scheme of the distribution of social and political power, all members of those societies should realize that their form of consciousness must be false.

The critical theory does not leave any room for an agent, once induced to engage in reflection, to deny that coercion ought to be used in this extremely broad sense. Against the pretensions of the critical legal theory based on ideological delusion, it can be argued that an agent should be able to reflect on the institutions that mark her society and conclude that the principles which guide that society are defensible. In critical legal thinking, coercion is treated as tantamount to or even synonymous with domination, and little attempt is made to distinguish justifiable from unjustifiable instances of coercion.[110] Construed this way, legitimation is not a problem to be investigated empirically to discover on what ground a form of domination is maintained or justified. In classic sociological accounts, such as that supplied by Weber, such possible grounds are discussed in light of empirical and historical analysis.[111] By contrast, legitimation in the critical legal sense has been employed without sufficient differentiation.

From the point of view of the radical legal critique, coercion is ever-present, politically problematic, and always pathological. Moreover, the realization, if critical legal accounts were to permit it, that a liberal democracy could still be acceptable to many of its citizens, even after they ponder the meaning of central legal concepts, is an important lesson of reflection. The foundations of both critical theory and critical legal writing have tied reflection closely to social transformation. The latter would be expected to occur once agents are induced to think about their interests and realize the extent to which these have been denied in their current political context. Indeed, there is such a degree of propinquity between reflection and the desire for social change that critical theorists tend to view the relationship as one of logical compulsion. So, for example, according to the radical critique, agents by and large are supposed to be unaware that the basic principles of property law are neither 'natural' nor 'objective' and they must be encouraged to conceive them as artificial or contingent products of social and political processes.[112] Once this insight is achieved, agents will come to view such principles as self-chosen. In the final step of the process of enlightenment agents will decide to change the principles fundamentally to bring them into line with their improved understanding of their real interests. This stirring portrait of the revolutionary potential of ideas is far-fetched. There is no reason to infer that once a citizenry realizes that it makes its own laws it must change them entirely. While a critical theory might inform members of a society that their legal system is flawed, it remains to be seen whether the system will indeed be transformed. The social and political practices underlying legal change require more than recognition of new ideological frameworks.

Another critical legal tack has been to point out the extent to which law involves a dangerous process of reification. As a logical phenomenon, reification has been defined as 'the fallacy of regarding an abstraction as a material thing.'[113] It is a type of category mistake. This seems straightforward until we examine how the process is criticized in radical legal literature. A good example is the claim that a legal rule is a 'series of reified politics.'[114] Here we have a metaphor masquerading as an explanation. On this view the tendency in law to establish some authoritative guideline that leads to like cases being treated alike may be a subversion of political discussion and agreement. 'Reification' here functions pejoratively. The heart of the idea is that we are prone to making category mistakes about legal phenomena. What we thought was a matter of law – a judge, for example, initially setting down or later appealing to the rule that contracts that offend public policy are unenforceable – turns out to be a usurpation of the democratic political process. By including a judge-made rule to govern situations where the basis of the action contains an element of immorality (for example, a suit to recover a gambling debt), the legal system in effect removes the issue from public dispute. But the critique of legal rules in this regard applies to more than the common law practice of establishing and following precedents. It is also a critique of constitutional law-making and the enactment of ordinary legislation.

What this argument misconceives is the role of rules vis-à-vis human activities. Some rules are the outcome of politics: at some stage closure occurs and the discussion is succeeded by a popular decision. Closure is just as authentic an activity as politics itself. It is not a nasty, avoidable corruption of the practice of politics; at some stage discussion must crystallize into decision. This is not to say that every accusation of reification or objectification by critical legal writers is ill-founded; the possibility of mistake they discern is real enough. The threat is most clearly exemplified in the language of rights, where some confusion can result from denoting large areas of human experience as involving a right, the basis, pedigree, or source of which is not always apparent but must be worked out through rigorous philosophical examination.[115] Nevertheless, reification arguments, as illustrated above, are in danger of literalizing metaphorical expressions.

A particularly severe problem in the critical legal account of ideology is how an agent is supposed to step outside a society's dominant legal consciousness. On the one hand, the critical legal account stresses the pervasiveness of the beliefs and assumptions that constitute the governing form. On the other, the mere realization that such elements are social and historical constructions operates to free the individual mind from its intellectual thraldom. The critical legal account also stresses the uniformity of beliefs among both the legal élite and the masses. This general argument can be challenged on the ground that liberal democratic societies are marked not by the blanket effects of a single way of viewing the world, but by plurality and fragmentation. As outlined above, early critical legal thinking ignored the possibility that, contrary to its hypothesis of a dominant consciousness, very few beliefs exert universal influence. Indeed, some sociological observers of Western democracies have claimed that the system of hierarchical domination is in fact maintained by vast diversity among mass consciousness.[116] Few beliefs are shared by all or even most members of a large industrial society. Effective social change is not barred, on this hypothesis, by the pervasiveness of rationalizing and mystifying ideas. Rather, the very heterogeneity of citizens' ideas about politics prevents strong oppositional movements from coalescing.[117] Even if it were plausible to see popular consciousness as essentially uniform, the mere fact of uniformity does not necessarily entail that both lawyers and all other members of a society have thereby been conceptually hobbled. The alleged connection between seeing the world through established legal categories and conceptual blindness is to some extent an exaggeration. If it were literally true, critical legal writers could not warn us about it.

'Consciousness' is a useful explanatory vehicle up to a point, but its literal implications would take us to the very brink of the thesis of ineffability. The problems described above intensify the need for more precise, theoretically acute investigations into the necessary and sufficient conditions for ideas to maintain their hold on those who think about the law. That common ideas or illusions are widespread and tenacious should not be assumed at the outset.

Another significant problem in critical legal theory is the power it ascribes to doctrinal analysis to free mass consciousness from the bonds that restrain it. This theory implies that by engaging in deviationist doctrine, as Unger calls it, our minds will be stretched and our vision of alternative political conceptions sharpened.[118] It makes a modicum of sense to take this view if, by legal consciousness, we mean the kinds of thinking to which legal élites are prone by habituation and indoctrination. The program of purposely engaging in discourse that offends established modes of thought makes less sense if legal consciousness is treated as all-inclusive. The suggestion that all of us, lawyers or not, should alter the way we approach legal doctrine or methods of adjudication is not novel. The critical legal theory of law is unique because it implies that consciousness, right down to the most basic conceptual categories, can be altered simply by our willing it. There is a huge leap from the assumption, justified though it might be, that many of our conceptions are socially conditioned to the claim that those conceptions can, through the mechanism of discussion and decision, deliberately be changed. Missing from this account is any consideration of how the practice of discussion itself is embedded with social conventions and understandings. Again, the problem for the radical, 'total' critique is finding a ground that is not liable to shift under the earnest scepticism that gives the critique its energy.

Although critical legal writers have understandably tried to deflect criticism that their critical theory amounts to a form of philosophical idealism, this charge is not easily evaded.[119] Reassurance that all the ideas necessary for transforming contemporary societies can be found in legal doctrine makes the critique especially vulnerable. First, popular consciousness is unlikely to find such doctrinal arguments accessible. This puts a premium on the revolutionary role of the legal analyst. Owing to the inherent value of widespread participation in defining the practical goals and institutions that should be nurtured, the critical legal emphasis on the lawyerly vanguard is problematic. Second, the claim that current consciousness contains the seeds of its own transformation implies that historical change generally is a totalizing experience. All the changes yet to come are latent in current legal doctrine and practices. This view takes for granted that in some way law is an intelligible whole: even its internal contradictions are necessary for the unfolding of a progressive outcome. In the absence of considerably more justification than we have been given, we are right to be suspicious of such a Hegelian, prefigurative approach. We do not have a vantage point that permits us to judge historical accounts under the aspect of eternity. No matter whether history is viewed as heading towards ultimate salvation or final damnation, the thesis that change is always immanent is extremely contentious.[120] The theory of consciousness would have to be substantially fortified to overcome a considered resistance to the grand claims implicit in this approach.

The hegemonic capacity of legal élites both to induce acceptance and passivity on the part of the masses and to provide the leadership for conceptual revolution was never definitively explored by early critical legal writers.[121] One of the dangers is that by granting such a crucial capacity to those engrossed in the law, the critical legal program breached its own strictures about the necessity and vitality of politics. Claiming that the principles for a better social order can be found entirely within legal discourse comes perilously close to removing the need for consciously making any political choices outside the ideological unmasking of legal doctrine. Far from being democratized, the process of discovering which values ought to count as the most important in a transformed society is already, in some sense, made redundant.[122] How deeply this criticism cuts depends, of course, on whether law is viewed as inimical to politics or as a mode of practising politics. As Chapter 5 of this book attempts to show, there is vacillation on this issue within the movement.

Critical legal theories about inescapable forms of consciousness are also susceptible to erosion by their own sceptical premises. The notion that all ideas are historically contingent can be challenged on the ground that it is self-defeating.[123] For that notion itself must be treated as merely contingent and, for the purposes of philosophical analysis, provisional or heuristic. This means there can be no end to the logical regression into which the critical legal account is in danger of falling. It does not help to point to an imaginary set of conditions under which knowledge is the product of intersubjective agreement by members of a society. When faced with an interpretive task, in which the issue is the best reading to place on legal doctrine, some values must already be available to provide rational support for the interpretation eventually selected. The choice comes down to that between, on the one hand, background values which are in some sense embedded in legal and political practice and, on the other, values that we might guess members of a society would adopt under perfect conditions of unconstrained communication.[124] The critical legal account would dismiss the first option as foreclosed because there are in fact no such shared values, or at least none that have not been corrupted in practice. Yet the alternative, transcendental solution, which is supposed to preserve a serious place for political and moral discussion in assessing what ought to be the shape of legal doctrine, appears too vague to provide any guidance at all. Reaching a counterfactual, ideal consensus depends so much on weighing factors that are specific and local, that it must be questioned whether such adjudication could ever amount to a process of principle. Every result achieved would always be defeasible in the light of changing conceptions of the good: the constructive aims of the process are continually overborne by the critical process.[125]

Conclusion

A major promise of early critical legal studies was that the exposure of liberal ideology in legal doctrine and in the operations of law in ordinary contexts would provoke a transformation of society. In retrospect this promise has proved to be both unduly optimistic as a social theory and weakly defensible in terms of its conceptual foundations. The naturalistic thesis about law, advanced by critical legal writers to explain the compliance of citizens, assumes little capacity or urge for self-reflection and also that all persons, contrary to their 'real' interests, frame the world in more or less the same terms. I have criticized the critical legal approach for failing to recognize that there is no single form of consciousness pervading liberal democracies. Rather, a salient feature of societies such as the United States is the degree of widespread difference in the way that citizens identify their multifarious interests and, in so far as any talk of consciousness makes sense, adopt distinctive modes of consciousness according to circumstances such as gender, ethnicity, race, and other features that have always been present, even if they have only recently gained political currency. Early critical legal writers not only ignored these differentiated forms of consciousness, they excluded the one difference which, given the leftist origins of the critique, might have been expected to occupy the foreground, namely, membership of citizens in different economic and social classes.

The critique predicated on a professional, legal consciousness has also turned out to be of limited utility. Insufficient attention was paid by early radical critics to the issue of how legal ideology, assuming it is formed within the circle of legal experts, spreads throughout society. The primary unexamined assumption in this context is that the critique has wedded itself to an account of ideological formation based on top-down imagery. If my assumption is accurate, then the achievement of social transformation through non-juridified, democratic politics looks remote; indeed, it appears contradictory to the basic premises of the critical project of intellectual emancipation.

In this chapter I have also taken early critical legal literature to task for misunderstanding the relationship between law and coercion in liberal societies. For the purposes of ideology critique, the radical critic is inclined to assume that current ideological traces discernible in the law could only have been adopted under coercive conditions. Reasoning backwards, the critique then tends to characterize the legal system itself as riven with domination and coercion. This conception of coercion is used broadly and loosely. The critique does not explore the possibility that reflection by agents on the underlying principles and actual practices of their legal system would result, not in exposing false consciousness, but in confirming the sense that liberal conceptions of democracy, the rule of law, and rights protection have progressive potential. Just as in Chapter 2 we discovered that critical legal writers underestimated the ability of contemporary liberal theory to respond to a critique alleging faulty metaphysics and an anaemic commitment to social justice, so in this chapter we can see that the radical critique has failed to develop an adequate framework for understanding how competing legal ideals form at least one ingredient in the cement of society.

Throughout this chapter I have drawn parallels between the recent radical legal critique and critical theory as it has evolved since the work of the Frankfurt School. By way of a brief postscript, it may be added that some modern critical theorists have discarded the concept of consciousness in favour of a reinvigorated systems framework for social explanation.[126] The legal system is viewed as interacting with economic, political, and cultural systems, rather than as a secondary source of legitimation and oppression. Among the dangers that systems analysts detect with reference to consciousness are the monocausal method associated with it, as well as its subjectivist premises.[127] For critical legal studies, the notion of an all-encompassing legal consciousness has been shipwrecked and for good reasons largely abandoned. Even if the concept of consciousness continues to be employed for the purpose of illuminating how law operates through a system of ideological images and assumptions, contemporary social research and empirical investigation have failed to resolve serious methodological questions about such inquiries. We still lack exemplary studies that show in what way citizens are passive subjects of legal structures, how legal ideologies are transmitted and reproduced, and how expectations of social transformation can be grounded on more than mechanical assumptions. The projects of critical legal studies remain, at best, programmatic statements, full of moral criticism but lacking the requisite empirical basis and any real resolution.[128]

4

Renovating through Counterpoint: Critical Contract Law

Perhaps the most deeply hidden motive of the person who collects can be described this way: he takes up the struggle against dispersion. Right from the start, the great collector is struck by the confusion, by the scatter, in which the things of the world are found. It is the same spectacle that so preoccupied the men of the Baroque; in particular, the world image of the allegorist cannot be explained apart from the passionate, distraught concern with this spectacle. The allegorist is, as it were, the opposite of the collector. He has given up the attempt to elucidate things through research into their properties and relations. He dislodges things from their context and, from the outset, relies on his profundity to illuminate their meaning.

Walter Benjamin, The Arcades Project

The great preponderance of critical legal writing published since the mid-1970s has not been unduly occupied with attacking legal liberalism on the elevated plane of political or philosophical abstractions. Critical legal authors have tended to concentrate on a task of a different order, which has seen them sift through the mass of governing principles to be found in specific branches of the law. Roughly, the pattern of analysis is that established doctrine is identified, its content is isolated and examined for implicit political or economic assumptions, and finally the doctrine is revealed as ideologically tilted in favour of what Mark Kelman calls its 'core privileged liberal values.'[1] The critical legal goal is – to use an inelegant metaphor – to 'trash' the existing legal literature that supports the principles at the foundations of a legal regime.[2] This chapter presents and assesses examples of the critical procedure as applied to contract doctrine.

Two reasons underlie my choice of critical legal writing on contract law for close inspection. First, previous discussions about the plausibility and implications of radical claims regarding the contradictory texture of legal doctrine have not paid sustained attention to a particular doctrinal area. Andrew Altman, for instance, assesses these radical claims without investigating the roots of the so-called principles or counterprinciples invoked by Duncan Kennedy or Roberto Unger in the history of contract doctrine.[3] On the view I present below, one of the pivotal questions to be asked of critical legal writers is whether their understanding of doctrinal development squares with the legal materials used as the basis of their generalizations. If there is some problem with the portrait they offer, one can expect their theoretical analyses of the subject to be blemished. A second reason for focusing on this area is that contract law offers a wealth of just the type of images critical legal scholarship revels in breaking. For the radical critic, both modern and historical forms of contract doctrine hide the real situations of people, particularly the subordinated and the powerless. According to this account, in the context of describing how the established law handles contractual disputes and contractual planning, the traditional literature tends to reinforce illegitimate hierarchies of authority and power. The assumptions that supposedly inform liberalism, described in Chapter 2, reappear in the principles guiding judges, lawyers, and other participants in the legal process. In the course of this chapter those principles will be made clear in the context of contract doctrine. It will then emerge that critical legal authors favour the adoption of countervailing values in an area where, it is claimed, both the common law and any relevant legislation have been dominated by liberal ideology. The discussion begins by considering the multiple sources of 'doctrine' as the term is used by radical critics. Doctrine is not confined to the currently governing law but covers as well many types of exposition and analysis that allegedly have been infiltrated by liberal modes of thinking.

The critical legal approach to contract law makes sense only when viewed against the background of previous attempts to construct a comprehensive theory of contract principles. One of the fundamental techniques of critical legal thinking is to 'historicize' the subject of inquiry. In this chapter I argue that critical legal writers see themselves as successors to early twentieth-century commentators on the faults of 'classical' contract law and theory – the 'classical' label was applied retrospectively to a particular period of modern legal development. The radical critique to some extent replicates the earlier, legal realist rejection of the main tenets of classicism and formalism. At the same time, critical legal writers have objected to many of the policies and values (such as the facilitation of transactions or encouragement of economic growth) favoured by their realist predecessors. The prevailing judgment within critical legal studies is that, with the demise of any illusions about the applicability of classical theory, modern contract law has reached an impasse. The controlling doctrines are viewed as lacking determinate force and have become so complicated and conflicted as to be incoherent. According to the radical critique, doctrinal indeterminacy and inconsistency undermine the conventional modes of legal argument and judicial decision making. On this sceptical view, these have become exercises that disguise a lack of rational authority. Once unmasked, the process of making and applying contract doctrine is supposed to become more ideologically transparent and more sensitive to inequalities of power. The middle section of this chapter deals with the prescriptions provided by various critical legal writers to resolve the impasse. The strengths and weaknesses of each prescription will be evaluated.

The chapter concludes with a set of reservations about the accuracy and ultimate direction of the critical legal assault on prevailing contract doctrine. Much of the criticism levelled by critical legal writers at classical conceptions of contract theory has been voiced before. Among the weaknesses of the radical contribution to the reinvention of contract law are its arguably tendentious retelling of doctrinal history and its emphasis on the indeterminacy and incoherence of established law. The portrait of a contradictory body of rules suppresses the degree to which some central contract notions, such as fairness, were expunged from certain periods of the evolution of contract concepts. In addition, the allegation that, because of the presence of internal tensions or inconsistent rules or principles, the whole business of legal argument falters, seriously exaggerates the standard of coherence among legal materials appropriate to this area of law. Competing doctrinal principles are not the embarrassing feature claimed by the radical critique; the presence of principles that seem to pull in different directions is in fact necessary to the growth and adaptability of the law. The alleged incoherence does not paralyse the processes of argument and deliberation; rather, it often both animates and frames common law reasoning. The chapter concludes with a sceptical examination of the dangers identified by critical legal theorists.

The body of material at the base of the critical legal characterization of contract doctrine is vast and varied. Just as the notion of legal consciousness has been invoked to help explain the pervasiveness of certain presuppositions and patterns of reasoning, so the concept of doctrine has been used by radical critics to cover many different means of presenting the key ideas of a legal subject.[4] Critical legal writers take into account much more than what courts have declared in judicial opinions arising out of disputes that involve issues traditionally assigned under the head of contract. Their broad sense of doctrine includes other forms of legal discourse as well. The black-letter treatise or the hornbook in contract law, in which an author systematically sets out basic principles and discusses their application in decided or hypothetical cases, is but one example. Others include contract casebooks, historical narratives or analytical treatments of individual topics in textbooks or articles, legislative enactments that alter or augment the common law, and officially sanctioned restatements. This expansive conception of doctrine would probably also include a lawyer's arguments as they appear in a factum or brief, where they are designed to instruct and persuade the court about the relevant principles. It would even embrace letters of opinion a lawyer might render to a client. Though critical legal writers have selected particular doctrines of contract law, such as the doctrine of consideration, for special critical treatment, in general their concern is with all the various forms of legal expression that purport to state what contract law is, to identify its purposes and implications and the policies upon which it rests, and to illuminate the relations among different principles and policies.

This broad scope is required to give the critical legal project the longest reach possible. According to critical legal authors, the covert political message of contract law is present in every one of the forms of discourse described above. Each medium serves to reinforce the root principles of the subject, so that the judge, the lawyer, the legislator, the professor, the business owner or manager, and the student are all operating under the same basic assumptions.[5] In this area we find a number of legal landmarks. First, there is the magisterial attempt to create an internally coherent system of legal thought found in Williston's comprehensive treatise.[6] Second, the prototype of legal casebooks was Langdell's compilation of leading reported cases in contract law.[7] Langdell's use of the case method has exerted a tremendous impact on the way in which several generations of law students in the English-speaking world have learned the rudiments of one of the fundamental subjects taught in the law school.[8] Third, the original *Restatement of Contracts*, sponsored by the American Law Institute, constitutes the paradigmatic attempt in the twentieth century to organize and lay out the constituent principles of an entire doctrinal area, taking into account both reported cases and the advice of acknowledged experts, academic and judicial.[9]

Within these different modes of asserting the underlying principles of contract law arises an interesting uniformity and consistency. In the first place, certain exemplary situations involving exchange transactions with regular legal consequences are described. Present throughout is the assumption that all conceivable factual configurations can be made to fit the model presented. This goal is most transparent in the works of Williston and Langdell, but it occurs to some degree as well in the writing, teaching, and advocacy of many of their successors.

As we shall see, critical legal authors argue that the idealized, classical structure of contract law is an impossible creation, one that failed to encompass even all the data available at its making. The structure was being undermined before the capstone was placed on it. The critical legal challenge of contract doctrine is to a significant degree a reaction against the very hope for the emergence of regulative and determinative legal doctrine. The discussion now turns to the evolution of contract law as it is manifested in the various sources of doctrine described above. It should be stressed that although the description that follows is derived predominantly from the critical legal point of view, in many important respects it overlaps with analyses advanced many years before critical legal studies arrived on the scene.

Critical Legal History of Contract Doctrine

It is crucial to remember at the outset that, in the critical legal scheme for understanding the historical development of a doctrinal area, the principles underlying that area are constantly changing according to the particular conjunction of various social, economic and political forces. Chapter 3, which dealt with legal consciousness, enlarges on the problem of explaining how legal forms correspond with other intellectual and institutional structures. From a critical legal standpoint, the denial of such contingency, however difficult it may be to articulate precisely its nature and operations, is a primary characteristic of modern legal philosophy.

In illuminating the essential features of the different periods into which the history of contract law has been divided, it is useful to consider a couple of examples of possible disputes calling for resolution under the applicable principles of contract. The following hypothetical cases are proposed not because they are in themselves striking or ingenious, but because they contain problems that may be conceived in different ways, depending on the premises of different doctrinal approaches. Reference will be made to one or the other of these cases periodically throughout the remainder of this chapter when clarification of an abstract point would be helpful. Reference to specific examples allows the reader to grasp more easily what is at stake in arguments about which theory should be preferred.

The Case of the Fugitive Rig: A, the lessee of a deep-sea drilling platform used in the North Sea oil fields, has brought the rig into harbour for refitting. One morning the platform slips its moorings and begins to drift further into the harbour basin and towards the only bridge connecting the two halves of the city. In desperation, A requests B, a tugboat owner and salvager, to deploy his tugs and capture the drifting rig. B, who owns most of the working tugs in the harbour that day, stipulates that the price for such an operation will be $500,000. A is shocked by the exorbitant figure, but feels he has no choice in the circumstances. He enlists B's tugs, which succeed in securing the rig and towing it back to safety.

The Case of the Mistaken Bid: A, the owner of a site ready for development, invites bids from general construction contractors. B, one of the bidders, receives bids in turn on different parts of the project from subcontractors and suppliers. These latter bids form the basis of B's proposal to A. B will rely on the lowest bid received on each part of the job. C, an electrical subcontractor, submits a bid to B, but in the process makes an error in calculating the cost of the job. C's bid of $200,000 is too low and C stands to lose $100,000 by carrying out the electrical work. Unaware of the error made by C, B relies on C's bid in the process of winning the competition for the construction contract. C notifies B of the error and indicates that he is withdrawing his bid. B eventually has D, another electrical firm, do the specified job at a cost of $400,000.

With these hypothetical situations to refer to, we can turn to discovering the process of change in fundamental concepts of contract law, especially as they have been characterized in the critical legal account.

The critical legal discussion of the historical background of contemporary contract doctrine reaches beyond the U.S. legal realists and past the grand synthesizers of contract law to eighteenth- and nineteenth-century conceptions of the basis of the institution of contract. In the critical legal account of the development of contract law, any events earlier than the final quarter of the eighteenth century tend to be ignored. The starting point is generally around the time of the Revolutionary War in the United States or the publication in England of Blackstone's *Commentaries*.[10] Further, the doctrinal events that attract the attention of critical legal writers occurred in the United States. The primary historical issue is how indigenous American legal concepts were derived from traditional English contract principles. This concentration is indicative of the basic orientation throughout the critical legal examination of doctrinal development. By contract law the critical legal expositor is inclined to mean contract law as evolved or evolving in one or more of the U.S. jurisdictions. We still await a full-blown comparative treatment of contract law from the critical legal perspective.[11]

On the critical legal account, two significant, different trends emerged in the late eighteenth and early nineteenth centuries. Both stand in contrast to the classical theory that arose subsequently. First, there was a gradual surrender of the tenets originally derived from feudal law. The importance of status or role in a hierarchical social system as the defining element in the duties and rights attached to each individual was diminished.[12] Instead, the law evolved to a point where it was taken for granted that individuals had some choice, making due allowance for interest, effort, and capabilities, in determining their role in a capitalist economy. Feinman has described in general terms the legal position prior to this shift: 'In the eighteenth century image, contractual liability was not sharply differentiated from liability arising out of nonconsensual situations, such as injury (tort) or status relations. Contractual obligation arose not solely or even principally from agreement, but from implied community standards of behavior.'[13] The standards to which Feinman refers were often determined and applied by lay juries rather than trained judges. The result was that eighteenth-century contract law evinced an anti-commercial bias.[14] The paternalism marking this system meant that juries would impose duties of good faith on parties in the negotiation of contracts. In the case of oppressive bargains, juries could refuse enforcement.[15] In determining the amount of damages to be awarded against an overreaching party, the jury was not bound to redress lost expectations resulting from the breach; the usual measure was instead the actual losses of the innocent party. The aim was thus to prevent unjust enrichment rather than to compensate a commercial party for consequential losses.[16] In this period the application of law need not be separated from considerations of morality. The jury could always bring its sense of fairness directly into play without being hampered by strict legal rules. The presence of custom was an effective counterforce to law.

A second significant pre-classical feature associated with the period around the beginning of the nineteenth century was the rise of a theory of contractual liability based on the intention of the parties. In particular, the focus of the courts was on the parties' actual states of mind at the moment of entering into the bargain. This development was arguably foreshadowed in Lord Mansfield's view that the purpose of consideration in the scheme of contract liability was primarily evidentiary.[17] Added to judicial anticipation of the 'subjective' or 'will' theory was the later fully fledged jurisprudential view represented by such continental writers as von Jhering and Savigny.[18] This account gave primacy to the individual will, so that the institution of contract was conceived as a matter of inward agreement or a 'meeting of minds.'[19] Both parties must at the relevant moment of contract formation have mentally assented in fact; mere mutual outward expressions of assent would not be sufficient for the contract to be enforceable later on.[20]

What has been called classical theory, by critical legal and other writers alike, departs from the both the paternalist and the will theories of contractual obligation. The key premises on which classical theory was built relate to the importance of consent, the standards of behaviour expected from contracting parties, the role of the jury in calculating damages, and the rise of the commercial contract as the norm.[21] When Gilmore wrote of the death of contract, he was referring to a general legal regime like that associated with classical theory.[22]

The growth of classical theory was motivated by the search for the essential elements of every valid contract. An adequate theory would have to specify whether a contract had been formed and, in the event of non-performance, what the legal consequences would be. A 'controlling paradigm' was fabricated.[23] Critical legal writers unanimously emphasize the political and economic assumptions that supported the theory. A representative summary of those assumptions is contained in the following quotation: 'Classical contract conceived of contract as a field of private ordering in which parties created their own law by agreement ... This notion of consent was grounded in a conception of the social world as composed of independent, freedom-seeking individuals, each of whom avidly pursued his own self-interest. Courts, accordingly, were to enforce the rights created by the parties' contracts and to refrain from imposing obligation where it had not been assumed.'[24] This description, based on the prevalence of individualist political values and reflecting the critique of legal liberalism dealt with at length in Chapter 2, is not unique to critical legal studies. Adherents of classical theory themselves frequently used similar terms to explain the foundations of their theory construction. Williston and Pound, for example, both acknowledged this background,[25] and the point was not lost on some early twentieth-century critics of the classical theory who, on this issue at least, did not want to give up the fundamental principle of 'private autonomy.' Thus, 'when a court enforces a promise it is merely arming with legal sanction a rule or *lex* previously established by the party himself.'[26] As stressed in Chapter 2, one should, of course, be cautious about automatically assimilating metaphysical theses of individualism or atomism and ethical theories of personal conscience or autonomy. Notwithstanding this reservation, in contract law as in other doctrinal areas, the critical legal approach has been to construe the ethical point of view founded on personal autonomy as a quintessentially liberal position, and to argue that it is in fundamental opposition to competing ethical positions based on community or solidarity.

The last quotation above, drawn from Fuller, appears to endorse the will theory of the early nineteenth century. In fact, in order to accommodate those instances where a contract was found to subsist, even though the parties might never have put their minds to a particular term or condition, both courts and commentators were forced to develop an 'objective' theory of contractual liability. The touchstone of this approach was not the actual mental assent of each party, for under that interpretation a party could successfully avoid a contract by privately expressing a mental reservation. Instead, the courts proceeded to consider, as one step in their inquiry, what would have been reasonable, in view of the circumstances proved in evidence, to infer about each party's promise. In the case where one party claims that a mistake had been made and, on equitable grounds, the contract should therefore not be enforced, the court will be obliged to ascertain the most reasonable interpretation of each party's respective conduct towards the other.[27] The subjective theory, with its rhetoric of the necessity of a 'meeting of minds,' also failed to reflect those types of contract in which the parties cannot plausibly be seen as legislating for themselves. By the early nineteenth century, employment law had already developed to the stage where no real bargain was negotiated between employer and labourer. Certain rights and duties were involved in the relationship that attached generally to cases of employment regardless of the state of mind of the particular parties at the time of hiring.[28]

The emphasis on individualism as the conceptual foundation for the doctrines of contract law is integrated by critical legal authors into a larger picture of the political and economic ideologies that gripped judges and commentators during the high tide of nineteenth-century classical theory. Critical legal writers have stressed repeatedly the connection between the assumptions of the classical contract model and the reigning system of laissez-faire economic thinking and utilitarian politics.[29] This purported connection is treated as more than a simple historical accident. The one is supposed to be entailed by the other, or at least the imperatives of capital accumulation required a judicial rationalization that incorporated individualist premises.[30] Hence we witness the courts' increasing reliance in the nineteenth century on rhetoric extolling the freedom of the individual (or of the business firm) to enter into bargains with other free and equal individuals or enterprises.

The classical conception of contractual freedom has three dimensions. First, the individual would ideally be able to contract with any other individual. Therefore constraints on economic conduct, such as state regulation of monopoly practices or agreements in restraint of trade, should be kept to a minimum. Second, the parties to a contract ought to be able, through bargaining, to settle upon the terms that will govern their relationship. The fairness of the exchange, for example, should ordinarily not be reviewable by the courts. Finally, no individual party should have foisted on it a relationship to which it had not consented. In other words, freedom from contract is as important as freedom to contract.[31] The doctrine of consideration was in part designed to ensure that only those promises which involve a bargain or exchange of real economic value ought to be enforced. In this way a connection is drawn between the assumed self-seeking interest of every contracting party and the need to prove some form of consideration.[32] The ideology of freedom in this context is part of a more general intellectual concern during the latter half of the nineteenth century about the liberty of the individual subject in a democratic state.[33] U.S. constitutional decisions such as *Lochner* struck the major chord of the era.[34] As we shall see, a central part of the reaction against the classical model of contract concerns involved this interpretation of autonomous conduct in a market economy where a priori reasoning about the relative equality of each potential contractor is really no more than a pious wish.

In a typical contractual transaction the two parties would create their bargain by making promises of future performance to each other and would set such terms as courts would not lightly disturb. The parties would thus contribute to the working of competitive markets and to an expanding economy. The classical theory took as its model contract, then, the purely executory bargain, where breach involves the failure by one party to perform its promise. The other party is envisioned as capable of going to court and asking for damages that make up the loss in the gains it expected to accrue from the contract.[35] By leaving it to the individual parties to plan their own business affairs, the state would not be responsible for determining how resources should be distributed within a particular society. In elucidating a body of coherent and logical doctrine, the courts were expected to facilitate planning and protect the security of transactions already undertaken.[36] The distinctive style of judicial reasoning thus required by the classical theory was one based on a developed set of clear rules that could be derived from the logic of the contractual relationship. Subsequent or potential disputes were resolvable simply by deducing what legal consequences flowed from the classical model as elaborated by courts in the form of settled rules. This is the essence of the 'formalist' approach, brought to its highest pitch in Williston's treatise.[37]

The nineteenth century also witnessed the removal from the jury of the power to set contractual damages. This task was assumed by judges. Again, the rationale for this development is found in the principle that the legal consequences of transactions should be predictable. Commercial parties could then make a reasonable calculation of all relevant risks. A judicially established rule limited the amount of damages awarded in the event of breach to an amount that covered those losses within the reasonable contemplation of the parties at the time the contract was formed.[38] Richard Danzig's book, for example, holds that this development illustrates how contract law itself became a standardized product, rationalized and marketed, and distinguishable from the 'hand-crafted' justice of the previous century.[39]

The result of these efforts to devise a comprehensive model against which all transactions could be compared was that the social and economic bases of contract law were largely forgotten or ignored. The classical theory was elevated to such an abstract form that its definitions ceased to reflect the nuances and variety of actual social and business transactions. The construct of a bilateral executory agreement, which raised expectations in each party about the benefits to be gained, became the Procrustean bed for assigning liability and distributing losses in all contractual disputes. Williston had occasionally adverted to the basis of liability as found in 'reasons of policy and justice,' which might have little to do with the professed intentions of the parties to a contract.[40] Furthermore, he was willing to concede that promissory principles were not the only possible way of conceiving how contracts are formed and enforced.[41] But in the main, for his immediate successors as well as contemporary radical critics, the pure classical system, balanced in structure and with strong lines demarcating contract from all other kinds of legal liability, is designed to marginalize any principles that do not fit within Williston's plan. Williston defined a contract as: '... a promise, or set of promises, for breach of which the law gives a remedy, or the performance of which the law in some way recognizes as a duty.'[42] Thereafter, all relationships not fitting this mould were treated as in some way pathological and difficult to deal with logically. It was remarked by early twentieth-century commentators that missing from the classical account is a vital historical or sociological element that would reaffirm the basis of contractual doctrine in the variety of transactions that parties actually undertake.[43]

The implications of the abstract classical theory and the doctrines developed in light of it may be disclosed by examining the hypothetical cases sketched earlier in this chapter. In the case of the Fugitive Rig, where a defendant might resist paying a clearly exorbitant charge for assistance in circumstances of necessity, the contract could be upset in court even on classical principles. There is little evidence of a specific principle in any era of the common law that a bargain must involve a fair exchange of economic values.[44] Nevertheless, and this is especially important when juries participated to some degree in setting damages, there is a strand of authority justifying a court to refuse to enforce a bargain that is grossly unfair. The precedents accumulated on this score are usually grouped under the heads of duress, fraud, or unconscionability. In the case of the Fugitive Rig, given our understanding of the interpenetration of moral and legal principles in pre-classical contract law, it would be easy to imagine a result whereby the owner of the tugs was denied the benefit of the full contract price. Prior to the nineteenth century, there was no overriding principle of freedom of contract to protect the integrity of the bargain struck by A and B. This result need not have been justified on the ground that A's consent to the contract price of $500,000 for B's services was somehow vitiated by the extraordinary peril presented by the escape of A's platform. Consent would arise as the principal issue only after classical theory had made it a necessary condition of all valid contracts.

According to the strict tenets of classical theory, A's promise to pay $500,000 to B is at least prima facie enforceable, assuming all necessary formalities have been satisfied. It is difficult to claim that A had no choice whether to enter into the bargain. It is conceivable that A could have rejected B's offer as too high, let the rig continue to drift, and incurred responsibility for the destruction caused thereafter. One of the goals of classical doctrine was to preserve such realms of choice and to reward those parties whose foresight leads them to take adequate precautions against potentially costly events. By enforcing the actual deal that A and B reached, contract doctrine would serve its purpose of informing other business operators about the legal risks inherent in certain activities and the steps that should be taken to shield the viability of the enterprise.[45] This sort of reasoning is consistent with classical theory at least – actual developed doctrine is another matter. Operating under the assumption that in the circumstances illustrated by the Fugitive Rig, the consent given by A could not have been truly voluntary, even courts in the heyday of classical theory excused the promisor from the obligation to pay the whole contract price. Instead, the courts tended to substitute a figure they judged to be reasonable in light of evidence about normal markets.[46]

The case of the Mistaken Bid exhibits no similar qualification to the stringent terms of classical theory. On the traditional analysis given by courts and treatise writers C, the subcontractor, is entitled to withdraw the bid for electrical work at any time until B, the general contractor, actually accepts C's bid. This would be the result even after B had relied on C's bid in making a play for the prime contract. In the circumstances described in our hypothetical situation, C's revocation would leave B responsible for the difference between C's mistakenly low bid and whatever it costs to have another subcontractor perform the electrical work. This legal result is consistent with classical theory's assumptions about the necessity for an agreement between the contracting parties. The fact of B's reliance on C's offer will make no difference to a court which adheres to the concept of mutual assent leading to a contract coming into existence at a precise moment. Judicial expression of the lack of a contract between B and C can be found in Judge Learned Hand's opinion in the 1933 case of *James Baird Co. v. Gimbel Bros., Inc.*[47]

Classical contract doctrine in cases such as this, where one party acts under the assumption that a contract has been or is capable of being formed on certain terms, is often analysed in terms of rules of offer and acceptance. The image of two parties engaged in preliminary haggling and then one making a specific offer that the other accepts, thus clinching the deal, has traditionally been among the first scenarios encountered in contract law courses. It forms one of the key building blocks in the classical structure. The following section reveals the deep dissatisfaction felt by contract scholars with this image, among others. By all rights, the criticism is so strong that the classical edifice should have crumbled from repeated assaults. After examining how classical theory has been qualified or repudiated, we will consider the possible explanations for that theory's continued influence on the work of judges and academics. The subsequent discussion will uncover the most significant issues dividing critical legal writers from other post-classical critics of conventional contract theory and doctrine.

Many factors contributed to the erosion of the classical system. At the level of received doctrine, it was noticeable by the time Williston finished his prodigious labours that his presentation of 'fundamental principles' was sprinkled with exceptions that made the projected task of devising a coherent account of those principles' 'wide range of application' impossible.[48] The attack on the purity and consistency of the classical system came from two directions simultaneously. Judges had decided contract cases in many instances by invoking doctrines that were incompatible with classical principles. These cases were so numerous that they could no longer be treated as anomalies or isolated instances of wrong-headed or anachronistic reasoning. Second, academic writers began to challenge the very underpinnings of classical contract theory. They questioned ultimately whether a single model of contract could possibly serve the purpose of guiding courts to assessments of contractual liability. Out of this two-pronged challenge grew strategies to replace the formalism associated with the classical doctrine. Critical legal writing on contract law shares the doubts expressed earlier in the twentieth century about the value of a uniform classical model. It has some trouble, however, with many of the doctrines, principles, and policies that have been suggested to replace that model. This part of the chapter describes the grounds on which classical contract law has been rejected by many analysts. It also deals with attempts to reconcile the traditional body of doctrine with more modern trends in contract thinking.

The first important recognition was that the principle of freedom of contract is not sanctified. The very process by which courts enforce some types of agreements and refuse to enforce others, in the latter case notwithstanding perhaps the parties' original intentions, shows that other principles compete with the idea of freedom of contract. Conjoining the ideal of freedom with the concept of contract does not, in one view, lead to any sort of indubitable axiom: '... "contract" is an instrument, not a value in itself, while "freedom" is a thing intrinsically desirable. It does not quite follow that the two are always bound in an indissoluble union.'[49] It has even been claimed that courts have extolled the principle of contractual freedom because they are emotionally bound to it. This attitude was supposed to constitute 'the main obstacle to progress' in developing a common law of contract that takes seriously the social and economic implications of established doctrine.[50] The work by Fuller, in which he demonstrated how the classical model's preference for expectancy rights was only one of several possible choices, each of which reflects a different economic policy, constituted a large step towards undermining the alleged evenhandedness of the law's intervention into private bargains.[51] Mere appeals to the inviolability of property rights or of freedom of contract (which in such appeals were often yoked together as coequal basic principles) fall flat unless more specific reasons of economic policy can be given to justify a particular legal result.[52] The classical picture of the private individual trying to engage in business and contribute to the common good by pursuing self-interested goals as free as possible from state regulation is not the sole ideal available, even for a commercially minded society. The dichotomy between private autonomy and collective control is misleading as a description of competing values if, as in the classical model, the principles are stacked so as to favour one side. The enforcement of private bargains by the machinery of the state meant that there is inevitably a public aspect to settling contract disputes and making the market work. Thus, the brave invocation of individualism as among the root principles of classical theory is (and always was, according to critical legal authors) a piece of sleight-of-hand.[53] The vaunted 'socialization' of contract law in the twentieth century was a response to the imbalance of doctrine evolved under the influence of classical theory.[54]

One of the fundamental principles of classical doctrine was therefore viewed as distorting the role and purpose of a system for legally enforcing contracts. The next challenge against the classical system arose from the realization that the assumptions about social and political life embedded in that system clashed dramatically with the actual circumstances in which contracts were used. While the classical theorist assumed that individuals were relatively equal in bargaining power, in initial resources, and in the capacity for forming rational preferences in their own self-interest, legal writers continually pointed out that these assumptions misdescribed actual human behaviour. Although the gap between what is assumed for the purposes of the theory and what is real could presumably have been demonstrated by examining social scientific data, what brought the point fully home to the anti-classical legal writers were such phenomena as the adhesion contract. This kind of standard-form contract arises where one party, usually a consumer, is presented with stipulated terms and little opportunity to negotiate any variation on them. Classical contract principles were either unhelpful or positively obstructive in formulating an adequate legal response to the proliferation of such business techniques. Instead of reflecting a perfectly competitive market in which all participants have more or less the same economic power: '[t]he essence of the adhesion contract is ... the fact that one of the parties has, at least for the purpose of the transaction in question, some of the powers of a monopolist.'[55]

Emphasis on industrial integration in twentieth-century business life in Western societies has led to broad generalizations about current doctrine as reflective of 'monopoly capitalism' as against the 'free-market capitalism' of classical legal mythology.[56] In other words, the ideal of competition has been subordinated to the goal of industry-wide planning in pursuit of economic stability and self-preservation. The actors in such a scenario include unions as well as substantial industrial firms. This development led one commentator, Clyde Summers, to see in collective labour relations the prime contemporary model of contractualism, a model that uses criteria that deviate significantly from the underlying assumptions of classical theory.[57] What has traditionally passed for basic contract law, that is, classical doctrine, has minimal relevance in the context of organized labour. Paradoxically, in Summers's view, only examination of those areas of bargaining and agreement traditionally excluded from 'pure' contract law allows any real sense of what is essential in contract doctrine to become clear.[58]

Summers's call for broader investigation into the actual forms contracts take, rather than the abstract requirements of a possible contract, finds echoes in other writing of the post-classical period. Of particular interest on this score are the attempts to study empirically the functions of contractual rules and the role of law in the conduct of particular businesses. Examples include Schultz's report on current attitudes within the Chicago construction industry in respect of certain bidding practices and legal rules;[59] Macaulay's sociological work on the automobile industry and relations between manufacturers and dealers;[60] and British studies of the role of legal remedies in business planning and the same firm offer problem studied by Schultz.[61] The general conclusion of these various studies belies some of the key assumptions of classical doctrine. As mentioned above, it is crucial to the classical view that the rules of contract law are necessary for economic transactions to flourish in modern Western economies. In contrast with this view, as Macaulay points out: 'The studies as a whole show that the *empirical* picture of the contract process in capitalist societies differs sharply from the classical model. Planning for the risk of nonperformance is none too careful, and disputes are seldom resolved by litigation or even by applying the norms of contract law outside of litigation.'[62]

The upshot of these empirical inquiries was portended a generation earlier by writers dissatisfied with the abstract ideals of the classical theory. Corbin, for example, reporting on the state of contract law in the 1930s, sought to emphasize that doctrine must have its basis in what people do: 'Each statement of a "rule" of law is a generalization drawn from this seething, pulsing background of life.'[63] Llewellyn, with his instinct for surmising commercial realities, concluded that the law of offer and acceptance, the cornerstone of Williston's structure, was of only marginal importance since: '... in the great bulk of transactions not carefully held unclosed until the final papers are signed, men do not know rules or consult lawyers, but go ahead and then (in the cases threatening litigation), change their minds or become dissatisfied with results, and consult a lawyer only to see whether he can – under the rules – get them out. That is: they are not much guided in their "operative" action by the rules.'[64] This cautionary generalization is in line with Llewellyn's proposal that we 're-canvass the *life-situation*' in order to construct a more meaningful law of contracts.[65] The advice has since been repeated by various writers, some within the critical legal studies movement and others outside it.[66]

A last recourse of those writers who remain more or less sympathetic to the classical project of a general, formal law of contractual liability has been to distinguish between 'core' principles of contract theory and the actual application of those principles in specific doctrinal areas. This describes in outline the method followed by Charles Fried, who has adumbrated a model of contract that retains at its foundation the idea that contract and promise are conceptually intertwined (the promissory principle).[67] Fried's approach must deal with the problem of how to incorporate a large body of case law that is plainly based on reliance or restitutionary principles into a system of promissory obligation. The strategy he pursues is essentially that of reclassifying awkward data. Reliance cases, for example, will not embarrass his conceptual scheme if they are assigned to the domain of tort law.[68] A more intractable problem arises out of the cases traditionally conceived of as matters involving mistake or frustration. Such cases are not so easily disposed of through reclassification. Fried has conceded that these are matters of genuinely contractual resolution, but argues nevertheless that in such cases the courts merely construe terms of the contract that the parties did not expressly deal with in coming to their agreement.[69] Fried's arguments have not commanded broad agreement among those writers unsympathetic to classical theory.[70] For critical legal writers, in particular, his scheme represents a throwback to the Willistonian enterprise of constructing a model which gives the illusion that settled formal rules can, for the most part, provide the solution to any dispute, with only a minor amount of interstitial discussion required about competing social, economic, or ethical policies.

One of the tangible results of the U.S. legal realist assault on the classical theory was the eventual adoption of the Uniform Commercial Code (U.C.C.).[71] This enactment, strongly identified with Llewellyn's influential views on commercial law, is a prime example of how the common law of contracts has been altered in direct opposition to classical doctrine. In particular, the scope permitted in the Code for appeals to standards of commercial practice represents a significant departure from the idea that individual private citizens can always legislate for themselves, regardless of the customary context that surrounded their transaction.[72]

The most significant evidence that the classical system has been shaken, however, comes from exploring the case law for instances of a court limiting or extending liability on the basis of doctrines not easily comprehended by classical theory. These cases can be grouped under the doctrinal categories of reliance-based protection, promissory estoppel, unconscionability, duress, and standards of good faith and fair dealing. In each area judicial developments in U.S. jurisdictions, at least, have reconfirmed the demise of classical theory.

The work by Fuller and Perdue pushed into the foreground a group of cases in which courts consciously abandoned their traditional position of awarding damages that reflected the expectation interest of the non-defaulting party.[73] The tendency of courts to gauge the plaintiff's loss on the basis of what was lost by way of profit because of the defendant's overreaching was, as Fuller stressed, not a 'natural datum.' It was a product of specific normative choices made by courts and theorists. In this area, as in other aspects of legal doctrine, 'it would be quite possible to reverse our conceptions in this connection of what is normal and what is anomalous, without doing any violence to the rules which ultimately determine what contracts are to be enforced.'[74] A theory of recovery based overtly on reliance, as opposed to expectation, might in some types of cases achieve the 'most equitable compromise of the interests involved.'[75] This would be especially appropriate where the parties to a contract are not trying to make the ultimate deal with each other, but instead are 'participants in a common adventure' where it is not obvious that one party should have its economic interest protected at the full expense of the other.[76] At any rate, the reliance approach, as initially systematized by Fuller and Perdue, manages to bring into the open significant questions of social policy and distributive justice that had been muted during the ascendancy of classical doctrine.[77]

The enlarged role for the doctrine of promissory estoppel offers a second area in which to study the way in which classical conceptions of contract have been whittled down by judicial innovation. As discussed above in connection with the case of the Mistaken Bid, classical notions of revocability would protect C, the subcontractor, in the event of a suit launched by B, the general contractor. In the United States this situation has been modified through the application of the idea of promissory estoppel. Intimations that the doctrine should be strengthened were recorded in light of a thoughtful analysis of the subsisting rule on firm offers (which was applied in the *Baird* case).[78] The judgment that promissory estoppel should be actionable in the case of the Mistaken Bid was based not on a classical dogma about the necessity for consideration to support a business promise, but rather on a 'great complex of evaluations, psychological, moral, commercial, political, [and] ideological.'[79] The decisive turn in the law of promissory estoppel was achieved by Judge Traynor's decision in *Drennan v. Star Paving Co.*[80] The subcontractor's bid in that case was held to be irrevocable until the general contractor had a reasonable opportunity to accept that bid after being awarded the prime contract. Once B, in our hypothetical case, had relied on C's offer, in the form of a bid, to make a proposal for the construction contract, C was obliged to keep his offer open until B could accept it and create a bilateral contract. The remedy to be awarded in cases where the subcontractor refuses to perform could be damages calculated according to several different formulas. In *Drennan* the subcontractor was held liable for the difference between its bid and the price the general had to pay another subcontractor to do the job. Applying such a measure in our hypothetical case, C would be liable for damages in the amount of

$200,000. This is probably an expectation measure. If the next lowest bidder after C had submitted a figure of $350,000, then regardless of whether B had eventually to pay $400,000 for the job to be performed, the reliance measure of damages would be $150,000.

The doctrine of promissory estoppel is not so robust in jurisdictions outside the United States. In England and in Canada, for instance, the general judicial position is that promissory estoppel cannot be pleaded as a cause of action, though it can be invoked as a defence to a suit on a contract.[81] The U.S. solution found in *Drennan* shows that the court will not insist that a contract must already be in existence for the doctrine to operate: the court is protecting the reliance interests of contracting parties during the negotiating period. This approach cuts a wide swath through the carefully tended classical conception of the model bilateral, executory contract under which no liability arises either before the contract is formed or unless a promise sued upon has been supported by some form of consideration.

According to the most detailed studies into the history of the modern application of promissory estoppel, especially in light of the inclusion of this concept in section 90 of the first *Restatement,* the courts have been rather confused about the elements that must be proved to sustain an action based on promissory estoppel.[82] There is no question that U.S. judges have realized that the doctrine applies to bargain transactions as well as to traditionally limited classes of gratuitous promises. Nevertheless – and this point will be significant in our later examination of the critical legal view about the tenacity of classical assumptions in contract doctrine – it has been noted that there is a 'disposition to treat action in reliance as proof of bargain rather than as an independent basis of enforcement.'[83] The doctrine of promissory estoppel thus tends to be run together with requirements of consideration without judges grasping that these two doctrines rest upon separate theoretical foundations. This conflation has serious consequences when a court is faced with applying the doctrine despite failure by the parties to satisfy the writing requirement under the Statute of Frauds.[84] Moreover, courts have apparently betrayed their uneasiness about the precise status of promissory estoppel by failing to arrive at a consistent approach to the question of the appropriate measure of damages where a case of promissory estoppel has been made out.[85]

The third doctrinal area that shows a marked departure from classical theory involves the defences of fraud, unconscionability, and duress. Arthur Leff has usefully distinguished the instances of 'procedural' unconscionability from 'substantive' unconscionability.[86] The purpose of the doctrine of unconscionability is to allow the courts, as agents of the state, to attempt to correct the imperfections of economic markets. This is a normatively defined role for judges. That is, they are not neutral in going about their task of revising bargains entered into by capable individuals.[87] Judges' politically charged role naturally irritates defenders of the classical notion that only procedurally defective bargains should be reviewable by the courts. This fits with the cardinal idea that lack of genuine consent vitiates a bargain. Substantive unconscionability, by contrast, is liable to turn courts into 'roving commissions' empowered to police the fairness of exchanges,[88] a result that would offend the classical principle of freedom of contract. In response, Leff would probably have argued that, first, the scope of the doctrine of substantive unconscionability depends very much on how it was defined in the U.C.C., and second, the individual cases where courts have refused to enforce a bargain because of substantive unconscionability will tend to have only a 'trivial impact' anyway.[89]

Alongside unconscionability, the doctrine of duress has been expanded to include cases which, under classical doctrine, did not negate the quality of a party's assent to a bargain. Academic discussion justifying this expanded doctrine has concentrated in particular on showing that economic duress should lead to the same legal result as physical duress.[90] Such an approach would be anathema to the classical conception that individuals must generally be held to their bargains regardless of market pressures at the time the bargain was made. Under this scheme, the market is the indicator of the true values to be assigned to promises, and ordinarily courts should resist the temptation to interfere with what the market has wrought. Exceptions should only be made where one party has overpowered the will of the other by, for example, unlawful threats of violence. Commentators such as Dalzell have parried this argument by claiming that situations of economic duress in fact reveal examples of the most genuine consent.[91] The real basis of the doctrine of duress should not be the criminal or tortious threats of the promisee, but rather the fact that the promisee has been unjustly enriched at the expense of the promisor owing, for example, to the promisee's markedly superior bargaining power.[92] These criteria invite the explicit discussion of ethical and economic policy issues that go far beyond the apparently factual issue of the nature of the promisor's consent. Such a novel approach to duress thus broadly conforms with the other reliance- and restitutionary-based doctrines discussed above.[93] As with the shift in the judicial understanding of unconscionability, this new trend in the doctrine of duress remains subject to criticism from writers who harbour a residual belief in the value of the classical model. Rather than concede that economic duress is a simple extension of the common law concept of duress, Epstein, for example, has claimed that the innovation is a 'repudiation' of the previous line of authority.[94]

Another aspect of the classical theory that has come under attack is the emphasis it places on understanding contractual relations as essentially single-shot transactions in which the contracting parties have no interest in common other than the benefits to be gained on each side from the performance of the other side's promise. This is not a recent recognition, though it has been systematically exploited as suggesting a counter-vision of the nature of commercial relationships. In the 1930s it had already dawned on Gardner and Llewellyn that policies of economic and social justice competed with classical principles such as freedom of contract. The point of contract doctrine ought to be to provide '... means for conducting a cooperative commonwealth on a voluntary basis, of reconciling group industry and economic justice with individual freedom and responsibility for results.'[95] Around the same time, Llewellyn was emphasizing that the growth of the credit economy, and the commensurate importance placed on reliance on promises that did not necessarily fit comfortably into the traditional schema of offer and acceptance, was accompanied by the emergence of a social structure that involved 'household units, groups, and classes' entering into deals. The single individual as the archetypal party to a contract was a 'vicious heritage' from classical theory.[96] The 'increasing interdependence among the members of society' was also noted by Fuller, who concluded that the rules of contract, such as the doctrine of consideration, had to be changed in response to social evolution.[97]

These themes provided the seeds for the later systematic treatment of contract law as essentially a relational, rather than a transactional, institution. The relational approach has been extended furthest by Ian Macneil, who incorporates the lessons drawn from the realists with the empirical pictures developed by investigators such as Macaulay. Instead of acceding to the classical view of contract as a locus of intense individual competition with the principal goal of achieving the best bargain possible, Macneil's model stresses the cooperation and trust which every contractual relationship involves at some level. Moreover, on his view contracting parties are not oblivious to the future, in terms either of the contract's performance or of the possibility of further exchanges with the same contracting party. Like Macaulay, Macneil accords due weight in this relational conception to non-legal sanctions in the context of contractual behaviour.[98] Recognizing how contracts actually arise and function would require a drastic revision of the economic and social presuppositions of classical theory. It would issue in new doctrines and new methods of teaching contract law.[99] The relational approach holds some attraction for the critical legal writer on contract law, who views it as a positive advance on both classical theory, shaped as it was by the pre-eminent values of individualism, and on the unsystematic insights of the legal realists, who did not follow up their observations with any attempt to uproot the deepest foundations of classical doctrine.

Post-classical Analysis versus the Radical Critique

The preceding remarks suggest several serious difficulties, from the critical legal point of view, with the contemporary state of contract law and theory. The single most formidable issue has been how to reconcile the inherited case law, which depends for its legitimacy on the kind of theory that guided Williston, with post-classical developments that con-sciously depart from that theory. The differences between the classical and post-classical theories have been exploited by critical legal writers to demonstrate both the incoherence of current contract doctrine and the inability of mainstream theories (dependent as they are on liberal pre-suppositions about social and political institutions) to transcend that incoherence.

According to the radical critics, the recurrent problem of incoherence cuts across any efforts to make existing legal materials intelligible. It vitally affects the work of the law teacher who must draw up a syllabus for a contracts course. It also presses on the lawyer who is obliged to present arguments in particular disputes about the existence or interpretation of an agreement. It vexes the judge who must decide whether an agree-ment is enforceable and, if it is, on what basis and with what remedial consequences. And, of course, it matters to the legal commentator who tries to present a rational account of decided cases and to explain their impact on the development of doctrine. The tension that exists between cases and theories stressing the necessity of promises and bargains and those stressing a theory of general obligation forms the central topic of the critical legal response to the inadequacy of much current doctrine and teaching with respect to contract law.

Various strategies have been devised to resolve this tension. A crude example is the judicial effort to stretch the notion of consent until in many cases it becomes a palpable fiction.[100] But according to one of the earliest and most subtle solutions proposed promise-based and reliance-based case law can happily be used as alternatives and courts, in adjudicating contract issues, can apply the valid elements of each approach.[101] One type of doctrine might simply be more appropriate than the other for particular contracts. In some factual circumstances, the most advisable policy might be to emphasize the general obligation to honour one's promises, while in others the important policy goal is to effect some kind of distributive justice.[102]

A second possible approach, related to the first, is to see the principle of compensation for losses due to justifiable reliance as a supplement to the basic promissory principle. This appears to be Fried's tack.[103] On this view also, the expanded doctrines of mistake, duress, and so forth 'limit' the subsisting promissory principles without destroying them. The principles of personal, private autonomy and freedom of contract retain their privileged position, although they are not unqualified by other rules and policies the courts have fashioned. On this view, the protection of the reliance interest is conceived as another private entitlement that can be recognized judicially without judges having to discuss issues of public policy with their political and economic ingredients.[104]

Another rationalization of the 'deepgoing antinomies in the structure of our system of contracts' is based on historical analysis.[105] The enshrinement of reliance as a basis for finding liability is justified by appeals to the pre-classical development of contract doctrine. A survey of the earlier case law, extending back into the mists of that era when contract doctrine emerged out of its feudal predecessors, suggests that cases in assumpsit involved circumstances when detrimental reliance, rather than consideration (as later required), was present.[106] Twentieth-century developments in the area of contracts enforced despite the lack of consideration thus have a pedigree that helps legitimate them as a part of contract doctrine. This implication, however, plays a limited role in critical legal analysis: it is not the fact that reliance was once perhaps protected by the common law that impresses the radical critic of classical doctrine. Instead, what is noteworthy is that the system of contract theory could once have rested on a fundamentally different basis. Whether or not that original notion of reliance was a matter that sounded in tort rather than in contract is a detail of history only minimally important to this view.[107]

From a critical legal perspective, these suggested solutions are hopelessly tied to presuppositions present in the original classical theory, which cannot be applied to contemporary economic and political conditions. It might seem that the legal realist emphasis on exposing the precise policies that support established contract doctrine would be more palatable to the radical critic. This strategy has been discussed under the labels of 'social conceptualism'[108] and 'critical functionalism.'[109] Whatever the difference in the name and characterization of an essentially realist approach, its authors ran up against the problem of defining the values a scheme of contract law is meant to serve. One set of proposed values included the goal of facilitating business transactions to foster the continued expansion of capitalist economies. This is not a value that a radical critic would easily commend, since such goals are part of the problem to be overcome.[110] Second, we have no assurance that commercial values are susceptible to a clear consensus.[111] Therefore, installing empirically discovered norms of business conduct will not achieve the neutral impact that writers such as Llewellyn were disposed to take for granted. Third, the suggestion that contract adjudication should be based on achieving particular social or economic goals can conflict with another aspiration of contract doctrine, namely, the promotion of certainty in the law.[112] Broadly worded standards directing courts to reach results that serve vaguely defined values of social or economic justice will likely encourage uncertainty. Fourth, the whole gamut of legal realist proposals about manipulating contract law to make it more responsive to actual business circumstances does not fit well with the evidence that has emerged about the limited or marginal impact of received legal doctrines. Lawyers and academics have, on this account, overestimated the importance of the disputes in which they typically engage.[113] Finally, and perhaps most significantly from a critical legal viewpoint, post-classical developments in theory and doctrine maintain some continuity with the classical conception of contract on a central issue. Regardless of whether it was Williston or Fuller who propounded rules and exceptions, both aimed to project a systematic theory that could be used to predict the outcome of cases and to account for all doctrinal results. Post-classical writers are likewise attracted by the conception of a single, sustainable theory that can explain all contractual commitments and liabilities made in contemporary societies. Hope persists that a body of rules or standards (whether its source lies in legal, political, or economic arrangements) can be propounded to justify the results reached in contract adjudication. Elaboration of a comprehensive contract theory continues to be asserted as an overarching aim, whatever the disagreements about the precise source of contractual obligation.[114] As we shall see, there is considerable ambivalence within critical legal studies about this goal, and at any rate, critical legal authors dispute the view that legal doctrine determines the results of all contract cases. It might provide a framework, but legal doctrine will not resolve any cases beyond the very easiest ones, because of the 'gaps, conflicts, and ambiguities' in the 'elaborated body of law.'[115] Just as contract doctrine cannot determine the results of many cases, it cannot explain them either.

Contract scholars and teachers have found it difficult to break the classical mould. Mainstream contract law has been dubbed 'neoclassical,' because it has achieved a 'partial accommodation' between the original classical scheme and its subsequent critiques.[116] Plausible reasons for the tenacity of certain normative and empirical assumptions, despite the supposed demise of the classical structure, have been offered by both Stewart Macaulay and Robert Gordon.[117] These include the symbolic and legitimating functions of contract doctrine; the self-interested goals of treatise writers, law teachers, and appellate judges; and the elements of mystification and indoctrination discussed above in Chapter 3. Elizabeth Mensch further suggests that classical theory somehow satisfied an aesthetic need by providing an elegant structure, though this claim is difficult to validate.[118] In general, the point is forcibly conveyed that post-classical thinking is not altogether free from the problems that beset classical theory. The escape route from the assumptions of that theory is revealed in the positive recommendations made by critical legal writers, to which our discussion now turns.

A Critical Reconstruction of Contract Law

The critical legal attempt to reshape the governing principles of contract law has moved ahead on two fronts. The first involves a reconsideration of how contract doctrine should be arranged so that adjudication is possible. Critical legal writers have also turned their minds to the question of what the content of that body of doctrine ought to be. Some critical legal writers emphasize that the best methods of deciding contractual disputes take for granted certain substantive principles and several have focused specifically on contract law to illustrate larger issues of legal liberalism. They are unanimous in rejecting the image of actual daily relationships projected through classical contract theory. The ensuing discussion focuses on a few of the key issues on which this disagreement is manifested and goes on to discuss the merits of critical legal proposals for stimulating social change through doctrinal dialogue.

Duncan Kennedy, whose work has had a deep impact on that of other members of the critical legal movement, has acknowledged that the collective project is not entirely without precedent: 'The ultimate goal is to break down the sense that legal argument is autonomous from moral, economic, and political discourse in general. There is nothing innovative about this. Indeed, it has been a premise of legal scholars for several generations that it is impossible to construct an autonomous logic of legal rules. What is new in this piece is the attempt to show an orderliness to the debates about "policy" with which we are left after abandonment of the claim of neutrality.'[119] The thesis that an orderly pattern of inconsistent systems of values (or at least rhetorical representations of those systems) will surface from the critical legal analysis of doctrine was promoted heavily by Kennedy while he was entranced by the possibilities of structuralist interpretation.[120] As noted in Chapter 3, he has since apparently altered his starting point and repudiated much of his early work.[121]

Once again, the most logical entry point to Kennedy's system is through the notion of the 'fundamental contradiction,' discussed earlier in relation to legal consciousness. Legal liberalism assumes that the core problem of contract theory (as in all other legal artifacts) is to reconcile the ideal of individual freedom with the necessity of some degree of social control. Classical contract theory can be conceived using a continuous scale that has, at its ends, the values of 'individualism' and 'altruism.' By individualism, Kennedy understands: '... the making of a sharp distinction between one's interests and those of others, combined with the belief that a preference in conduct for one's own interests is legitimate, but that one should be willing to respect the rules that make it possible to coexist with others similarly self-interested. The form of conduct associated with individualism is self-reliance.'[122] This contrasts with altruism, which on Kennedy's terms is: '... the belief that one ought *not* to indulge a sharp preference for one's own interests over those of others. Altruism enjoins us to make sacrifices, to share, and to be merciful. It has its roots in culture, in religion, ethics and art, that are as deep as individualism.'[123] Using the continuum that lies between these two polar concepts, Kennedy claims that one can gauge approximately the distance of judicial or academic approaches to contract issues from one ideal type or the other. For example, at the extreme individualist pole, a judge in the case of the Fugitive Rig would uphold the bargain between

A and B on the ground that no higher policy considerations supplant the principle that a party should be held to whatever bargain it chooses to enter into, thus protecting the policies of personal autonomy, regulation by market forces, and transactional security. This result accords more or less with a strict classical approach. The meaning of individualism is that other considerations, such as the moral duty to assist persons in distress, or a civic duty owed by B to help avert a likely catastrophe to the port city, have no effect on the adjudicative process. In fact, Kennedy argues that an extreme individualist approach proceeds on the premise that all values are subjective and arbitrary.[124] It thus serves no purpose to argue that the victim of a bad bargain has any 'rights' that offer protection against strict enforcement of the contractual terms. By contrast, if a court followed an altruist model in the case of the Fugitive Rig, then it would be unfair to hold A to all the terms of the deal. While B deserves something in return for its efforts to pursue and secure the rig, a more appropriate, lesser amount would be fixed by the court. Kennedy argues that there is no rational means to reconcile the conflicting values and doctrines comprised in contract law; instead, there are stark alternative extremes plus a number of intermediate positions that take on the colouration of the nearest pole.

In practice, of course, few decided cases ruthlessly follow individualist logic. But neither do they adopt the alternative extreme of the altruist point of view. Under the altruistic scheme, which again must be understood as an ideal construct (a person cannot be altruistic all the time and survive), every member of a society understands that all values derive from a shared sense of human solidarity. Each person participates in the continual process of defining social goals and purposes. This form of ethical and practical discourse is the means by which a common good is identified. Contractual disputes will, in a perfectly altruistic regime, be settled by reference to the values emerging out of that continuing discourse.[125]

On Kennedy's scheme, the development of contract doctrine can be depicted as the adoption at various times of positions somewhere along the continuum between individualism and altruism. In other words, all issues of contract law can be reduced to questions of what political, economic, and social values will prevail in a particular set of factual circumstances. The classical conception of a body of developed rules that can be applied without taking into account of the underlying values is a denial of the presence of the universal structural characteristics Kennedy was keen to reveal. Ironically, in repudiating the classical taste for formalistic order Kennedy claimed to discover a compelling order of another sort.

This analysis poses a crucial issue for someone who, like Kennedy, sees the results of altruistic reasoning in judicial and legislative achievements. For example, by rejecting strict individualistic claims for freedom of the worker to submit to whatever conditions of employment are offered, legal doctrine has evolved schemes providing for minimum wage protection, collective bargaining rights and union security, and workers' compensation. Nevertheless, Kennedy displays ambivalence about whether established legal doctrine, in so far as it tends towards the altruist pole and is therefore 'progressive,' is ultimately valuable. He has suggested that perhaps it would be better if such doctrines as promissory estoppel or unconscionability were ignored or at least treated in 'an aggressively formal way, in order to heighten the level of political and economic conflict within our society.'[126] Then, presumably, the debate about which political and economic values ought to govern would acquire a sense of urgency. There is also a tinge of revolutionary ardour in this recommendation for pushing classical strictures to their ultimate conclusion. Kennedy values not merely debate but also the actual wrenching of power away from those who have historically used contract doctrine for their material benefit.

The substantive side of Kennedy's structural analysis thus contains a utopian ideal which would, in his perfect world of widespread communitarian feeling, supply the ends on which adjudicative dispositions would be based. The formal aspect of Kennedy's program is similarly contrasted with the classical model. Rather than aiming to develop determinative rules that by themselves would allow a judge to infer the proper result in a contract suit, he commends an alternative scheme in which courts deploy standards, principles, or policies. The latter orientation would permit a judge to refer directly to a particular substantive objective in the law of contracts. If the goal of the received doctrine is that a value conferred unjustly in a promissory estoppel situation should be disallowed, a judge should be able to assert that goal without having to cloak it in the guise of deduction from neutral premises.[127]

One of the chief virtues of a formalist system comprised solely of rules is that individuals involved in exchange transactions can be confident that their interests are not defeasible so long as the transaction conforms to the enabling rules of contract doctrine. The adoption of standards would seem to sacrifice this function of contract law. As we have seen, such advance knowledge is supposed to be guaranteed by classical theory.

Against this must be placed the empirical studies, also described above, which tend to marginalize contract rules as an influence on contract planning and performance. There may be little point, therefore, in stressing the need for a rule-based adjudicative system. A system based on standards would do no worse and perhaps would perform better than the formalist model, since judges would have more freedom to recognize the complex circumstances and customary understandings that surround a transaction or relationship. Moreover, there are now so many exceptions to the pure principles of classical doctrine that increasing the use of broadly worded standards would not seem at all anomalous.

Such is the outline of Kennedy's analysis and prescription. It contains some striking elements, but it also suffers from some crucial omissions. First, the imagery of a continuum that connects individualism and altruism is itself charged with political meaning. Kennedy aligns individualism with liberalism, so that the features of the one reflect those of the other. His account is weakened somewhat by the acknowledgment that there is no essential or necessary connection between the two.[128] Further, on Kennedy's definition individualism is, at least in miniature, a theory about human nature and primary liberal virtues. As argued in Chapter 2, this definition does not correspond with actual liberal commitments.[129] The normative background to contemporary liberal political theories involves respect by the state for each citizen as an individual, but it also is interested in ensuring equal respect for citizens. The latter commitment is, on Kennedy's definitions, more in keeping with what he calls altruism. If, as has been argued in Chapter 2, liberal theory can plausibly contain both so-called individualist and altruist orientations, a great deal of Kennedy's scheme becomes pointless.

A second serious problem is found in the argument that one can project a society embodying the altruist model of substantive harmony without having any pre-determining values in mind. To describe a society imbued with the values of fairness, free political dialogue, economic equality, and so forth is already to have chosen specific values that members of that society cannot reject without incurring the risk of losing their identity as a cohesive community. Moreover, Kennedy grants that a perfectly altruist society could conceivably be a totalitarian nightmare.[130] This concession should render us wary of his general position that altruist values are ordinarily to be preferred. A better tactic on Kennedy's part might have been to concentrate on describing something less than an ideal type. In other words, specification of the conditions necessary and sufficient for the achievement of a regime that would satisfy critical legal standards of procedural and distributive justice might have been more persuasive as an 'alternative vision' to classical doctrine. By adopting the tactic of imagining a community that self-consciously and collectively chooses the values its law will be geared to protect, Kennedy has left his discussion of the substantive content of contract law curiously bereft of substantive values.

Another flaw in Kennedy's reformulation is the separation he imputes of the ideal categories of rule-based and standard-based adjudication. At the abstract level of describing the essential differences between these approaches, the distinction seems clear enough. But once we encounter actual examples of judicial interpretation of contract doctrine, the line becomes blurred. When a judge in a case of mistake, for example, refuses to enforce a contract on the ground that the parties could not possibly have agreed about the identity of the subject matter of the transaction, that result by itself does not tell us whether the reasoning was based on a rule regarding lack of certainty or on a standard formulated by looking at the relevant commercial customs or economic criteria of loss-shifting. It is not difficult to imagine a case in which a judge explicitly resorts to one doctrinal rule rather than another on the basis that the one chosen better fulfils the policy which, as the judge understands it, supports the just result. It is also possible to imagine situations, contrary to Kennedy's scheme, in which a court applies a contract rule strictly, even though the rule has an altruistic motivation. Consider, for instance, the case of a sophisticated teenager who subscribes to a compact disk club, receives the free initial offering, and then refuses to satisfy the other parts of the subscription agreement. Assume the club sues the teen, and the court refuses to enforce the contract against the defendant on the ground that the teen was under the minimum age required for contractual capacity. This result naturally defeats the justified expectations of the plaintiff retailer. In terms of Kennedy's scheme, the judge is using rule-based reasoning, adhering strictly to the law regarding the age threshold, despite any evidence that the teenager was fully aware of the conditions set out in the subscription offering and could reasonably be expected to grasp their legal significance. Although the reasoning is rule-based, the goals served are not individualistic. Rather, the court is altruistically concerned with protecting the interests of children, that they might not suffer from commercial manipulation.[131] In other words, even individualistic forms of reasoning can be used to preserve altruistic ideals. Because of the presence of both types of reasoning and both types of goals, contract doctrine already allows a fair degree of the sort of flexibility Kennedy seeks to build into his theory of adjudication. We should not forget that formalism, the object of Kennedy's attack, is an ideal conception that does not reflect the developed body of current contract doctrine. Contemporary contract law, in both its principles and its normative underpinnings, eludes the categories that Kennedy seeks to impose on it.

Another radical critic, Karl Klare, has premised his recommendations for the reconstruction of contract law on a dissatisfaction with the ordinarily narrow ambit of appellate reasoning. There are impliedly two methods to cure the defects of contract doctrine. The first operates in the law school classroom. From his review of contract casebooks, Klare has concluded that the available materials seal off legal knowledge from other sources of scholarship. What is needed, in view of his belief in the 'impending demise of the casebook method,' is a new form of training that would expose students to 'historical, socio-economic, and political literature and to diverse modes of political analysis and argument.'[132]

The second type of useful activity, according to Klare, would be to concentrate on effecting large-scale political and economic change. The goals animating such change would not be known at the outset; they would instead emerge in the process of social and political experimentation. Klare's emphasis on the notion of 'praxis' is tied to this image of theory and legal practice modifying each other dialectically as different projected arrangements are tried out, tempered, and then discarded for something better.[133]

The implication of Klare's recommendations at this second level is that we must be agnostic about the substantive content of contract doctrine. The stress again is on process and learning from one's experience of a novel situation. This orientation is difficult to incorporate into any recognizable setting in which adjudication could take place. On the one hand, Klare's scheme implies that doctrine is always moribund, that there is no specific value in legal reasoning, and that courts are probably unnecessary for settling contractual disputes. In this sense Klare adopts an extremely anti-doctrinal position. On the other hand, it may be that adjudicative processes should remain, but that political or economic doctrine will replace what the judge feels are constraints imposed by law. If the second of these alternatives is the fairer interpretation, studying case law would presumably have little value. We ought to take our politics neat, so to speak. Therefore, it may be important to study political and other relevant sorts of theory not as an adjunct to legal materials, but as their substitute altogether.

In the work of Roberto Unger we are presented with the choice between rejecting contract as well as other legal doctrine in favour of an apocalyptic vision of social and economic life and seeing how traditional doctrine can be 'internally developed.' Unger claims that internal development is the more logical of these two paths: political prophets are only successful when they can appeal to the existing 'anomalies of personal encounter and social practice.'[134] Moreover, entrenched schemes of constitutional government make it difficult to achieve a total reshaping of social and political institutions. It is therefore more prudent to pursue change by using available forums (such as, presumably, the courts, legal periodicals, or law classrooms) that allow some expression of fundamental political disagreement with established structures of power and authority.

The principal task of Unger's notion of critique is to reveal the discontinuities between the ideals enshrined in law and the actual arrangements in Western liberal societies. Unger's conception of 'deviationist' or 'expanded' doctrine closely resembles the observations recorded by Kennedy and Klare. His recommended method of critique questions the connection between legal doctrine and its supposed effects and provides alternative interpretations of basic doctrinal principles, such as freedom of contract.[135] Both approaches were in fact already present generally in twentieth-century challenges to classical contract law. A further way of understanding deviationist doctrine is to see it as emphasizing the possible range of social and political values to choose from in deciding how we want our institutions to be structured. Deviationist doctrine, then, provides an opportunity to elevate apparently narrow legal issues into political disputes of great social magnitude. Traditional legal doctrine, including the area of contract, has become ossified because the use of precedent in formalist adjudication disguises the political content of all litigation.

For one of his two major examples of deviationist analysis in action, Unger draws upon contract doctrine. His aim is to beat 'the received theory at its own game of persuasive generalization.'[136] Unger purports to reduce the entire body of contract doctrine to one pair of principles and a corresponding pair of counterprinciples. His argument is designed to show how the 'deviant' counterprinciples can plausibly be changed into 'dominant' principles. One example of this process involves the principle of 'freedom to contract' and the counterprinciple that 'the freedom to choose the contract partner will not be allowed to work in ways that subvert the communal aspects of social life.'[137] To illustrate the workings of the counterprinciple Unger refers to doctrines regarding protection of reliance and restitutionary interests and especially to rules restricting the finding of contractual liability in non-commercial settings, which operate to limit the liability that would otherwise be imposed under the dominant principle of freedom to contract. But the bifurcation of cases according to one or the other of these distinct legal categories provides a clue to a more general picture of the social assumptions that govern contemporary law. By separating commercial exchanges from intrafamilial ones, contract doctrine has established two separate realms of human interaction. There is the world of commerce, in which the parties' self-interest should dictate the terms of the bargain. In this realm, the spirit of competition reigns. In the contrasting world of family and friendship, communal and fraternal values antithetical to those of commerce should prevail. On Unger's view, contract is at present treated as antithetical to community. He claims further that this result both impoverishes the concept of community and treats contract as essentially involving distrust, competition, and selfishness. Unger would offer a 'countervision' that 'incorporates the analysis of explicit statements into a more comprehensive framework that also takes into account the merit and measure of the promisee's reliance and the moral quality of the promisor's claim to discharge.'[138] Unger's countervision bears a marked likeness to some of the principles that have crept into contract doctrine in the past half-century. Citing a case on all fours with the case of the Mistaken Bid,[139] Unger concludes that an application of expanded doctrine would lead to the result that the loss might be split different ways depending on the peculiar circumstances of each case. At any rate, the reliance measure of damages, and not the expectancy measure, would be controlling. In other words, judges such as Traynor were already engaging in their own version of a technique similar to Unger's deviationist doctrine (excepting the precise formula for calculating damages) a generation ago.

What is there to be gained from tracing through and adopting Unger's procedure of treating counterprinciples as the norm and seeing what legal consequences flow? It seems to depend on one's initial position. If one's basic premises are in line with classical contract theory, then following Unger's method will indeed reveal a host of insights into the limits its principles impose on our conception of the social world. An intellectual conversion might be the result. If, however, one is familiar with the range of developments that have already occurred or are on the brink of occurring in contract doctrine since the classical model was at least partly shrugged off, the results of Unger's deviationist doctrine will appear fairly pallid.[140] In many cases, his purportedly all-powerful method seems only to duplicate the best examples of incisive contract analysis to be found among realist and post-realist critics and judges. We could for instance point to Llewellyn's or Fuller's intuitions about the nexus between legal rules and commercial behaviour; Dawson's or Hale's rearrangement of the design of thinking about coercion, duress, and contractual freedom; Macaulay's studies of commercial planning and non-legal sanctions; and Macneil's elucidation of relational concepts and their social context. All of these developments have attenuated the classical model, but they are largely ignored in Unger's presentation of the essence of established contract learning. More importantly, the work of many of the writers listed above is more precisely defined than Unger's. They have grasped the dangers of letting the ambition of building a grand theory overpower the instinct for detailed analysis.

Clare Dalton, in her lengthy treatment of the current principles of contract, relies avowedly on Kennedy's example of dichotomous analysis.[141] Her discussion is organized around the task of illuminating how various dualities operate to make contract doctrine inconsistent and indeterminate. Dalton claims that specific principles in that doctrine are favoured over other, competing principles. For example, contract law has traditionally been considered, under the sway of liberal political assumptions, a matter of regulating the interests of private individuals. Public control of contract institutions is supposed to be tangential to the main purpose of giving maximum scope of expression to individual autonomy.[142] One of Dalton's objects, deconstructing the distinction between the public and private spheres, indicates that she too is choosing as her target, initially at least, the stock principles of classical theory. These supply what she calls the current 'principal vision' of contract doctrine.[143]

Dalton's main criticism of the many ways in which modern contract doctrine has handled such issues as duress, unconscionability, and the duty of good faith is that technical issues regarding how to make these doctrines square with established law have obstructed the overtly political debate they invite. She focuses in particular on the *Restatement (Second) of Contracts*[144] which, like its predecessor, perplexingly includes several bases of liability (bargain, donative promise, reliance, promissory estoppel) and several sources of excuse from obligation (unconscionability, duress, mistake, impossibility), but fails to provide an adequate rationalization to make those doctrines compatible. Dalton thinks that the confusion caused by this abundance of principle is vividly illustrated in the way casebooks are compiled and in complex hypothetical problems faced by students at examination time.[145]

Dalton employs the example of a cohabitation arrangement which has broken down to illustrate the difficulty in convincing courts to abandon conventional forms of doctrinal analysis. The Anglo-American common law has long refused to recognize any contractual liability arising out of situations where the parties to an alleged agreement are either members of the same family or are in some similar relationship where they are not perceived as being 'at arm's length.'[146] The possible bases for such liability would seem to be either an express agreement (oral or in writing) or a claim in restitution. After canvassing the possible doctrinal and policy arguments that would favour or deny the enforceability of any promises made in that context, Dalton concludes that traditional categories are simply too hidebound to allow an adequate resolution of the pertinent issues. She therefore turns to a radical analysis based explicitly on the question of how power is exercised in cohabiting arrangements and what ought to be the state's response, through the courts, to a whole set of emerging modern problems.[147]

This final manoeuvre in the context of Dalton's argument is revealing. It seems to imply that developed doctrine by itself is so indeterminate that we cannot expect from it any specific guidance about how to resolve particular disputes. Because contract doctrine is a rambling structure with incompatible elements, no definite answer can be given to the apparently straightforward question of what law will govern in a reasonably complex set of factual circumstances. Dalton's deconstruction of the attempt to summarize the law in the *Restatement (Second)* appears to convey the lesson that assertions about what the law is always teeter on the brink of an opposite characterization. The result of this deconstructive essay is not especially satisfying, for we are still left with questions about whether adjudication must therefore be perpetually unguided by principles of general application. There is a serious lack of connection between Dalton's analytical insights and the image of transformed contract doctrine that is supposed somehow to reflect a more just way of resolving disputes.[148] As discussed below, the problematic idea that doctrinal incoherence in some way represents a flaw that vitiates the reasonable application of a received body of principles is common to several critical legal writers discussed in this chapter.

Assessing the Radical Critique

This section summarizes and assesses several general issues that arise in critical legal attempts to diagnose doctrinal maladies in the modern law of contracts. These issues may, for the sake of discussion, be divided into two groups: first, problems related to the critical legal method of characterizing existing doctrine, both historically and ideologically; and second, problems associated with proposals for a radically revamped conception of regulating contractual behaviour and expectations. The former group of issues occupies the bulk of the discussion here. The second group of problems is addressed at length in Chapter 5, which is concerned in part with the degree to which doctrinal change can be revolutionary.

Some of the most important questions about the version of the development of contract law offered by critical legal writers concern its historical accuracy and its so-called liberal underpinnings. On the historical issue, there is no doubt that critical legal accounts, such as Horwitz's, appear to present a powerful case for concluding that in some respects much contract case law in the mid-nineteenth century differs significantly from case law dating from a century earlier. The important issues are the extent to which the later jurisprudence is representative and in what sense certain assumptions and motivations can be said to have 'dominated' the thinking of legal élites in the eras being compared. They are thus in part evidentiary problems requiring an assessment of whether Horwitz's generalizations are founded upon a preponderance of relevant evidence. As A.W.B. Simpson has pointed out, the issue is often whether a single doctrine can be said to have been created or to have prevailed in a particular period.[149] It is difficult to conclude that an anti-commercial bias, for example, was rampant or even influential in the eighteenth century. Nor do many nineteenth-century cases fit comfortably with the critical legal account that accentuates the insidiousness of classical assumptions. Moreover, classical doctrines were attenuated by judges throughout the so-called classical period, often on the basis that public policy or values such as 'fairness' were significant factors in reaching the correct judicial decision. For example, the doctrines of unconscionability and duress were not simply abandoned for a half-century or so. They remained part of established doctrine. It may be (though this observation is suggestive rather than conclusive) that some confusion has arisen between fairness of the substantive contract and fairness of the process leading to the formation of an alleged contract. Even during the second half of the nineteenth century, when classical theory was supposed to have ignored the criterion of adequacy of consideration in fixing liability, doctrines remained that warranted courts' solicitous concern about the fairness of compelling one party to perform its end of a bargain. These are most noticeable in the form of equitable doctrines, relating for example to agreements such as mortgages.[150] Fairness as one ground of decision making was not abandoned across the board.

The criticism of over-generalization also applies to the critical legal claim that a single form of judicial approach or reasoning marks a particular era. On the face of it, the critical legal argument that the late nineteenth century was especially notable for an unprecedented reliance by common law judges on the ideal of a rule-based 'formalistic' approach seems powerful. But to describe the rule-based method as simply involving the 'mechanical application of general principles to reach decisions in particular cases' is remarkably unenlightening.[151] Even after such a loaded descriptive term as 'mechanical' is elaborated, it remains unclear why formalism was not a vice of any era in the common law that has paid some deference to the concept of controlling precedents, or indeed, of any civil law system based on codified first principles. What Kelman calls the 'deductive temperament' requires much more refined analysis than what has been offered in critical legal discussions of late-nineteenth-century contract doctrine.[152]

Kennedy's definition of formalism also turns on characterizing the application of rules as a 'mechanical' exercise. In his scheme, the 'decision process is called rule application only if the actor resolutely limits himself to identifying those aspects of the situation which, *per se*, trigger his response.'[153] Lawrence Solum shrewdly comments on this passage that Kennedy has defined mechanical rule application in 'such a way that only a completely determined decision will count as a decision that is not indeterminate.'[154] That is, Kennedy sets up formalism as if it embodied the claim that all cases are easy cases – only one possible result squares with the legal materials available to the court. Instead of viewing the formalistic tendency as dependent on an exaggerated belief in law as a closed system that guarantees certain results (a claim already undermined by the time legal realists cited cases where the results could not have been reached by pure deduction), Kennedy treats formalism as the only sort of rule application possible.[155]

In addition, we may also justifiably doubt how it is that Langdell and Williston are seen as the arch-systematizers of a field that had been undergoing doctrinal organization and rationalization for centuries. Contract law as a body of ascertainable doctrine was certainly not invented by Langdell, whatever the implications of Gilmore's tidy picture. Many of the elements of consent, promise keeping, and consideration, however inchoate, were present in discussions of contract doctrine long before the turn of the nineteenth century.[156] Scholars have always been interested in organizing these issues under a general theory.[157] The theoretical impulse itself should not be taken to mark a particular era. Nor has that impulse diminished, even among critical legal writers, a point that is elaborated below.

One of the forces behind the critical legal tendency to classify developments in contract law according to more or less definite time periods is the desire to discover a new 'orderliness' (to use Kennedy's term) latently present in their material. Critical legal writers frequently begin their analysis by describing dichotomous concepts or principles. The most general pair is Kennedy's 'fundamental contradiction' discussed in Chapter 3. Other examples of fundamental distinctions found in contract law are public/private, form/substance, general/particular, and contract/tort, used by such writers as Dalton and Feinman.[158] After isolating these pairs, the critique tries to show how doctrine is shaped by a wavering conception of the boundaries that lie between the poles of such opposing concepts. Legal liberal doctrine is supposed to be inconsistent or incoherent because at any time a critic can challenge, for example, whether a legal issue arises in the public sphere or the private sphere, whether a legal requirement is a matter of form rather than substance, or whether a case should be settled by the application of classical contract rather than contemporary tort ideas.

The Achilles' heel of this line of argument is the charge of incoherence. Because competing values lie at the root of contract theory, developed doctrines are bound to take, on the critical legal view, more than one form; in fact, they might take incompatible forms. The contemporary situation, in which promissory forms of obligation contend with reliance or other non-promissory forms, is therefore the understandable result of a system of thinking that is not all of one piece. When radical critics claim that the system is so riddled with contradictions that it lacks coherence, it is useful to ask what standard of coherence is being applied. The critical legal picture is that of a system of ideas or body of doctrine containing propositions that cannot all be true at the same time. Consequently, it is concluded that the system or doctrinal corpus collapses from incoherence. A necessary connection can never be established between the background doctrinal principles and a particular act of judicial decision making, in the sense that contract doctrine causes the judicial result.[159] Given the large number of doctrinal formulations, allowing each case to be argued different ways, and the lack of consensus in other background conditions, legal reasoning does not have the methodological power to reach predictable outcomes.

When critical legal writers emphasize the incoherence of legal doctrine, they stress at the same time the remarkable degree of coherence within general forms of consciousness. In other words, though there might be little determinate linkage, from a critical legal perspective, between doctrinal rules and the disposition of individual cases, there is arguably a strikingly significant degree of linkage between the rules and the normative beliefs or assumptions forming the background ideological structure. The radical critics have not turned their considerable skills to the issue of whether contemporary legal consciousness is as monolithic as the early forms of critique made out.

The charge of doctrinal incoherence seems to be aimed at those theorists who claim that legal decisions can always be predicted on the basis of contract doctrine alone. For theorists of adjudication who do not argue for determinacy in this narrow, causal sense, the radical critique has little bite. The review provided earlier in this chapter of competing values and doctrines in contract law turned up numerous commentators who had no illusions that contract doctrine is coherent in this sense. But they do not believe that the body of doctrine must as a result be abandoned as the product of a worthless enterprise. The process of adjudication may be understood as an attempt to approach the ideal of coherence, to make decisions in which the results are best justified on the basis of the materials available, even if it is understood that the ideal of perfect coherence will never be reached.[160] On this view, the standard of coherence that governs the practices of lawyerly advocacy and judicial decision making is not based on logical consistency within a closed system of axiomatic premises. Nor is it modelled on treating contract doctrine as if it were fashioned by a single person who aims at comprehensiveness and ruthless consistency. Contract doctrine is an evolving body of rules and principles, built up over several generations and representing the product of many different minds, operating with perhaps conflicting primary assumptions. The contrast between these two ways in which we might talk about the development of a theory should warn us against thinking that coherence is a virtue in precisely the same way in every field. In the case of law, where doctrine is formulated through collective input, variety and incompatibility among the principles or values may not be deficiencies; rather, they might stimulate further growth.[161] That is, there is a positive side or 'calculated process' (to use John Eekelaar's term) to the incoherence which, according to the critical legal account, saps the ramifying body of doctrine of any explanatory strength.[162] Once framed in this fashion, the alleged incoherence of contractual principles is hardly a bugbear theorists should fear. In fact, although critical legal writing repeatedly stresses this flaw of inconsistent guidance, one would have to be historically and politically naive to believe that, in a society which prizes pluralism among the values held by its citizens, all doctrine could or ought to be retailored into a coherent whole.[163] For that would ultimately lead to the suppression of competing values and conceptions which, according to critical legal writers, is the problem with established doctrine in the first place. It is also worth noting that the allegation of fundamental incoherence has not led critical legal authors to ignore doctrinal materials. Instead, those authors have continued to lavish attention on many different areas of doctrinal study as they search for more complex and politically interesting features of existing legal regimes.[164]

A second way of conceiving the incoherence of contract doctrine is to invoke the notion of a specific legal liberal view of human relations. By this account, individualism is a shorthand term for denoting the dominant set of ideas that determines the basic premises of doctrinal reasoning. In Kelman's terms, classical contract theory, by valourizing certain liberal values, is devoted to preserving the autonomous choice of each person to determine which relationships she enters into, to keep or dispose of acquired property, and to be free from constraints imposed on the ground that some other individual or some public agency claims to know what is better for the interest of that person.[165] On the individualist thesis, contracts are motivated by competitive instincts rather than considerations of cooperation and trust. The parties to a bargain assumedly want to aggrandize their own positions by giving up the absolute minimum value necessary to accomplish the exchange. Courts are created by states to serve the bare function of keeping this spirit of competition from degenerating into a war of one party against the other. Contract law thus harnesses basic anti-social instincts tending towards distrust and selfishness. It is vital that the critical legal account renders such a picture as the background for all liberal theories of contract, for it can then provide a contrast to more enlightened conceptions of how people might be encouraged to interrelate. One problem with this approach, of course, is that various forms of liberal thinking have pointedly repudiated the crude image presented by individualist assumptions. There is nothing to stand in the way of founding a liberal theory on a notion of the desirability of economic equality, so that the best contract doctrine can include strictures against one party using its superior economic power to coerce a weaker party in a deal. Such a liberal construction of equality would be straightforwardly anti-individualist. A second example might involve a liberal conception of distributive justice. There is nothing inherently contradictory about a liberal theorist preferring the use of contract litigation to achieve a redistribution of resources in a society so that some of the wealth of the most affluent class is given to a member of the worst off. This example side-steps the issue of whether such redistribution might not be better accomplished through a general taxation system rather than piecemeal litigation.[166] The point here is to emphasize again that liberalism cannot be conflated with individualism and, indeed, many contemporary versions of liberal theory are antithetical to it.

Critical legal doubts about both contract law and the content of liberalism converge on just these issues, for it has been claimed by Hugh Collins that the incoherence of contract doctrine reflects the incoherence, or at least the multiplicity, of different types of liberal moral and political theory.[167] The dispute among contract theorists over the proper conceptual basis of contract institutions is said to result from the internal inconsistencies in constituent principles of liberalism. The contract theory based primarily on promissory obligation, for instance, is supposed to correlate with the liberal value of individual autonomy. By using the convention of promising, a person is able to make responsible choices which, for the most part, should brook no interference. On Collins's view the competing contract theory based on reliance principles is also inspired by liberal notions. In this case, the interest protected is the prevention of harm to others caused by avoidable conduct. Like the two contract doctrines, these two liberal principles are assumed to conflict with each other. We are thus, it is claimed, faced with an 'antinomy,' to use Unger's vocabulary. We are precluded from adhering to both doctrines or both principles at one and the same time.

Collins's argument is problematic. First, either the principles or the doctrines could be shown to be free from a fundamental conflict, which has been argued above. Second, even if they were in conflict, that conflict does not necessarily lead to such incoherence that we would be compelled to abandon both pairs of doctrines and principles. On the first method, we might say that the notions of promise and reliance are not 'opposed' in the sense that they are mutually exclusive bases for conceiving how liability is assigned in a contract case. Promissory estoppel, for example, is supposedly a reliance-based doctrine, yet by definition it always involves the giving of a promise (actual or notional). That is not a perfect example, because such imputed promises show that a specific promise is not invariably made. A better approach might be to claim that promise is the core concept from which the idea of reliance radiates.[168]

The next alternative would be to subsume promissory forms of obligation under the general category of obligations based on preventing unjust enrichment. In such a scheme, contracts based on promise would form a species of a larger legal genus titled something like 'obligations.'[169] Or they might be brought together under a notion of 'consent' that is broad enough to encompass both promise and reliance on another party's conduct.[170] In any event, it is not obvious that the ideas of promise-based and reliance-based liability are mutually exclusive. The theory that liability should never be based on promissory conduct between the contracting parties would, in fact, be the opposite of the promissory theory. It would be difficult to find any writer who adheres to this extreme opinion. Promise and reliance may be competing conceptions, but they are not logically or conceptually irreconcilable.

A better way of understanding how any inconsistencies are registered and dealt with is to look at actual legal practices, based on the available materials, which are especially abundant in U.S. law. The critical legal account on this score is thin. According to Dalton, who tends to rely too heavily on the *Restatement (Second)*, as if that text contained the final word on the subject of the two bases of contractual liability, 'neither text nor commentary addressed the knotty questions of how their coexistence should be imagined.'[171] She goes on to claim that, so far as any structure can be inferred from the treatment contained in the *Restatement (Second)*, the bargain or consideration principle is treated as the norm, while the reliance principle is the exception.[172] What Dalton neglects to inquire into at any length – she refers briefly to the excerpts of cases contained in the single casebook on which she draws for examples – is the plethora of cases in which these two principles contend for recognition. She thus errs by trying to elaborate specific legal concepts or principles as if they determine actual legal practices, such as those involved in arguing and resolving contract cases, rather than the other way around. It is sounder theoretically to analyse the relationship between, and respective weight of, different principles by examining how they arise in deliberative practices rather than to search for a single master concept of law which is supposed to back up the claim that a legal principle is indeed a valid principle of a particular legal system. The process of theorizing is better conducted a posteriori than a priori.[173]

The process of a posteriori deliberation will follow something like the following pattern, which has been carefully explored, as part of a larger philosophical project on practical reasoning, by Susan Hurley.[174] In the circumstances of a particular dispute, the court will sense some conflict between two contending principles. In our hypothetical case of the Mistaken Bid, C's erroneously calculated bid (construed as a promise) does not give rise to liability because B did not accept it before C's withdrawal. The requirement of acceptance in order for a contract to be enforceable provides a means of enforcing promises selectively. It ensures that parties are free to negotiate without one party snapping up the other's offer without the latter's knowledge. The requirement of acceptance serves the goal of certainty of transactions: parties will be able to predict when a contract has been formed and when its attendant obligations have arisen. On the other hand, the doctrine of reliance prevents C from taking unfair advantage of a predicament in which C's error was not known to B at the time B was making its bid for the main contract. The relevant policy here is that B should be compensated for the economic loss resulting from B's reliance on C's estimate, when C refuses to perform the work because the estimate turns out to be too low. C should have realized what might happen to B's position in view of the risk of C's error. The two doctrines of a bargain based on acceptance and one based on detrimental reliance seem to point in different directions. In summary, the court proceeds to this point by identifying the alternative principles and articulating the purposes underlying each.

In the next stage of its deliberation, the court will examine the developed law and the principles that appear in the reasoning of those cases to determine their bearing on the instant case. Hurley calls this the stage of gathering 'background data' to see how 'settled outcomes' give reasons for the next stage, which requires the court to theorize in order to arrive at a coherent resolution to the conflict in issue.[175] U.S. contract law is, as noted above, particularly rich in such data. In these intermediate stages the court will try to determine the relative weight, given the specific circumstances of the case of the Mistaken Bid, of the competing principles. For example, it might be treated as relevant to the issue of weight that, in the type of business in which B and C participate, the kind of promise that C makes (the lowest bid on electrical work) is always relied on by general contractors such as B. The weight might be different for other cases, involving, for example, gratuitous promises in a noncommercial setting. Because the data show that C's kind of promise is invariably relied on without specific notice being given to or expected by C, the policy of protecting B against injurious reliance probably outweighs both the policy of protecting parties like C against having their offers snapped up and the policy of certainty.[176] Where this issue has been settled by actual decisions in some jurisdictions, these resolutions become a factor that can be added to the deliberative matrix. If cases have been resolved in favour of C's position, a court has to look closer to determine whether there are distinguishing features in those cases that augment or diminish the weight in favour of one principle or the other. As Hurley claims, any theoretical underdetermination that existed prior to this process of moving back and forth between gathering data and trying to find a theory which best resolves the instant case does not entail radical indeterminacy. The deliberation involved in giving reasons to justify one outcome or the other breaks any ties that may have obtained prior to the instant case being decided.[177] At the conclusion of the process, the principle that is not used to decide the case is not, of course, invalidated on that account.

The foregoing description is more textured and more accurate than Dalton's in terms of understanding the deliberative context required to resolve disputes involving two competing principles, both of which are valid, at the foundations of modern contract law. For a court merely to invoke one principle or the other would be a necessary condition to render a legitimate decision, but such an invocation would not be sufficient or conclusive. Bare application is not enough. As Hurley's analysis reminds us, and as has been pointed out elsewhere by Neil MacCormick, to reach a particular resolution the court must also engage in a practice of rationalizing each contending principle, elucidating its purpose, and taking into account perhaps consequentialist reasons supporting the application of one principle over another in a specific context.[178] Whether or not the metaphor of determining the respective 'weight' of each principle is illuminating, the general point is clear.[179] Coherence is a noble ideal and under its inspiration judges inquire into the values and policies underlying specific principles, but this aspect of the common law system is not subverted by the presence of two principles that pull in different directions. A participant in the legal process might concede that both principles are warranted simultaneously without necessarily feeling trapped in a dilemma. Those principles are not logical contradictions. They may conflict with each other in the sense that, on the facts of a particular case, a judge might be faced with finding reasons to apply one principle rather than the other. That those principles may have arisen at different times, so that a later principle perhaps meshes better with the contemporary political and economic climate, is one criterion that might come into play. The critical legal account has focused intensively upon the classical background to contract law and, except for passing references to the emergence of monopoly capitalism, has seriously failed to take adequate notice of modern developments in which consumers, employees, and other parties to contracts have received special solicitude from judges and legislators. Recognizing such developments leads to the signally important fact that values underlying contract doctrine have already been partly changed in a way that stresses communal rather than individual interests.[180] A reader of much critical legal writing on contract law might be forgiven for thinking that classical conceptions of the subject and its constituent rules reign unchallenged in the process of resolving contractual disputes.[181] Yet, as we have seen in the case of the Fugitive Rig, for instance, a judge guided by the doctrine of duress will predictably stress the role of the law in protecting persons against avoidable economic harm resulting from a contract made when the promisor was at a severe disadvantage because normal market conditions were absent. This type of decision seems to interfere with the tug owner's autonomy, but that inference may be only apparent. An argument could be made that the net result of the case law on duress is to reinforce the overall value of letting persons take responsibility for their conduct in situations where the circumstances are largely within their control, or are at least foreseeable. Even if this argument is fatuous, it is not immediately evident that, in cases decided using the doctrine of duress, the principle of individual autonomy has been submerged so deeply that it cannot rise to the surface in other disputes. On the contrary, it will doubtlessly continue to be pleaded in subsequent cases of alleged duress. The choice of one principle in a particular case does not inevitably destroy all other contending principles.

The distinctive critical legal emphasis on the idea of incoherence appears plausible only if it can be shown that conventional contract theory fails to encompass the whole of the relevant data. Thus, doctrine may be deemed incoherent because it fails to account for all the conflicting precedents, or liberal theory may seem incoherent because it incorporates incompatible assumptions. At least in part, the goal for critical legal thinking is to expose and cure these elements of incoherence. One of the preferred methods of accomplishing this goal is to show that the principles underlying contract law can be manipulated to favour results opposite to established doctrine. The next step is to demonstrate how, by reminding ourselves of the 'counterprinciples,' we can achieve a better point of view. More possibilities of how human transactions can be promoted and eventually thrive will be realized. The critical legal account is thus supposed to provide guidance as to how the process of adjudication can be sharpened and made more sensitive to the normative basis of legal doctrine. The logical extension of this argument would seem to be to replace the notion of adjudication altogether by an overtly political process. This route has not generally been followed, because critical legal writers have concentrated on manipulating doctrine rather than simply eliminating it.[182] They envision doctrinal criticism as at least an initial step towards realizing the system of shared values to help overcome the alleged dilemmas of liberalism.[183] Doctrinal critique can perhaps prepare the ground for a subsequent general debate, in which communication will be free from the distorting effects of unequal power and unexamined assumptions.

The ultimate goal of the radical critique seems to be a society-wide agreement on the values that ought to animate contract adjudication and contract behaviour. The most significant omission in critical legal writing on contract doctrine thus far has been the identification and nature of these values. As Feinman admits, 'at present, we have no compelling utopian vision, no theory which leads inevitably to the correct decision in each case.'[184] Generally, the process of identifying the central values of contract theory is postponed to the time when intersubjective agreement can be reached. The hope seems to be that the values then chosen will differ significantly from those attendant on current theory, which in some sense have been imposed by corrupt political practice and maintained by legal mystification. The sort of theory on offer by critical legal writers is therefore essentially empty at its core. The values promoted are defined primarily by opposition with currently dominant ones.[185] The problem with doctrinal critique, therefore, is that it can provide only allusive hints about the shape of a more just political and economic order. It self-consciously refuses to advocate substantive values in any way except as an heuristic device. Two paradoxes are created from the political agnosticism of early critical legal writers. They form the subject of the next chapter, which examines critical legal projections of the shape of things to come.

5

Darn That Dream: The Communitarian Vision of Critical Legal Studies

But the wise know that foolish legislation is a rope of sand which perishes in the twisting; that the State must follow and not lead the character and progress of the citizen; the strongest usurper is quickly got rid of; and they only who build on Ideas, build for eternity; and that the form of government which prevails is the expression of what cultivation exists in the population which permits it. The law is only a memorandum.

Ralph Waldo Emerson, 'Politics'

This penultimate chapter is about two paradoxes found in the radical critique of legal institutions and legal learning. The first, the paradox of engagement, takes the form of critical legal authors calling for an appreciation of law as deeply political while refusing on principle to disclose in detail their substantive political views. The second paradox, the paradox of postponement, arises from the view that, although law is entirely a matter of political choice, the critic has no business commending the values that ought to shape a legal regime. Critical legal writers have been committed to what has been called, in another context, the 'perpetuity of contest.'[1] Legal values and institutions must be selected through a process that operates at a grassroots level. The regular presence of these two paradoxes, if only in the background, in the critical legal literature, might account for the perceived degree of threat the critique has posed to teachers and practitioners of the law. A cryptic political agenda, by the very fact of its concealment, inevitably invites suspicion.

Ultimately, while the radical critics have claimed to expose the hidden ideological content of contemporary law, they have adopted a strategy which justifies providing only the barest outline of a progressive legal regime. The language of communal aspiration, of government by the acclamation of fundamental values, and of the separation of citizens into intentional political cultures, has been used to try to persuade the audience for critical legal studies that the era of post-liberal politics has dawned. But where the radical literature finds illumination and hope in this morning of political reconstruction, many of its readers, including those who share left convictions, see only indiscernible shapes and ominous shadows. This chapter will focus on the alternative ideas proposed to form the foundation for a better social order.[2]

Critical legal writing has generally been reluctant to provide explicit accounts of the nature of a post-liberal society. Its proponents have referred episodically to alternative values or alternative institutional arrangements within the context of legal adjudication. Missing, however, is an extended treatment of how revised conceptions of law will fit into a wholly transformed society.[3] Doctrinal commentaries are not of course obliged to include tidy, synoptic descriptions of utopian arrangements. Since much critical legal writing has taken the form of such commentary, expectations should not be too high. One of the most ambitious attempts to delineate the essential features of a post-liberal polity, Unger's *Knowledge and Politics*, antedates much of this doctrinal critique.[4] That text, along with Unger's voluminous tracts from the 1980s, presents many of the major problems of understanding how the business of critique translates into social reconstruction. It should not be taken for granted that critique by itself constitutes a mode of reconstruction, although there are grounds for believing that some critical legal writers hold this to be true. One of the central conclusions of the present chapter is that such an opinion is wrong. There are many ways to practise politics while engaged in legal debates, in whatever forum, but the academic criticism of existing legal arrangements is not a sufficient condition of revolutionary change. Although critical legal studies was dedicated to achieve such a transformation, the envisioned society has never become clearly apparent.[5]

By isolating the two paradoxes at the beginning of this chapter, I am characterizing the failure of critical legal exponents to stimulate political transformation as a systematic failure. The critique has been largely prevented from achieving its goal of a post-liberal regime by its reluctance to assert a defensible scheme of political values or of the arrangements that are meant to serve them. The paradoxical quality of this failure arises from the widespread conviction that the critical legal project makes political debate the core of legal education. This conviction, or in some quarters this apprehension, should be set off against a reading of critical legal texts intent on discovering the elements of a distinctive critical legal politics. What this search turns up is a surprisingly non-committal stance towards fundamental political questions. Escaping the paradoxes identified is a difficult process. What might be asked of the members of the movement, and what members might demand of one another, is more political discussion and activity, not less. The object would be to take a stand, to develop and defend political conceptions of legitimacy, obligation, equality, power, and the protection of minority groups, as well as gender and social justice – to become fully engaged in political discussion, rather than leaving political matters to be decided within an imaginary or future society. The mood of the debate ought to be assertive instead of subjunctive.

There has been a sense within the movement that critical legal writing need not always be aimed at the final form of a transformed society. Indeed, the approach of nearly all critical legal writers has been more modest. Their concern has been to suggest particular values, perhaps underplayed in precedent or current law, that ought to be accorded priority in further doctrinal development, or novel patterns of argument that would displace the notion that adjudication should be conceived as a matter of finding and applying reasonably definite and determinative rules. These procedures received labels like 'advocacy scholarship.'[6] There is no pretence of neutrality on the part of the radical critic. Once proposals are made, however, the test of their validity must lie, at least in part, in the kind of society to which they would lead, or in the context they would occupy in a quite different system. At this point the critical legal discussion too frequently leaves off, for it is part of the nature of the critique that the final determination of the shape of a post-liberal society is to be left to an authentically democratic decision. It is not something to be imposed in advance.

Nevertheless, some of the claims of critical legal writing with respect to the way in which post-liberal values differ from their liberal counterparts are susceptible to scrutiny. Included in the credo of critical legal study are beliefs in experimentation and imagination. The problems posed in this chapter arise out of the question of how current Western societies may be reconstructed along fundamentally new lines. Critical legal writers have claimed that reform is an inadequate response to social ills, for it fails to resolve the basic contradictions endemic in liberal legal thought.[7] To be persuaded of the need for a new set of arrangements and values however, we need to know precisely what they are. The purpose of this chapter is to bring critical legal proposals for revolutionary change out into the open and to assess the merits of each. The watchwords of critical legal discourse in this regard have been 'community' (and its cognates); genuine or radical democracy; and intersubjective concern, debate, and deliberation. The compelling idea is that the room for discussing and choosing among political values must be made as large and public as possible. The selection of fundamental values is not a task to be left to the political enclaves of courts and legislatures.

The discussion begins with a brief account of those features of liberal democracy in practice and theory that have led to the legally sustained oppression of many members of supposedly democratic societies. We then turn to a detailed portrait of what various critical legal writers envision as an alternative basis for social and legal order. The chapter concludes with an extensive discussion of the difficulties inherent in the critical legal attempt to aid in the theoretical overthrow of existing institutions. These difficulties are so serious as to bring into question the ultimate success of the critical legal attack on conventional doctrine and theory.

The Occlusion of Debate in Liberal Society

One of the main criticisms made by critical legal writers of established ways of thinking is that the collective political imagination in contemporary liberal democratic societies has been systematically stunted. Citizens, however, persist in believing that existing institutions reflect the best of all possible worlds. They fail to realize the defects in their practices and in the theory by which such practices are explained. As discussed in Chapter 3, raising to the surface of consciousness an awareness of these defects is one of the crucial emancipatory goals of the critical legal movement. The critical legal project also involves the promotion of communitarian values and processes. Before describing the virtues of the critical legal alternative to legal liberalism, it is useful to outline the failures of current structures.

The institutions of representative democracy have for the most part been repudiated by critical legal writers. On the critical legal view the use of representatives in societies too large for direct political participation threatens democratic ideals. Representatives in popular assemblies might exercise independent judgment, contrary to the wishes of their constituents. They might also view themselves as representing only the majority, or the largest single minority, within that constituency.[8] In societies where the mass of citizens participate in politics only to the extent of casting a vote every few years during elections for the various levels of government, democracy as practised is a mere shadow of its ideal form. This regrettable situation, in which most members of society are politically apathetic, cannot even be justified on the ground of expediency. As one critic (from outside critical legal studies) notes: 'For most liberal democrats, representative government is not at all a concession to the difficulties of practical political life, but is itself the ideal.'[9]

Radical critiques of modern liberal democracies question whether they really amount to democracies in anything but name. A form of government in which non-participation by most citizens is tolerated or even encouraged is not truly democratic. Political participation ought to involve more than just filling out a ballot. Ideally, all citizens ought to be given maximum opportunity to engage in meaningful debate in many different forums (not just traditional political assemblies) over values that affect them.[10] The vocation of politics should not be restricted to those seeking representative office; it should be practised by every person who wants to be a citizen rather than a subject.[11] Political participation has not, however, been conceived in this way by liberal writers.[12]

Debate over fundamental values has been generally withdrawn from public gatherings that involve ordinary members of a society and has been carried on instead at the level of legislative deliberation, bureaucratic administration, or legal adjudication. This development has minimized the importance of the private individual's statement of personal values. Thus, according to critical legal thinking, while liberal democracies are supposed to devote themselves to the recognition of individual preferences, the system actually works against taking into account such preferences. Decision making on many fundamental issues is effectively insulated from widespread contribution.[13] The critical legal attack has been directed in particular at the claim that courts possess some privileged insight into the shared values that form the basis of a polity and its ideal social practices.[14] This liberal view has been challenged on the grounds that there are no such values and that the liberal account itself assumes the lack of shared values as one of its major premises.[15] Ceding the job of protecting the moral basis of our society to judges is interpreted by critical legal writers as a tacit admission by liberals that the public is not to be burdened with the problem of deciding issues affecting the common good.[16]

The critical legal account has made great play out of what it sees as a principal assumption of liberal thinking: that there is no widespread, shared conception of what is to be prized in contemporary social and political life. No single value or set of values commands general respect. The values held in fact conflict with one another and there is no meta-theory available by which to sort out which values are defeasible in light of superior ones.[17] The radical critic takes this premise and tries to turn it back upon any liberal effort to construct a moral or legal theory that purports to show how communal life is possible despite a lack of consensus on values. The insidious assumption of radical individualism is supposed to be threaded through the foundations of political practice and legal doctrine. Critical legal writers refuse to accept this state of affairs as inevitable or as part of the human condition. The failure of legislators and courts to arrive at an adequate conception of the common good does not mean that such a conception cannot be fashioned by other, non-liberal political means. The invocation of the ideal of communal dependence and dialectic is intended to show how shared values may be achieved. This ideal, which includes at its core an overriding concern for the public or social good, is supposed to provide a release from liberalism's 'predatory and vicious conception of politics.'[18]

One of the critical legal objections to the liberal doctrine of individual rights is that the relationship between persons and the community in which they are active is reified. Instead of trying to understand and describe the particular circumstances of a person seeking meaning and fulfilment in a deeply social context, the courts, by relying on a rhetoric of abstract rights, ignore the peculiar aspects of specific cases.[19] Only a formal sort of justice is achieved. The language of rights again serves to reinforce the separation between the public role of the citizen and her private life. Most rights protected under liberal regimes are directed at freeing the individual from interference by others, and particularly from state action. Self-fulfilment is thus implicitly assumed to be a matter of freedom to do as one chooses in the private sphere, where the virtues of fellowship, love, and cooperation are supreme. By contrast, the public sphere is perceived as a threatening, competitive, and impersonal environment.[20] The distinction between the two realms has developed historically, and the boundaries shift constantly.[21] Nor should it be assumed that the public sphere is delimitable simply as a matter of state activity. The evolution of liberal capitalist society into corporate-welfare forms has broken down the conventional distinction of public authority from private business.[22] The critical legal goal has been not to reinvent these categories by contrasting community with autonomy, but instead to arrive at a conception of community that incorporates the criteria of what is to count as autonomy.[23] Freedom is to be achieved through, not despite, the matrix of group activity.

In a liberal legal system, legal doctrine does not seize on the possibility that there are alternative conceptions of human relationships. Instead, legal 'ideas constrict the horizons of the possible by establishing within consciousness the boundaries of legitimate authority.'[24] Thus law 'mediates' political issues by purporting to resolve them in a 'neutral' manner without the messy contentions involved in power struggles among political interest groups.[25] From the critical legal point of view such mediation is merely a ploy designed to mask the extent to which law itself is a political process deeply imbued with the stains of illegitimate power and corruption.

The critical legal account is ambiguous about whether law has contributed to the gradual disappearance of communal ties and affections. The imposition of the state, at least in its liberal democratic form, may be seen as a response to liberal assumptions about individual egoism and struggle. The liberal justification of government is based on the need for an agency able to regulate effectively the competitive relationships that spring up between individuals who seek to maximize their own utilities. In the process, activities that were formerly controlled by communitarian notions of reciprocity, custom, and fellowship became subject to legal forms of regulation. This is one of the conventional arguments made in support of a certain type of anarchism, which as an ideology is aimed at demonstrating the dispensability of the state and its apparatus.[26] One possible driving mechanism behind the critical legal emphasis on communal values is the characterization of law as contributing to the alienation of the modern individual. The liberal state and its legal forms estrange members of the same community, who are blocked from realizing their common interests. There is a faint echo here of Marxist literature on alienation as a widespread social consequence of capitalist economic relations.[27]

Other critical legal authors argue that law as a mediating factor actually reduces or eliminates alienation. This argument has been given its most detailed exposition by David Trubek: '... the "mediative" perspective prepares us to grasp the full complexity and contradiction of legal life, and to avoid a series of errors that can stem from more simpleminded approaches. The mediative perspective asserts that a significant feature of legal life in liberal, capitalist societies is the simultaneous assertion and negation of basic ideals of equality, individuality, and community. The legal order neither guarantees these ideals, nor does it simply deny them: it does both.'[28] In this portrait of the operation of law, politically dominated classes are reconciled with the established social order in part because legal institutions succeed in capturing communal as well as self-seeking aspirations. The message of legal rhetoric is thus loaded with inherently contradictory values that both befuddle and appease the powerless. There is naturally a cost associated with the mechanism of mediation, and it takes the form of political quiescence. The vast majority of subjects in a liberal democracy are denied clear-cut choices. Entrenched power holders also reap advantage by keeping legal doctrine 'complex' in the sense adopted by Trubek. Even on this latter theory, the radical critique is valuable for dispelling illusions. Although individuals may not be alienated in the classic, Marxist sense, they must still be freed from an intellectually captive state.

One way to achieve the desired emancipation is to make available the 'visions' or 'images' that reveal the shape of a non-liberal social order. The critical legal account on this score is, like the Platonic, strongly visual.[29] The usual critical legal agenda has been to point out the ubiquity of liberal assumptions about social life and then to speculate on the shape of society built on different assumptions. The employment of 'irreconcilable visions of humanity and society' has generated illuminating doctrinal deconstruction in one part of the critical legal project.[30] The object is not to find a 'balance' between opposing schemes, for critical legal thinking is wholly averse to the image of a balance in reaching judgment,[31] but to retrieve conceptions that might have been suppressed owing to the dominance of single set of assumptions. The critical legal goal of describing the conditions that prevail in a social order conjecturally different from the existing one has been stated in deep philosophical terms. The problems of arranging a social order that gives due weight to the communal aspirations of all its members can be framed, on this way of thinking, as a philosophical problem involving the tension between recognition of self and understanding of others.[32]

The crucial idea behind the radical adjuration to take up the activity of polity-building is that there is no permanent or necessary political order. Readers of critical legal literature are invited to engage their political imagination and construct the system that approaches our progressive ideal. Of course, critical legal writers have not provided a startlingly novel insight into the possibility of unfettered theorizing and human control over political forms: a similar level of recognition can be traced back at least as far as the Sophists, and Plato later provided an example of the thorough exercise of speculative political vision.[33] Correspondingly, reification, in the sense of a belief that the current state of affairs is natural, outside of time, and immune to manipulation, is not a uniquely liberal mode of thought, although critical legal writing often makes it appear that way.[34]

A Communitarian Understanding of Law and Society

In this section of the chapter we begin with a brief consideration of what might reasonably be demanded of critical legal writers in the way of details about a post-liberal society, and then turn to the different ways in which that society has been conceived. It will become clear as the various modes are presented that they are not perfectly congruent with one another. Given that the members of the critical legal movement are not knit tightly together by subscription to any particular party dogma, such variety is not surprising.

The question of whether a societal blueprint is possible can be answered firmly in the negative, at least so far as providing a blueprint means describing in minute detail the institutions, practices, and values that will go to make up a society that rejects liberal principles of social order. As argued above, critical legal writers have refused to be drawn into the game of imagining the precise contours of a progressive polity. There are at least two serious problems, from the critical legal perspective, associated with any attempt to indulge in 'blueprintism.' In the first place, no single form of social life is logically bound to succeed existing liberal democracies. Critical legal thought does not fall into the Hegelian trap of arguing that political history follows a developmental pattern that will culminate in a specific, transcendent state.[35] Secondly, to the extent that transformation does occur, it will most likely be the result of incremental progress. No apocalyptic change is guaranteed by the radical critique of law. Instead, critics of social theory and practice are content to arrive at, and pass on to others, glimpses of utopian possibilities in the material being examined. A critical program, in other words, does not necessarily dictate a comprehensive form of ideal social order.[36] Finally, to provide a description of the particular institutions in a post-liberal society would be antithetical to one of the core themes of critical legal thinking. As we have seen, emphasis on the importance of universal participation in setting the values that will inform a society is a familiar motif in the radical literature. Critical legal writers have thus been limited in their activity to detecting the inconsistencies, empirical mistakes, and logical fallacies found in the liberal premises that justify existing legal and political practice. Radical critics would violate their own strictures on the democratic determination of social forms if they tried to spell out the specific values that ought to be given priority in a transformed polity. The social problem is not merely one of providing a legislative program for a community created *in vacuo*. Rather, the task is to aid in the birth of a new psychological as well as political and legal orientation. Promoting a new form of individualism, in which every member of a society is enculturated with traits of economic initiative and enterprise or given scope to pursue the widest range of opportunity,[37] would amount merely to a successor form of liberalism. The real transformation will arise out of a change in widespread consciousness whereby all members of a society grasp how individual welfare and freedom are tied indissolubly to the common good. Such a shift in consciousness cannot be mandated. Furthermore, once it occurs, there is no telling in advance how it will issue in new structures of legal or political practice.

With the foregoing constraints in mind, it becomes clear that critical legal thought is utopian only in a special sense. Although critical legal writers stress the role of imagination and speculation in political discussion, the point is not to discover a single, timelessly perfect set of political principles. Such an enterprise imposes closure on further discussion and experimentation. Interestingly, to the critical legal eye, practitioners of law-and-economic analysis espouse such a truncated theory. Their assumptions about rational self-interest and about efficiency as the product of legal entitlements and unimpeded markets represent the sort of intellectual fallacy critical legal thought strives to avoid.[38]

The critical legal refusal to assert more than the general direction of a progressive legal theory and practice has assumed two significant alternative theoretical forms. The first is to make opposition to current structures and practices a matter of principle; the second is to describe the search for post-liberal premises as a pragmatic exercise. By elevating the practice of opposing governing conceptions of rights, of the rule of law, and of constitutionalism to a guiding precept, critical legal writers have tried to accomplish two tasks. First, they have attempted to bring systematically to light the suppressed possibilities buried within legal and political discourse and to make those possibilities live options once again. Even though a radical critic might have some sympathy for certain aspects of liberal doctrines and institutions, the critical program requires that critic to subject all the outgrowths of liberalism to fundamental scrutiny.[39] Second, by belonging to an 'oppositional community,' that is, to a group of like-minded inquirers who share doubts about how much justice any current legal system can achieve, critical legal writers hope to provide a model for the shape a post-liberal community might take. Such a community will be composed of members who are united by a common target of criticism and who are in a position to demonstrate to some extent in their own relationships and critical projects the virtues of undominated intellectual exchange.[40] Members of the critical legal movement ought thus to recognize their own interdependence and live up to the communitarian ideals of care, mutual assistance, and opposition to all forms of hierarchy, domination, sexism, and racism. Examination of the critical legal literature reveals the repeated invocation of these ideals.[41]

The second theoretical explanation of why only a vague outline of post-liberalism is possible might be labelled 'pragmatism.' According to this view, individuals are the authors of their own social system and are capable of giving meaning to legal ideas. They should not be concerned with whether their inherited ideas are true, at least in some positivist sense. As Trubek notes: 'While positivists look for the facts because they are the "true" reality and determinists think the facts represent the "only" reality, pragmatists seek to explore the way our provisional worlds work so that they can determine the consequences of the concepts we employ and the projects in which we are engaged.'[42] If the critic's goal is to commend the virtues of a society based on the values of community rather than individualism, the pragmatic course of theorizing requires the critic to suggest concepts or arrangements that might be adopted by a genuinely democratic polity. But this activity does not include a licence to construct particular institutions; it is essentially limited to testing the social effects of proposed concepts. Since that kind of test is only practicable in light of the actual circumstances of a future society, the radical critique's pragmatist aims are really no greater in scope than oppositionism.[43]

In following sections of the discussion make an initial attempt to isolate and describe some of the approximate shapes critical legal thinking has assumed on the issue of which non-liberal values lie at the foundation of a new social order. It bears emphasizing that most of the suggestions made in this respect have occurred primarily in the context of doctrinal criticism, not in that of constructing a systematic social theory. The significant exception is Unger's work, the early parts of which at least nominally served as the basis for much subsequent critical legal thinking. The first four sections that follow relate particular visions of how a progressive community may be shaped using the full powers of our political imagination: the socialist, the local, the civic republican, and the intersubjective communication visions. I then turn to Unger's conception of the ideal organic community.

Socialist Organization

As has been noted several times throughout this book, it is difficult to judge the extent to which the critical legal project is a Marxist project. An assessment would depend to some degree on an analysis of the Marxist, neo-Marxist, or post-Marxist elements in leading critical legal texts.[44] But it is clear at least that critical legal thinking is sufficiently leftist that, in its account of the economic foundation of the existing legal order, capitalism is seen as historically the concomitant, if not the necessary economic form, of liberalism. In particular, capitalist relations of production are seen as responsible for the destruction of the communal virtues of cooperation and fraternity. Moreover, the effects of capitalist organization have been gross inequalities of economic and political power within liberal democracies. The development of class distinctions is assumed to be inimical to the requirements of a just community. The latter insight is, of course, not unique to Marxist-inspired critiques of modern social organization; it can also be found in writers such as Rousseau, who are difficult to position on any contemporary political spectrum.[45] The general consciousness that allows class relations to appear legitimate has been the subject of much critical legal discussion.[46]

There is no comprehensive, sustained description in critical legal writing of how socialism provides the guidelines for a future progressive society.[47] Instead, only hints appear within critical legal literature that such a model is the most desirable solution. There has been no attempt within that body of writing to point to any existing or past experiment with a socialist government as instructive or worthy of emulation. On the contrary, Gabel has acknowledged that his conception of socialism has nowhere been fully tried.[48] The relevant remarks by critical legal writers consist for the most part in noting the conjunction between socialist ideals and the values of equality, common ownership of public goods, and accessibility to power. There is also no indication among these writers that socialism is likely to be a realistic political option in, for example, the United States. Critical legal theorists refuse to descend to the level of participating in actual party politics, and instead conduct their analysis on the basis of the principles judges might be persuaded to apply in adjudicating cases of great moment. Mark Tushnet, for instance, has pointed out a possible socialist interpretation of the U.S. constitution. The idea behind this proposal is that the seeds for such an interpretation are already present in the developed case law.[49] But these seeds are acknowledged by Tushnet as rare elements within the body of public law; generally, 'socialism is not on the agenda of contemporary public law scholarship.'[50] Tushnet's observation is borne out in particular by the critical legal analysis of the judicial interpretation of collective bargaining legislation, where it becomes clear that liberal conceptions of work, labour, and capitalist control still predominate.[51]

Perhaps the principal reason that socialism has not been chosen as the automatic model for a post-liberal society is that critical legal writers are concerned with issues that transcend the organization of productive relations within a polity. Productive relations are without question an important issue to be addressed in the process of transforming current modes of thinking, but they are not the dominant issue. Critical legal writing often stresses a concern for conceiving new forms of life that have little to do with productivity or markets. Also important, of course, are questions about who should control the distribution of goods and entitlements within a particular society. The version of socialist thinking that would assign this task to an overseeing and coercive state is bound to antagonize those critical legal writers who advocate an idea of community that renders such state functions unnecessary and possibly pernicious.

Local Organization

A grassroots emphasis on the general shape of a progressive community is not opposed to socialist ideals of economic, political, or educational equality. It rejects, however, according to the large, powerful state the role of guarantor of such values and it rejects paternalist state intervention into the course of life individuals or small groups choose to follow.[52] This rejection is not rooted in libertarian concerns; critical legal objections to such a megalithic role for the state have to do with promoting the ideal of democratic group decision, even down to the level of politics within the family rather than being based on some notion of absolute or generally inviolable individual autonomy.

A second rationale for favouring a concept of localized, decentralized community is prompted by the critical legal theory of mediation. One effect of this process is that political discussion is channelled through representative, bureaucratic, or legal institutions. Popular deliberation is held to be either unworkable in practice or untrustworthy, in that reason is sacrificed to mass will or opinion. By setting the debate within a local context, in which the persons participating can gain a concrete grasp of the issue and the consequences that will flow from the different possible decisions, a type of democracy can be achieved that transcends liberal notions. This process would satisfy a cardinal critical legal aim, to reduce 'abstract universals to concrete social settings' and thus to 'expose as ideology what appears to be positive fact or ethical norm.'[53] To illustrate how this process of direct decision making can help resolve basic tensions within liberal legal thought, Tushnet has cited the First Amendment protection of free speech in the U.S. constitution. By conceiving of this protection as a fundamental right that should presumptively prevail over any state action that attempts to circumscribe it, liberal constitutional thinking runs into deep trouble with such potential rights claimants as Nazis or pornographers.[54] In a localized setting, the arguments that could be made on behalf of the effects on communal life would be more obvious. The particular historical circumstances and social consequences of the activity in question would not be refined out of the adjudicative process. Instead, the concrete impact on group life would be retained as a focal issue. To make this sort of decision procedure possible, Tushnet and other critical legal writers seem to adhere to a conception of community that would permit direct, political resolution of disputes that touch immediately on the lives of those in the community. Although they do not specify the optimal size of a community in which this kind of politics could flourish, it would have to be much smaller than anything comparable among contemporary Western democracies. It would certainly be smaller than any U.S. state capital and may indeed be something in the order of an urban neighbourhood or rural village. Tushnet has suggested in passing a concept of federalism that would help communities deal with larger coordination problems, but that suggestion introduces a host of new problems that communitarian democracy cannot easily handle.[55]

The ideal of a local community as the primary social unit also appeals to that strand of critical legal thinking that would limit the application of law. Part of a critical understanding of law is the realization that there are many ways to structure relationships other than on legal models. The notion of customary regulation of social practices is important as an antidote to the claim that all relationships can be analysed using legal criteria. Once it is accepted that modern liberal societies tend to fragment into smaller communities that contend over national policies, the way is paved for adjusting conceptions of the relevance of legal control and sanctions.[56]

Critical legal writers have not directly addressed the question of whether representative or bureaucratic institutions should be incorporated into a progressive society. The logical implication of their claims about the necessity for widespread, direct participation in the determination of controlling social values is that those institutions should either be fundamentally reformed or jettisoned.[57] Participation in local public affairs does more than enable the individual citizen to become more capable of understanding and contributing to national political life.[58] Local participation is both a good thing in itself and necessary for a genuine democracy to work. This critical legal thesis is potentially radical, because 'local' in this context can be interpreted to extend beyond community-wide politics, to smaller constituent settings such as the workplace, the school, and the home. In all of these contexts members must be able to contribute to any debate concerning the values that should be implemented within that specific setting.[59] If the communitarian impulse were followed to its ultimate conclusion, there may not be such a thing as national politics. A further implication of this stress on the value of local participation is that politics potentially becomes an all-pervasive activity. Critical legal writing so far has been concerned to shine a strong light upon the convenient uses of the liberal distinction between public and private spheres. Under liberal ideology, the private world of family, personal relationships, and love becomes the most satisfying for individual development, but is treated as beyond politics. To counteract this division of experience, critical legal writers have doubted altogether the value of the traditional liberal conception of the private realm. I will have occasion below to question whether this is not going too far.

Civic Republicanism

The critical legal appeal to a notion of civic virtue as the motivating force in a workable conception of community has been essentially based on history. It links up with the vision of a local polity discussed in the preceding section. In both, the value of citizen participation in political activities is underscored. However, the civic republican ideal is largely restorative.[60] That is, the critical legal use of this concept has been to reintroduce into the discussion of political values many of the goals and aspirations that once held centre stage, particularly at the time of the debates surrounding the formation of the U.S. republic.[61] The vital elements of this earlier tradition that bear some meaning for current critical legal attempts to describe, even if opaquely, the form of a post-liberal society have been identified by William Simon as equal 'proper-tied independence' and by Richard Parker as 'relative equality, mobilization of the citizenry, and civic virtue.'[62]

Interest in the possibility of reviving civic republicanism as a model for a revised notion of politics roughly coincided with the work of historians of political theory who have emphasized the degree to which the tradition of civic virtue survived for several centuries, even though it was eventually eclipsed by conceptions of politics derived from Hobbes and Locke.[63] The origins of the republican tradition can be traced ultimately to Aristotle and the criteria he laid down for realizing human (in his restrictive terms, of course, men's) potential through participation in the public life of the *polis*.[64] Resort to the ancient Greek *polis*, however, has always led to the problem of idealization, whether the writer be Dante or the German philosophers of the nineteenth century.[65]

Critical legal writers themselves have referred only indirectly to the civic republican tradition,[66] providing little explicit indication how the ideas associated with that tradition can be realized under the conditions faced in a modern society. They make instead vague allusions to the 'classical conception of citizenship' or to the 'intersubjective nature of social life.'[67] The historical evolution of the tradition is an interesting and complicated topic in its own right. It has been, of course, heavily influenced by the specific historical circumstances that accompanied its growth as both reflected and structured by changing emphases in the vocabulary of political discourse.[68] Pocock identifies its modern incarna-tion as a product of the period 'after the civic universe had collapsed,' when Machiavelli sought to provide guidance to the ruler who might try to shape political events through prudent action.[69] This description conveys little about the kind of political principles that constitute repub-licanism. The original ideas had to be refracted through the work of such later theorists as Harrington and Rousseau before they began to take on the shape of a body of thought that emphasized the values of widespread civic participation and held that individual morality was intimately linked with the moral health of the whole community. In Pocock's words: 'The "Machiavellian moment" of the eighteenth cen-tury, like that of the sixteenth, confronted civic virtue with corruption, and saw the latter in terms of a chaos of appetites, productive of depend-ence and loss of personal autonomy, flourishing in a world of rapid and irrational change.'[70]

The civic republican tradition provided an important backdrop to the efforts of the U.S. founding fathers to establish the legitimacy of opposition to the theory and practice of eighteenth-century British politics. As Pocock comments, 'Not all Americans were schooled in this tradition, but there was (it would almost appear) no alternative tradition in which to be schooled.'[71] One of the interesting consequences of the discussions leading up to the establishment of the various state and federal constitutions in the 1770s and 1780s was an eventual abandonment of the strict premises of the civic republican vision. Instead of creating the decentralized conditions for a multitude of small republics of virtue, the early U.S. constitution builders rationalized the creation of multiple forms of central representation and administration.[72] In Pocock's description, theorists abandoned the idea that citizens were capable of perceiving the common good, and substituted instead the idea that they could only perceive their own particular interest.[73] In the final analysis, '... the republic asked too much of the individual in the form of austerity and autonomy, participation and virtue, and the diversification of life by commerce and the arts offered him the world of Pericles in place of that of Lycurgus, a choice worth paying for with a little corruption.'[74] The allusion to political corruption as the contrast to civic virtue helps explain one of the more notorious comments made in critical legal debate, in which Mark Tushnet accused Laurence Tribe of this peculiarly eighteenth-century vice.[75] It is a slightly ironic criticism, since on a civic republican model, a scholar's desire to serve in a more public capacity, such as in the judiciary, is not by itself corrupt. In fact, such an ambition is probably more defensible than remaining simply a private individual. The issue really turns on how 'austere' (to use Pocock's adjective) one's notion of a republic is. In a significant sense, critical legal writers' infrequent appeals to the notion of civic virtue recall the tactics of orators of the late Roman republic, who spiced their arguments with invidious comparisons to some early period of the republic, glorious for the selfless devotion of its puritanical and patriotic heroes.[76]

The Device of Intersubjective Rationality

The fourth type of vision propounded in critical legal writing differs from the first three in that there has been less of an attempt to explicate the notion of community by reference to the affective values of solidarity and fellowship, or to historical paradigms. The problem posed under this fourth head is to imagine a situation in which members of a community might be enabled to reach some shared conceptions of the communal good and thus overcome the liberal premise that no such conception can or should become dominant. The critical legal interest is in defining the necessary and sufficient conditions that attend the process of making such decisions.

The analogy occasionally drawn to show what critical legal theorists are seeking is found in Habermas's description of the ideal speech situation. This is a very technical construct and difficult to understand. It has been appropriated even though critical legal writers have done little to demonstrate the relationship between their projects and Frankfurt School critical theory.[77] If they had explored that relationship, the curious result might have been a deeper explanation of the varieties of opinion within the Frankfurt School. Adorno's views on the purposes of reflection and the evaluation of social and cultural practices form a strong contrast with Habermas's more recent work on the same issues.[78]

Habermas's theory of the ideal speech situation is intended to serve an evaluative or normative purpose. It is a device for determining what reflective agents might agree are the types of consciousness that could only have been developed under coercive conditions. Reaching this conclusion is the same as casting off that consciousness. To achieve the level of understanding at which such a rational reconstruction can take place, Habermas has to provide the philosophical justification that in some sense every communication presupposes the possibility of a form of life free from unwarranted domination.[79] This is a transcendental undertaking: 'Like Kant's transcendental philosophy, universal pragmatics aims at disclosing conditions of possibility, but the focus shifts from the possibility of experiencing objects to the possibility of reaching understanding in ordinary language communication.'[80] Although Habermas is aware of the transcendental tack this project takes, the information used to test the reconstructive hypotheses is gathered empirically by observation or by report of language users. The practical value of Habermas's construct is evident in this summary of the ideal speech situation, for it '... will serve Habermas as a transcendental criterion of truth, freedom, and rationality. Beliefs agents would agree on in the ideal speech situation are *ipso facto* "true beliefs," preferences they would agree are "rational preferences," interests they would agree on are "real interests."'[81]

For critical legal purposes, the practical or ethical side of Habermas's project has been exemplary. It seems to offer the prospect of a rational, consensual grounding for values within a community. It would therefore defeat the challenge of relativism posed by liberalism, namely that no such consensus is possible, because all moral values are ultimately subjective and based on the individual agent's self-interest. The ideal speech situation presupposes that agents are capable of engaging in unconstrained dialogue to reach agreement about ethical values. Habermas's discursive model does not presuppose any particular principles, leaving that sort of normative content to be produced through general discussion. Moreover, Habermas has not given much indication of the institutional aspects that would satisfy the requirements for an ideal speech community, beyond pointing out that some form of democracy is necessary.[82]

The notion of a radical form of democracy permitting discussion of public issues directly, without the interposition of liberal institutions, is one of the links between Habermas's ideal and the critical legal project to emancipate all citizens from illegitimate forms of domination. For critical legal theorists, legal structures, insofar as they rest on assumptions about subjectivism, the value of individualism, and the legitimacy of some forms of inequality, represent the very constraints that make rational consensus impossible. Loosening the grip of liberal thought is a necessary step in the realization of a progressive form of community. This can be done at the level of consciousness, in the critical legal account, because undermining the preconceptions that hinder citizens' agreeing on a conception of what is in the interest of all of them is a matter of persuasion and rational interchange.

It is important to recognize that the critical legal use of this model does not promise to disclose the form of the good in the Aristotelian sense.[83] Rather, like Habermas's transcendental scheme, the device of intersubjective rationality is designed to show how members of a community can reach some consensus on moral issues. Habermas applies his formulation generally, that is, across all types of communicative action. Critical legal writers are especially interested in the bearings of this attempt at philosophical reconstruction upon the choice of ethical values. The following description by Habermas is brought into relation with the activities of legal and political discourse: 'Coming to an understanding is the process of bringing about an agreement on the presupposed basis of validity claims that can be mutually recognized. In everyday life we start from a background consensus pertaining to those interpretations taken for granted among participants. As soon as this consensus is shaken, the presupposition that certain validity claims are satisfied (or could be vindicated) is suspended, the task of mutual interpretation is to achieve a new definition of the situation which all participants can share.'[84]

Habermas's explanation of how normative conceptions can be shared and, in the event of breakdown of consensus, refashioned so as to extend the continuity of the communicative community, has proved powerfully suggestive for critical legal writers. Just as Habermas has aimed his critique at the methods of positivist understanding, based ultimately on a form of solipsism, some critical legal writing would wish to see the device of intersubjective understanding replace the individualist assumptions of liberal social theory.[85] With this radically socialized account of the normative foundations of law and other forms of human understanding and action at its disposal, critical legal writing has tried to illuminate (or at least intimate) the ideal conditions under which social decisions should be made and legitimate authority exercised. Judges can presumably call upon definite principles in arriving at judgments in difficult cases of practical morality, and in creating laws legislators can consider what sort of life is best to lead.

This type of argument has ordinarily been made in less philosophically ambitious terms by critical legal writers. Some treat the mechanism of 'conversation' or 'dialogue' as the key element in surmounting liberal legal conceptions.[86] These authors rarely invoke the authority of Habermas,[87] and their pattern of argument invites some very serious questions and reservations. Habermas has used his refined system of universal pragmatics for the overtly political purpose of testing claims for validity and legitimacy.[88] This complicated procedure does not appear to have any counterpart in critical legal analysis. The ideal speech situation is rather adopted as a suggestive analogy; no full-fledged justification is offered for how it may be put to use to decide among contestable legal claims. Instead, critical legal writers are content to stress the virtues of rational discussion *tout court*, where it is not distorted by differences in power, status, or education among participants. They attempt no systematic presentation of the criteria for accepting and weighing evidence or for determining what 'consensus' means in situations of disputed moral questions. If a transcendental test is possible, then to some extent a group may arrive at a rational conception of the common good that should be applicable for all communities in the same situation. That is, one should be able to universalize the form of the good. This result, however, would offend the central critical legal theme that different communities should be free to determine their own governing values: no universally valid principles apply across communities. A further difficulty arises in the critical legal use of the notion of a set of counterfactual conditions for possible communication. Habermas's conception is an evaluative device. It is not necessarily meant to provide the model of an attainable society,[89] but is rather a standard for measuring the principles that an actual society might adopt. In this sense, it bears a curious resemblance to the theory of the 'original position,' hypothesized by Rawls as a method for isolating the conditions of justice in modern societies.[90] The critique of Rawlsian theory from the left has condemned the idea that 'disembodied individuals,' with no self-knowledge of their history or possessions of wealth or personality, could be used as an heuristic device for distinguishing principles of justice.[91] In other words, the abstractness of the procedure and its a priori nature are serious faults. To adopt Habermas's transcendental procedure may amount to the commission of a similar fallacy. This is not to say that Rawls's and Habermas's theories are on all fours with each other on any material issues.[92] It is only to point out that radical critics are in danger of falling into what some have claimed is a liberal trap.[93]

A final query to be raised in this context is whether a major philosophical theory is needed to justify critical legal claims about the possibility of intersubjective agreement and understanding. As we shall see below, in a significant sense the developed law already constitutes one mode of a 'community of understanding.' In the process of legal interpretation, there might already be found a 'parable of conversation' which Tushnet thinks ought to be central to the task of arriving at shared moral conceptions.[94] Limiting notions of what it means to make and defend a claim, to appeal to a recognized principle, and to present evidence in support of a claim are all part of the social practices that constitute the process of adjudication. In the hands of critical legal writers who depend on a variation of this notion, the ideal speech situation would largely incorporate conditions already embedded both in legal and other contexts where rational arguments are deployed.

Unger's Early Theory of Organic Groups and Later Description of Empowered Democracy

Roberto Unger occupies a singular position within the critical legal movement and two odd features distinguish his involvement with the project. First, the frequency of citations to his synthetic reconstruction of liberal social and political theory would indicate that his publications of the mid-1970s proved to be an essential part of the groundwork for the task of identifying and criticizing the liberal presuppositions of laws and legal institutions. Yet, as mentioned in Chapter 2, Unger's work generally and, in particular, its excursion in the 1980s into specific proposals for the recasting of contemporary societies in both Western capitalist and developing countries, has been little remarked on by other critical legal writers. The second feature worth noting is that Unger's own discussion of the alternatives to existing social structures and to reigning social theory takes conspicuously little account of the great volume of critical legal efforts to describe the flaws of the modern legal imagination. Unger appears to have followed his own trajectory, one which makes only incidental reference to the somewhat parallel course inscribed by fellow members of the movement. His is a solitary enterprise in the service of high, communitarian ideals.

The need remains for a thorough assessment and appreciation of Unger's work. Such an overview would have to trace through his writing themes and arguments that have become richly textured as they have been treated in philosophical, political, historical, psychological, and comparative contexts. I do not undertake that ambitious analysis here, but concentrate instead on some key ideas first adumbrated in his work on the interrelationship between epistemology and political theory and later given a detailed exposition in his three-volume treatise, *Politics*.[95] Unger has made some advances beyond the initial position set forth three decades ago and the comparison of his earlier and more recent work can be used to create a contrapuntal effect. With his restless intelligence and dialectical flair, Unger has so far been his own ablest critic.

The point of departure for Unger's earliest treatment of the shape of post-liberal social arrangements is the way in which the concept of community contrasts with that of autonomy.[96] The liberal tradition is wedded to the value of individuals as the basic units of society and their being accorded an alienable form of autonomy. From this notion flow many of the principles that shape existing institutions. Liberalism's pronounced emphasis on the value of autonomy has, according to Unger, both distorted social life and hampered the possibilities of a continuous process of revision and transformation of our form of social life. Community, in this part of Unger's discussion, bears heavy religious overtones, but as he candidly admits sacred and secular thought are inevitably mixed in his vision of the alternative ideal to current modes of theorizing.[97] Not only in the invocation of such terms as immanence and transcendence, but also in characterizing evil as a deprivation, Unger is following well-worn tracks of religious argumentation, in the latter case drawing obviously on Augustinian theodicy.[98] His description of Christianity as evolving from a hierarchical order to a recognition of the primary value of autonomy (exemplified in the Protestant Reformation) reveals that his picture of the growth of liberal political thought has analogies in many areas of social life.[99]

The method of analogy is crucial for the justification of Unger's project. It provides a bridge between philosophical speculation and political practice. The one endeavour supplies the theory which the other attempts to realize through the process or faculty of prudence.[100] Prudence, with its connotations of practical reason, represents the method of giving content to what theory has determined is the good. It becomes a necessary component in the life of post-liberal community.

The significance of community is revealed by Unger's original attempt to describe a doctrine of organic groups. It is through these groups that the antinomies generated by liberal thought can be resolved. Organic groups constitute the hope for an escape from the institutional paralysis that currently bedevils liberal democracies. Unger's conception of such groups is not the only way a community might possibly be envisioned; traditionally, adherents of various political persuasions have epitomized their respective theories by defining an ideal of community and distinguishing it from the reigning social order.[101] Unger's vision purports to be more penetrating, however, for it seeks to show how the relation between individuals' selves and their community can be metaphysically as well as politically explicated. Unger invokes notions of the concrete universal (with its Aristotelian and Hegelian echoes) and species nature as exemplified in each person (in this respect echoing the early Marx).[102] His recent treatment of the theme of how a regenerative form of society might be imagined explicitly denies many of the premises that inform one type of Marxist social theory and philosophy of history. Unger has been careful to counterpose his own thinking on the revisable nature of our social contexts with what he calls the 'deep-logic' or 'deep-structure' social theories that would envision ready-made sequences of social orders. Deep-logic theories are correct insofar as they deny what Unger calls the pervasive 'naturalistic premise' about society. In Unger's words, deep logic theory 'represents a denial of the conditionality of social worlds.'[103] But such theories err in failing to capture what has actually occurred in modern social evolution and, more importantly, in placing limits on agents' capacity to rearrange the formative contexts of their own history. These formative contexts are, according to Unger, always capable of being 'put up for grabs.'[104]

In his earlier writing, Unger refrained from giving many details about the optimal size, internal organization, external features, or productive relations of the imagined community. His discussion of prudence dictates that it is left to each organic group's collective judgment to determine such features.[105] He mentions only that the membership should be small enough that the choice over shared values can be accomplished and that members can come to know one another outside their occupational roles as producers within the community.[106] In addition, Unger specifies a need for plurality and diversity of sub-groups within the community, and for a democratic process for resolving differences,[107] thereby allowing values to come to be shared by group members. Those who disagree with the choice of values should be able to leave one community and re-establish themselves in a more congenial one. Freedom of expression and free movement between groups become, in Unger's view, essential liberties for communitarian politics.[108]

This organization into communities, which become the basic political units out of which nation-states may be formed, does not entail that all life occurs in the public realm. Unger appears to place significant value on keeping some matters outside the public sphere, though precisely which issues are private and which are public at any given time will depend on how boundaries have been shifted around as each community evolves.[109]

On Unger's view there is no highest form of community, no utopian vision of the pre-eminent form of social life. In *Knowledge and Politics* he offered a doctrine of organic groups solely as a 'regulative ideal,' not as a recipe for any future society.[110] Furthermore, his doctrine does not automatically spell the doom of the state. Unger seemed prepared to allow the possibility of political action at the levels of national society and beyond. This possibility remains an admitted defect of his theory and can only be remedied by the eventual institution of a world state. As this aspiration approaches too near the utopian vision Unger rejects, it appears that communitarian goals must be content with something less than radical transformation for the time being.[111]

Unger's communities require experimentation before any accurate judgment can be made about their efficacy and the likelihood of their resisting a potential slide into undemocratic and oppressive political forms. This is the third level of judgment identified by Unger: what one learns in practice will inevitably modify what prudence dictated on the basis of theoretical insight. The concept of community can provide a means to overcome the major drawback of liberal thought, namely domination. This progress is conceived by Unger in metaphorical terms: he employs the figure of a spiral to illustrate the reciprocal relationship between domination and community.[112] There are no universal ends; there is no ultimate resting place for the transformation of social life. A person's imaginative capacities cannot foresee what any final good might be. The use of the spiral to represent progress in the direction of individuals realizing the infinite possibilities of their species nature is meant to capture an advance beyond limited liberal thinking. In other contexts, Unger relies upon an image that lies beyond one's field of vision to illustrate the quest involved in escaping liberal modes of thought.[113]

To this point in the description of Unger's project, primarily as it was presented in its earliest phase, the emphasis has been on how social and political institutions generally might be arranged so as to achieve the intellectual and practical liberation he envisioned. His project began as a treatment of certain jurisprudential issues and then assumed the much larger proportions of a 'total critique.' Unger later spelled out at length the implication of that critique for law. Just as in *Knowledge and Politics* he traced the rise of certain modes of thought that culminate in the liberal vision, so in a companion volume, *Law in Modern Society*, he performed the Weberian task of delineating the transformation of societies through various stages of development, examining in particular how modern Western social life can be significantly contrasted with that of other cultures in different eras. Unger's analysis formed the prolegomenon for his commendation of a legal system that rejects the limitations imposed by the prevailing doctrine of instrumentalism.[114] The consequences of this doctrine, and of various ethical, political, and economic theories nourished by it, are the disintegration of community and the ascendancy of the view that society is an association of individuals. What Unger calls 'positive law' is the outgrowth of the still-ruling ideology that the rule of law provides freedom and order in the predominantly individualistic Western societies.

In contrast to such liberalism is Unger's early vision of how to reconcile the inherent contradictions at the root of Western legal thinking. Against the instrumentalist doctrine he places the doctrine of consensus and its attendant value of anti-hierarchic and anti-bureaucratic solidarity.[115] The concept on which Unger relies to explicate the goal of his radical revision of fundamental legal thinking is that of 'custom.'[116] This he derived from an analysis of how tribal societies (considered as an ideal type) differ from liberal societies. In the former, social relations are based on a communal bond, solidarity and, most importantly, a common vision of the good. This means that there is only a minimal role for explicit rules and bureaucratic structures in regulating conduct. Instead, members of the community have an ingrained sense of the proper relationship between themselves and others as well as a socially conditioned sense of self. Custom accomplishes in the legal context what communitarian political activities achieve for the state as a whole. Again, the lesson is that there is no natural or immanent order in society to which systems of positive law more or less conform. Unger detects to some degree the germ of a recognition of such a communal underpinning in all law. Distinguishing black-letter law from senses of equity and solidarity manifested in all legal systems, Unger characterizes the latter as 'latent and living law' and as the 'elementary code of human interaction.'[117] In Unger's view, underneath legal formality and bureaucratic instrumentalism are buried primary ideas that shape any social order. On the argument in *Law in Modern Society*, they deserve to be raised to a fully conscious level in which they provide the model for all law. The values of community, which provide the background to this more enlightened regime of law, reconcile freedom with the rule of law. Unger once again compares those values with their opposite by means of a spiral. In this instance, the opposite doctrines are those of instrumentalism and individualism.[118]

At some time between his earlier work on the epistemological foundations of social and political theory and his later attempt to portray the essential features of a post-liberal and post-modernistic society, Unger apparently recognized the need to revise his own understanding of the possibility and limits of utopian theorizing. Without actually repudiating his earlier writing, he later approached the task of social reconstruction from a standpoint that acknowledged the necessity of some description of institutions and processes. Although the soundness of his work ultimately rests on the theoretical premises sketched out in *Knowledge and Politics* and more recently in *Social Theory*, Unger seems to have felt compelled to do something more than simply 'invert' the existing structures of social life, which is the strategy of utopian dreamers.[119] The shape of his imaginative reformulation of contemporary social and political institutions was first disclosed in a long essay on critical legal studies[120] and subsequently developed at greater length in *False Necessity*.

The potential for destabilization has emerged as a cardinal virtue in Unger's scheme.[121] He is interested in the possibilities of citizens being free to reconceive perpetually the social structures within which they live. Unger claims to have developed a program that will ensure not a violent revolution that would smash our current institutions, but instead their continual revolutionary reform.[122] His notion of 'transformative activity' involves the unending and purposeful redesign of 'formative contexts.'[123] One of the most curious aspects of his theory is that he no longer envisions the demise of liberalism under the burden of its own contradictions, an event he implied was to be welcomed in *Knowledge and Politics*. Unger's recent tack is to cast his program proposals as the institutional forms liberalism always promised but never delivered. Similarly, he has advocated his vision of empowered democracy as the rational successor to both mature communist regimes and the political styles of developing nations.[124] This resurrection or redemption of both liberal and leftist ideals involves applying our imagination to determine what forms such traditional institutions as markets, rights, and democracy might take in different social contexts. Unger has pointed out that the terms of such reconstruction are already present in some form.

Although generally critical of the school of thought that reduces law to a reflection of moral imperatives embodied by the existing order, Unger is himself pushed in the direction of using his envisioned legal system to protect four fundamental rights: destabilization rights, immunity rights, market rights, and solidarity rights.[125] The first category is necessitated by the desire to ensure that established institutions do not become entrenched to the point of resisting further change. In Unger's scheme, the purpose of immunity rights is to protest each individual's sense of security. Market rights protect citizen's claims to a fair share of social capital. Solidarity rights are the legal expression of the expectations held by members that communal values, such as mutual reliance and vulnerability, will be respected. These limited categories of rights are commended by Unger as a practical necessity, and they are not to be confused with the conception of legal rights prevalent in existing liberal democracies. Inherent in that conception is a zone of discretion surrounding each rightholder that is inviolable and deserves protection by the law.[126] The paradigm of such rights is the 'consolidated property right.' Even entitlements not analogous to property ownership have been fitted into current legal systems according to this Western vision of what a right amounts to. The possibility of solidarity or community offered here, as elsewhere, is meant to provide a countervision to the aspect of domination exhibited by traditional ways of legal thinking.[127]

The institutional details supplied by Unger in *Politics* are vitally important to the issue of whether critical legal thinking can lean towards or is even capable of providing an alternative scheme of political association that reflects radical principles. By comparison with his early work, in which many issues of practice and institutional form were left unexplored, Unger has lately struggled with such questions as the basic forms of production, the distribution of wealth and power, incentives and the creation of opportunities for participation in politics, the uses and limits of representative democracy, and the agency by which radical social change can be achieved. He has tried to give concrete form to the type of economy that might best be used to promote the emancipatory ideals of freedom from dependence and domination. His retrieval of the petty bourgeois form of commodity production and exchange is certainly a clearer conception of a key element of communal life than the vague intimations made in his earlier work.[128]

A further divergence from the theory of organic community portrayed in the assault on liberalism in *Knowledge and Politics* is the scope Unger allows within his imagined polity for institutionalized conflict. His writing on 'personalist politics' and on modern theories of personality have led him to challenge the notion that communitarianism is built on the belief that members of a social group should come to share certain basic values. He has emphasized instead that the communal ideal ought to incorporate a model of human association that 'recognizes the benefits of conflict and insists upon the priority of heightened vulnerability and mutual acceptance.'[129] This ideal is supposed to be consonant with the power of each individual to engage in the transformative activity of context breaking. Where the social portrait created in *Knowledge and Politics* was that of a small, self-sustaining community of devout believers in a common faith, the image of political cohesion presented in *Politics* is characterized by profound tenuousness, ceaseless suggestions of unorthodoxy, and new forms of protection for economic competition – this is pluralistic liberalism with a vengeance.

The institutionalization and personalization of what Unger calls the capacity for 'negative capability' (here uprooted from its Keatsian origins) is meant to indicate and serve the indeterminate varieties of social transformation.[130] The most concise summary of the vision propounded by Unger is found in his text on criticizing legal doctrine:

> The program I have described is neither just another variant of the mythic, antiliberal republic nor much less some preposterous synthesis of the established democracies with their imaginative opposite. Instead, it represents a *superliberalism*. It pushes the liberal premises about state and society, about freedom from dependence and governance of social relations by the will, to the point at which they merge into a larger ambition: the building of

a social world less alien to a self that can always violate the generative rules of its own mental or social constructs and puts other rules and other constructs in their place.

A less contentious way to define the superliberalism of the program is to say that it represents an effort to make social life resemble more closely what politics (narrowly and traditionally defined) are already largely like in the liberal democracies: a series of conflicts and deals among more or less transitory and fragmentary groups.[131]

This vision appears at first blush to be an astonishing reversal of the critique worked out in *Knowledge and Politics*. The explanation lies perhaps in Unger's failure in his earlier work to state clearly how the communities were to be organized or how they might be expected to relate to one another. Little space was given to considering the model of democracy that might best be followed in those communities.[132] All Unger could do by way of excusing this omission was to point to the need for experience and experimentation. However, if he wishes to avoid the charge of advocating inherently authoritarian social structures, he cannot continue to eschew prescriptive treatment. Hence, his scheme has reverted to the language and goals of liberal democracy, albeit on a supposedly higher plane. If Unger is correct in holding that the 'naturalistic premise' is on the wane and that the notion of society-as-artifact and the slogan, 'it's all politics,' must be pushed through to their logical conclusions, he has implicitly diagnosed one of the main drawbacks of the radical critique in respect of legal doctrine. The next question is whether his own program, encompassing a proposed large-scale organization of government, the economy, and the workplace, alongside a theory of undominated personal attachments and social roles, completes the radical agenda.

In his earlier work Unger failed to treat in any detail the problem of the state. He appeared to have in mind some notion that the state and civil society (in the form of communities) are necessarily separable, but he neglected to clarify how the one relates to the other. The situation is in some respects similar to the dilemma faced by Lenin in the period during which he wrote *The State and Revolution*.[133] Lenin was forced to reconcile the assumption of state power by his victorious faction with the ideal, to which he paid lip service, that all power would be distributed among the workers' soviets. While purporting to preside over the demise of the state, Lenin was really engaging in the tortured logic that tolled the death knell for politics as a democratic activity. The soviets resemble to a significant degree the organic groups postulated by Unger. One would have thought that the ultimate consequences of the vision of politics he harboured in his earlier writing meant the eventual disappearance of the state as yet another doomed liberal institution. But Unger appears to have retreated from the brink of this conclusion, thereby avoiding the need to explain why the state and its legal apparatus serve to obstruct the realization of a genuinely organic community.

As noted above, in Unger's earlier work the organic group appeared to be anarchical, acephalous, and for the most part untroubled by the problems of bureaucratic authority. His later work arguably proposes a quite different scheme that purports to improve on political arrangements preferred by classical liberals, libertarians, social democrats, and traditional Marxists. In *Knowledge and Politics* the concept of the market is identified as a prime liberal notion that would be superseded in a post-liberal reconstruction of society. In his earlier discussions of contract doctrine Unger focused on market imagery as a principal defect in current conceptions of how interpersonal relations ought to be regulated. It is therefore curious to see him subsequently arguing for the protection of market rights for each individual. These are something less than the rights in property that have served liberal political theory as the supposed paradigm of all rights. Nevertheless, the market right, such economic structures as the 'rotating capital fund,' and certain principles that resemble anti-trust measures naturally lead to questions about the vision of a small community Unger formerly appeared to have harboured.[134] This community no longer appears to be the self-limiting, deeply spiritual, and harmonious body or polity dedicated to fostering such affective relations as love rather than rivalry. The shift may possibly owe something to a new tone of gradualism that has crept into Unger's writing. It may no longer be necessary in his view for society to be reconstituted by the intentional separation of persons into small communities. Instead, the road to post-liberal redemption lies along an internal change in our existing institutions so that they are held to the standards originally promised by liberal apologists. It is incumbent upon other critical legal writers, who have tended for so long to cite Unger's *Knowledge and Politics* as the last word in the demolition of liberal political thought, to take account of this evolution in Unger's work. No adequate account has yet appeared.[135]

It should be borne in mind that Unger's scheme has been deliberately fashioned to keep alive the central issues of political debate and struggle, not to impose closure on them. In the foreground throughout his discussion in *Politics* is the necessity of constructing institutions that preserve and even enhance the possibility of a collective reconstruction of social life. This is the nerve of Unger's social theory and program. But there is tension within his recommendations for reconstruction. The details of the program appear to touch on the central problems of politics. Unger's task, however, is not to solve those problems, but to envision a context in which they might be solved. In other words, while questions of rights, property, governmental competence and authority, and privacy appear finally to have been explained and a defensible conception of each has been arrived at, the real lesson of *Politics* is that only a setting can be described for these questions. It is still up to the citizens of each polity to put the institutions of that setting to use in determining how their lives shall proceed. The possibility of mistake, corruption, élitism, or authoritarianism continues to loom large. After describing his program of empowered democracy Unger acknowledges that: 'Both our happiness and our virtue depend upon the particular institutional forms we give to the search for plasticity. Just as the quest for empowerment through plasticity may enable us to live out more fully our context-transcending identify, so, too, it may subject us to a despotism less messy or violent but more thoroughgoing than any yet known.'[136]

The net result of Unger's expansive treatment of political and social theory, including its legal dimensions, is that genuinely democratic debate must be postponed until the institutional structures he commends have been adopted through collective mobilization. The critic's role is confined to suggesting or prophesying the actual forms political life might take. The rhetoric of prophecy is the dominant form of discourse Unger has chosen for himself. The role of the prophet is not, however, well suited to addressing the immediate concerns of political debate or practice. The prophet's address is directed at future generations who might be disposed to learn from someone who possessed a privileged vantage point in the past. By redefining politics as the proper concern of futurity, Unger has given the cleverest expression yet to the paradoxes of engagement and postponement.

Problems with Reconstituting Community

As the discussion to this point has tried to make clear, the use of such terms as 'community,' 'communal,' or even 'common good' is largely meaningless. The terms themselves do not disclose any particular program for social or political transformation. To be useful as an analytical or programmatic tool, a conception of community must be elaborated in sufficient detail that the contrast between critical and liberal theory becomes vivid. This elaboration may even require the use of such devices as exaggeration, invention, or fancy. Wolin, for example, sees the concept of community as a time-honoured technique of political theory, a conscious attempt to 'transcend history.'[137] It has also been used for other purposes: for example, as an analytical device in literary criticism and literary theory.[138] The preceding sections of this chapter have outlined some of the possible visions found within critical legal thought. The discussion turns now to the difficulties associated with the scope and meaning of those proposals. Specifically, the problems treated include: the indeterminate outlines of the critical legal use of community as a normative concept; the question of whether the radical critics ignore elements of communal value already present in conventional legal practice and theory; doubts about whether the civic republican ideal can be retrieved; the scope for meaningful political debate in the projected post-liberal community; and, finally, the question of who are to be the designated agents of the transformation, and the way in which the answer to this question reflects upon the current institutional role of radical critics of the law.

Progressive or Conservative Communitarianism

An appeal to a communitarian ideal can be used by theorists whose political orientations may be fundamentally opposed.[139] Critical legal writers can, in standardly leftist fashion, trace the breakdown of communal ties and values to historical changes in economic relations during the early modern period. The invocation of those values is part of the project of restoring to the arena of political debate all of the possible conceptions of social order. The pattern of argument is restorative, though not necessarily nostalgic. By the same token, conservative thinkers have occasionally appealed to the same presence within our political experience of a strong sense of community and of the significance of the collective good. This appeal can be plainly sentimental, as in Tönnies's idea of replacing Gemeinschaft with Gesellschaft, or it can be based on an overriding sense of a living tradition that should never be suddenly overturned.[140] The latter view is essentially Burkean communitarianism.[141] The critical legal approach is to stress the virtues of solidarity, intersubjective communication, and cooperation, but of course the radical critics are sternly opposed to any reconstitution of society based on such communal notions as differentiated power, hierarchical dependency, or the dominance of tradition as a bonding or legitimating force. These static conceptions of social organization are part of the critical legal target.

In addition to the communitarian conception, another tendency of modern social theory vies with the critical legal use of community. Sociologists in the twentieth century sought to find communal notions lurking in contexts other than the general social life of a nation or other grouping. The substitute for communal bonding is to be found at the macroscopic level in large organizations like the corporation or an administrative bureaucracy.[142] This conception of a communal setting within a larger liberal, individualist society is not compatible with the critical legal picture of alienation in the modern state. Employment in a corporate or public sector bureaucracy is no adequate substitute for full participation in a genuinely democratic political process, where members of a community are able to define their own conditions of productive activity without the distortions of authority and unequal power.

These examples show that the concept of community can be, on the critical legal account, as vulnerable to abuse and misconstruction as any other political notion. Tushnet's comments on the notion of community extending through several generations of constitutional history exemplify how such a misconception can take hold.[143] In his analysis, the theory of constitutional 'interpretivism' is attacked on that ground. A theory of non-interpretivism, such as that advanced by critical legal writers, would point up the active creation, rather than the mere inheritance, of a community of understanding.

It should be noted that the distinction between the conservative or nostalgic version of communitarianism and the radically creative or transformative version of critical legal studies is not always properly separated in critical legal writing. In that literature an earlier historical period sometimes appears to provide, in the type of relations among persons at a local level or even within a closed community, the model of a post-liberal grouping. Unger's two earliest books on social theory are particularly at fault in this regard.

It does seem that some specific strategy lies behind the critical legal appeal to communal virtues. This appeal has at least four sides. First, it is grounded in the empirical claim that individual selves do not develop except within a social setting, and that the social influences pressing upon them are determinative of personality. Second, men and women are both naturally political animals in the sense preached by Aristotle

(although he excluded women from his generalization). Only by participating in the public daily life of the polity do persons fulfil their potential as rational agents. Third, at this juncture, given the liberal emphasis
on individual autonomy and the subjective basis of values, the radical
critic must redress the balance by emphasizing the significance of communal values. Finally, harmony itself becomes, to critical legal thought, a
vital social desideratum which, if promoted sufficiently, will lessen the
need for coercive control through legal instruments. The object is to
find the conditions under which conflict can be controlled or, better yet,
transcended.

Taken together the foregoing reasons seem to constitute the best
interpretation of the critical legal emphasis on community as a political
conception. The problem that remains is whether liberalism cannot
share some of the premises critical legal writers claim as their own. In
other words, if a liberal theorist can advance the notions of the social
development of individuality, the importance of political participation,
the communal nature of morality, and the ideal of a relatively harmonious society, the sting is to a large extent removed from the critical legal
attack.[144]

On Legal Communities

As we have seen, one of the great ironies at the root of the radical
critique of legal doctrine is the degree of uniformity imputed to the
members and theorists of liberal democracies, who are all thought to act
under the same delusive consciousness. Yet the critical legal account also
attributes a radically fragmented nature to the values held by those same
individuals. The situation loses its ironic cast if one agrees with the
critical legal claim that the uniformity of thought has been achieved by
illegitimate means. That is, the values held by most citizens are imposed
through the forces of hegemony rather than being freely chosen. Not all
communities of interpretation or understanding are ipso facto desirable
or progressive.

The critique based on consciousness requires an almost total sacrifice
of the prescriptive ideal of a continuous legal culture. For a theorist to
rely upon the notion of enduring values that underlie the articulation of
principles, particularly by judges, is to commit the unforgivable sin of
freezing potential public debate over those values. To carry this radical
argument to its ultimate conclusion, we might say that the community
which must reinterpret its own tradition is never the same community

afterwards. A change of identity is always achieved, because interpretations will inevitably fluctuate as socio-political conditions change. On even the most minor issues members must continually work to destroy and then to reconstitute their community. It seems a reasonable question whether the notion of perpetual flux does not subvert the idea of community altogether.[145] It is not sufficient simply to assert this conception without greater elaboration as to the degree to which it reflects actual social or legal practices. The pre-eminent example of this kind of evaluative procedure is Dworkin's work in the 1980s on law as interpretation.[146] A further instance of a discussion of the claims of community in the context of U.S. constitutional law (bearing particularly on the doctrine of substantive due process) is to be found in the writing of Laurence Tribe.[147]

The variety of senses in which contemporary laws already reflect or arguably might be interpreted to reflect a communitarian spirit requires further investigation. Legal structures based on liberal assumptions may not be entirely in the ascendant now, nor possibly have they ever been in the way claimed by radical historians of the common law. One could cite literature to this effect from both within and without the movement. The evolution of contract law provides examples of the recognition by courts of the necessity of interpersonal bonds of respect and trust.[148] Tort law, it has been claimed, should encompass a concept of a remediable harm to be called 'destruction of community.'[149] Constitutional law, particularly as it incorporates notions designed to protect rights of free assembly, can be made as compatible with communitarian ideology as it can with frankly liberal conceptions of free individual expression as the mark of a healthy society. The dialectic between competing social visions is discernible within these and other doctrinal topics. Critical legal writers, in their frequently demonstrated capacity as scriptor ludens, might even make imaginative play with the 'common' law as multitextured communality.

A point of real difficulty for the radical critique is reached where claims are made for the inevitable closure a legal system or body of principles is supposed to involve. On Unger's notion of a formative context the legal principles employed to create and secure institutional arrangements are 'characteristically ambiguous and contradictory.'[150] Although dominant principles reflect a model of human association that informs all parts of social relations, also present are recessive principles that tend to influence the application of so-called determinative rules. Unger therefore concedes the partly communal content of existing bodies of doctrine. On his view of the process of 'internal argument' (which he relates to a general point about the practice of routines), it ought to 'incorporate more of the characteristics that we traditionally attribute to visionary thought.'[151] This recommendation depends on a theory about how normative argument tends to work within a settled framework that is never, insofar as the activity is 'normal,' subjected to fundamental challenge. Such a conception of the way legal argument proceeds rests heavily on the assumption that liberal legal theory is necessarily embarrassed by elements of incoherence, contradiction, or inconsistency. But not all 'rationalizers' of contemporary systems of common law, as Unger has called mainstream legal theorists,[152] would see the same implications in the claim that a body of developed legal doctrine contains ambiguous or competing principles.[153] Non-radical theorists are generally not naive positivists nor are they blind to the relationship between legal rules and other values in our particular social contexts. It may be that critical legal writers have a different sense from mainstream theorists of the defining characteristics that separate the pathological and normal so far as legal argument is concerned.[154]

If one acknowledges, as Unger has, that current legal doctrines contain the seed of new frameworks for political and personal change, what impact does this recognition have on the necessity of deep social change? Evidently, projecting the countervisions of communal aspiration and mutual vulnerability and reliance is not sufficient as a campaign for mass political enlightenment. Something more is required. This is the point at which the radical critique must question whether intellectual experiments in discovering the suppressed possibilities of political and legal history are enough. Some strategy for the collective mobilization of the citizens either of existing states or of conjectural polities that have yet to coalesce must also be formulated.

The critical legal project can play perhaps two instructive roles in this respect. First, it may offer an example of how continual progressive revolution applies to the attempt by movement members to unite into a community of their own. But in what sense have centrifugal forces overwhelmed conjunctive ones? Have the values that animated the movement at its founding changed significantly? Is the history of the critical legal movement that of a single community extending over time or is a successor community now destined to submit to the forces of fragmentation and realignment? Are movement members not torn between allegiances to the several communities in which they participate (take, for example, the law professor who at once belongs to a departmental or university community, a local community, a national community, and a community of law scholars, as well as to the Conference on Critical Legal Studies)? Most citizens are interested parties in several layers of community life, from the local and specific to the national and international: they are multiply constituted, in the communitarian view. How are the resulting various duties and responsibilities of conscientious citizens to be fitted together? By looking at these questions, the critical legal movement might find its own laboratory for social experimentation. The observer might focus on the types and degree of conflict and consensus, the activities of critical legal writers as civic participants, and the sensitivity and sensibility of each towards the mutual vulnerability of both members and non-members of the movement. All of these issues would be important in calculating the chances of success of the radical project in its goal of fighting dependency and domination.

Secondly, critical legal writers might examine their own strictures on what is to count as an emancipatory exercise in legal analysis. The lines between internal argument, in the sense in which 'normal' legal discourse takes place; context-smashing argument; and revolutionary argument may not be as easily drawn as some radical writers suggest. Critical legal writing, in practising doctrinal criticism, has often resembled the most acute form of internal argument, particularly where it reveals a number of incompatible assumptions behind a legal rule. Most of the criticisms of legal structures have consisted of revealing the controversial content that legal rules, by their appearance as settled directives, tend to disguise. In its paradigmatic form, the radical critique raises alternative principles to prominence and tries to put them into a political perspective that either denies that they are consistent with the liberal impulse or else reveals the meaning they bear for a reconstructed social and personal life. This strategy is something less than revolutionary. The critic does not reject outright the pull that established legal doctrine exerts. The bulk of critical legal writing remains closer to the best samples of internally critical argument that have distinguished legal academic commentary than it is to context-revising argument. One of the points of serious critical commentary, regardless of political motivation, is in some sense to resist the given and to attempt to understand doctrinal questions in light of higher-order inquiries into value and purpose. While a normative activity, this should not necessarily be construed as inherently radical.

Retrieving the Republican Vision

The principal difficulty with the critical legal attempt to summon out of Western political thought the ideal of civic republicanism is that the ideal is not self-evidently free from the taint of liberal assumptions. The example of Rousseau illustrates this point nicely.[155] Rousseau wished to devise a theory that would demonstrate how a 'close communion' among persons in an egalitarian society could be achieved so that members would become dependent on the society as a whole and be freed from personal dependence on each other.[156] But he based his theory on assumptions about a hypothetical social contract into which persons in their pre-citizen capacity entered for prudential reasons. As an Enlightenment thinker, Rousseau held the contracting parties' autonomy and rationality to be primary requisites. Thus, Rousseau's version of republicanism, which is perhaps the purest account of the political value of civic virtue and expression through concerted action, is shot through with certain liberal features that the radical critique would ordinarily repudiate. This example should put us on notice that republicanism by itself is not entailed by wholly communitarian premises.

Mark Tushnet has been impressed by the possibility that contemporary legal liberal commentators can continue to draw on republican notions, even if only rhetorically, but he has expressed doubts as to whether civic republicanism is in fact recoverable.[157] The goal ought to be instead to create a social order that is democratic in a way that perhaps has no historical precedent. Tushnet gives cogent reasons for dismissing the relevance of a republican vision. For instance, he sees a failure in that tradition to provide any content to the public values it defends.[158]

The most important judgment that could be made about the relevance of the republican tradition, from the critical legal point of view, is that as an historical phenomenon it cannot be expected to survive the conditions in which it was born and developed. Roman republicanism was not the same as Florentine civic humanism; similarly the debates of 1776 could not be held under the conditions operating in the United States in 2002. The continual change of socio-political circumstances means that institutions must adapt and even transform completely.[159] This perspective has been summed up as follows: 'The partition of sovereignties and obligations tacitly implied in the classical language of republican politics is no longer possible for us. Today, the price of that highest of republican virtues – patriotism – would be the destruction of all cities. Today, the uninterested consequences of our consumption choices within the city gates are visited on the whole ecology of the globe. We have inherited a language of political allegiance which no longer speaks for the needs we have, not as citizens, but as members of a common species.'[160] This sanguine observation would imply that the age of nationalism is at an end, though events in central and eastern Europe and elsewhere over the past decade hardly square with this assumption.[161]

Next, there is a problem with the privileged place civic republicanism accords to political forums as the locus of the good life. In societies in which limits are imposed on political membership in the community, in which there are significant barriers to participation in institutions of government (for example, because of the division of labour), or in which politics is defined narrowly as an activity that does not affect 'private' spheres of life, the republican ideal will be unattractive. Those who tend to be excluded from public deliberations on historical systemic grounds, like women, are unlikely to agree that the public arena is the best place in which to realize the good.[162] Nor will a strong commitment to universal political engagement tidily fit into a society dedicated to moral pluralism. Some theorists thus reject what they call 'civic humanism' as a viable democratic ideal.[163]

Finally, it should be said that classical republicanism or images of civic virtue are not themselves adequate foundations for a theory of community, as opposed to a theory of democracy. As Philip Selznick has pointed out, '[c]ivic virtue is best understood as a way of fulfilling the *promise* of community.' It presumes that a community already exists.[164] Civic republicanism is not itself a master key that will unlock the potential for the communal reorganization of existing social structures. At best, it offers only a partial vision that lures us in the general direction of progressive redefinition of our practices, and not a consuming vision that provides the sum of all values required to secure the common good in a post-liberal age.[165]

Discarding Political Issues in the Name of Transformative Politics

This section touches on a very sensitive topic within any radical proposal for reconstructing the entire shape of an existing society. By noting the conflict-ridden, interest-dominated conception of liberal politics, critical legal writers imply that a new harmony is attainable only if certain assumptions about human relationships are abandoned. One problem arising out of this radical prescription is whether the vitality of politics generally, not just that associated with liberal democratic structures, is being suppressed in the process of such transcendence. The sticking point on this issue is reached when critical legal writers plead for the replacement of current 'forms of life' by a new moral order, without detailing the specific contours of this order. As we have seen, radical writers have held back on principle from attempts to describe which particular values or principles will animate the progressive society. This refusal to interfere with the decisions that require democratic determination may arguably amount to an abdication of political theory. Politics, as conceived on this model, is a concrete, local, community-wide process that gives no special authority to the critical legal commentator, who renounces any claim to political expertise or special insight into what the common good might be.[166] Attempts to specify the principles of justice that ought to govern political and legal decision making, such as found in Rawls's theory, are condemned for foisting a specific conception of political values onto a polity when the members of that polity should be free to work out through discussion their own version of just principles based on circumstances known intimately and peculiarly to them.

This renunciation takes in a great deal of what we conventionally think of as political theory. Gone is the need for arriving at a defensible conception of distributive justice. Critical legal writing is generally suspicious of the tradition by which liberal theorists (encompassing all classic and modern liberals as well as libertarians and social democrats) set out to provide a rational account of the conditions under which economic goods are both initially held and thereafter redistributed, either by voluntary, private transfers among individuals or through the intervention of the state.[167] Critical legal thought favours a radical notion of equality, but the institutional consequences of this political preference have yet to be treated systematically. A second issue concerns the many dimensions of the radical conception of equality. In addition to economic equality, critical legal writers have been wary of imposing a precise notion of political, legal, or educational equality. As on many other contestable political ideas, their strategy has mainly been to provide an oppositional voice. The defects of the reigning liberal conception are thus stressed without the radical critique's alternative becoming much more visible. Our understanding of their position is based to a great extent on inference rather than on positive assertion. This same observation applies to the inchoate discussions within the movement about the place of fundamental rights in a transformed society. This problem bedevils leftist critiques generally, but so far no distinctive critical legal solution has appeared on the horizon.[168] Critical legal writing on this area is searching for the outline of a new theory of communal rights, rather than property rights, as the conceptual paradigm.[169] But for the most part, as at least some critical legal authors acknowledge, the move-ment lags behind other contemporary projects in redefining the post-liberal underpinnings of protected rights.[170]

The critical legal description of the communitarian ideal also omits discussion of the central political problems of legitimacy, authority, and obligation. These are in some sense understood to be issues uniquely associated with liberalism. Once individual citizens see their interests as essentially intertwined with the good of the community, such issues are supposed to dissolve. Yet, as our close examination of Unger's theory revealed, each community, in so far as it wishes to preserve the possibility of dissension and destabilization, will inevitably encounter exactly these issues. Unger's later attempts to define new categories of rights presum-ably have something to do with such a recognition. To deny that these problems will persist is, in an ominous way, to try to exclude perennial political questions from the arena of political discussion. In this sense it might urgently be asked whether the critical legal attitude to a new era of unconstrained political discussion is not a modern version of Plato's attempt to make mass politics unnecessary because a community is so distinguished by its harmonious structure.[171]

As recent essays in the foundations of law illustrate, radical theorists hold no exclusive patent on the use of a conception of community. John Finnis has discussed how an understanding of the 'most intense form of community,' friendship, can be used to come to grips with the idea of political obligation and with Finnis's special interest, the traditions of natural law.[172] Dworkin's recent work also depends, in explaining legal and political obligation, on an analogy between the conditions of frater-nal association and those of political association.[173] Both Finnis and Dworkin follow in an ancient tradition whereby 'friendship also seems to hold political communities together.'[174] These attempts to discover sug-gestive possibilities for what ought to be the content and values of a legal system illustrate how peremptory was the critical legal dismissal of most modern jurisprudential writing as apologetic liberalism. Writers outside the radical camp have continued to appropriate communitarian values in support of their own proposed configuration of the purpose, limits, and potency of liberal democracies.

Other problems with the communitarian aspects of critical legal think-ing have been raised by feminist commentators. While certain socio-logical and normative assumptions might arguably be shared by communitarian critics of liberalism and, for example, cultural feminists, this does not mean that communitarian themes have been wholly embraced by feminists who also have criticized liberalism.[175] They may be attracted by the way in which communitarian understanding promotes other-regarding behaviour and the importance of connection, but feminists have recoiled from framing their visions of a progressive society in terms similar to those prescribed by, say, Alasdair MacIntyre.[176] Feminists object to strategies based on nostalgia for a golden age of morality in which women were excluded from political life. In addition, the radical challenge to law represented by critical legal studies has not treated the subordination of women as a problem distinct from inequalities or discrimination generally. The critical legal work of Unger, for example, is relatively silent about the values that might differentially matter to women. One of the primary forms of community, the family, has frequently been invoked by Unger and other communitarians as a paradigm unit of association, rather than criticized as a problematic institution. At one level, the family is a primary site for women's oppression, although it has also formed the context in which some of women's deepest attachments are found. Another danger discerned by some feminists is that the desire for community denies differences among individuals and groups. Thus, communitarian politics could lead not only to the oppression of cultural, racial, or religious minorities, but also to an intolerance for gender heterogeneity. Communitarianism continues to share with liberalism an ideal conception of the polity as unified and universal: this ideal conflicts with feminist conceptions of politics founded on gender identity.[177] Moreover, communitarians tend to be preoccupied with political equality, to the exclusion of social inequalities. Granting women the franchise is an insufficient resolution; what is required is a re-examination of the division drawn by legal doctrine between the public and private realms.[178] From a feminist viewpoint, communitarians emphasize only the positive aspects of what Sandel refers to, or even celebrates, as the encumbered individual. While it is useful to contrast the liberal image of the disembodied individual with the richer understanding of the self constituted by membership in a community, feminists have cautioned that the communitarian analysis ignores the problem of power. Communities should not be pictured solely as safe and reassuring environments. They not only enable individuals, they also impose on them. While they can be a source of meaning, they can also be a source of alienation for the individual seeking to order her life coherently. Power is significant in the production and maintenance of the socially constituted subject.[179] On all these grounds, feminist writers have evaluated, and in significant ways subverted, the oppositional pairing of liberalism and communitarianism.[180] In so far as critical legal thinking has leaned towards a communitarian critique, it is exposed to substantial feminist challenges.

For the host of reasons reviewed above, the merits of the radical political alternative are open to question. Like Hegel, critical legal writers posit an ideal situation in which: 'The happiest, unalienated life for man, which the Greeks enjoyed, is where the norms and ends expressed in the public life of a society are the most important ones by which its members define their identity as human beings. For them the institutional matrix in which they cannot help living is not felt to be foreign. Rather it is the essence, the "substance" of life.'[181] The question comes down to whether this attractive ideal spells the beginning or the end of significant political debate. From the critical legal perspective, the arrival of a communitarian alternative allows citizens to begin to address in a proper, public-minded spirit the institutional issues of social order. The communitarian vision is achieved at a cost, however, in that the range of questions we ordinarily think of as political par excellence has played no part in shaping this community. Everything is up for grabs, yet the community is settled. One would have thought that a degree of consensus on basic values, rather than a mere working out of a few details of principle, is required at the time the community is formed. The paradox of postponement is both startling and unnerving.

Who Are the Agents of Transformation?

How does critical legal thinking on the organization and practice of legal education serve to illustrate larger claims about how real community can be achieved? It becomes clear from surveying even a small part of the original critical legal literature that radical critics view the law school as the public space in which the seeds of social transformation are being sown. The sweeping change required by a communitarian theory is not automatic; the causal force is not simply an inevitable conjunction of circumstances arising from the demise of capitalism and its attendant legal order. Although historicism is an integral part of the critical legal understanding of social institutions, it should not be confused with economic determinism. That is, the human subjects who operate and make choices within history remain the focus of political analysis. The individual agent has not been dissolved in favour of existing ideological or class formations. This leaves room for the possibility of revolutionary creativity.[182]

There are two ways of picturing the triumph of a new political and legal order, one of them more benign than the other. On the first scheme, the immediate cause of the projected transformation would be a widespread shift in consciousness under which communitarian ideals and values would gain intellectual ascendancy over liberal assumptions. This might eventually be a mass shift, but initially at least an élite cadre of theorists would have to introduce these ideals into legal, political, educational, and workplace forums. They would remind their audiences of the serious and apparently intractable social problems under liberal democratic regimes: poverty (especially among women and children), illiteracy, hunger, homelessness, and racial conflict. Radical critics have assumed that their delineation of inequalities will create dismay, though whether it will lead as well to an interest in carefully probing the causes of these social problems is difficult to predict.[183] The issue is complicated by the relatively hazy treatment critical legal writers have accorded to the important notion of consciousness.[184] Nevertheless, there is no doubting the significance of the process whereby a change at the level of ideas will be accompanied by institutional transformation: 'If society is in some sense constituted by the world views that give meaning to social interaction, then to change consciousness is to change society itself. This is the central tenet of the CLS creed, the grounding for its belief that scholarship is politics.'[185] Framing the issue this way means that critical legal thought has already assumed that the answer to the hoary question of how the theory of a shape for transformed society will relate to a revolutionary practice. On the critical legal account, the activity of theorizing, in which fundamental liberal legal assumptions are challenged, *is* putting into practice the ideals identified with the successor society. This interpretation permits the university teacher to see writing, lecturing, and dealing with colleagues as fundamentally important political contributions.[186] Emancipating students' and colleagues' minds from the grip of liberal political notions is, like psychoanalysis (to which critical legal writers sometimes compare their project), not just preliminary to the task of devising a new way of treating human relationships: the unmasking of constricting thought structures amounts to an achieved reconstruction.[187] Social transformation interpreted as a drastic change in consciousness thus leads to a new recognition of the communal values of fellowship, cooperation, and dedication to the common good. If all or most persons are assumed to have come around to this recognition, there is no call for specifying the social or political arrangements that will reflect those values. The enlightened community can be assumed to resolve the practical and political difficulties for itself in such a way that no severe friction will disrupt the shared recognition of intersubjective dependence and solidarity. This conception of revolution via persuasion and rational discussion is one of the major motifs in critical legal thinking; it is clear that the agents of enlightenment will be anti-liberal law teachers, lawyers, and judges. The success of their efforts to identify the failings of liberalism and to articulate the values of communal life will depend on their capacity to show the dark side of existing institutions and of current legal doctrine. The normal modes of discussion (law review articles, classroom instruction and discussion, treatise writing, conference and seminar participation) are assumed to be sufficient for the revolutionary task. Once the image or vision of a post-liberal community is presented, critical legal writers appear to assume that it will inevitably convince everyone to abandon their liberal presuppositions and to change their form of life.

A second possible mode for understanding how the communitarian change will occur has been less dependent on the pure persuasiveness of the dialectical or immanent criticism of liberal theory. It also implies less of an armchair or lectern role for the legal commentator as revolutionary agent. This second scheme depicts the building of a reconstituted community as a matter of first overthrowing, through some sort of violence, the established legal and political order. The proponents of this view would criticize the first scheme as the result of an obsession with the romantic view of spontaneously arising, harmonious communities.[188] The second view, by contrast, takes seriously the idea that the constitution of a community must nearly always involve some form of coercion or even violence, against both the enemies of community and its members. Critical legal writers such as Tushnet may at one time have seen the prospect of furious mass upheaval involving physical and personal destruction. There are hints of this possibility in his work. Or it may be that the term 'violence' is being used in a more neutral, social scientific sense, in which, for example, it may be defined as 'action that deliberately or unintentionally disorients the behavior of others.'[189] On this definition, 'antisocial' or hostile behaviour may qualify as violence. Efforts by critical legal law teachers to upset the established patterns of teaching and collegiality within their university faculty would therefore be an example of violent behaviour, possibly construable as a type of provocative terrorism, again in a social scientific sense, which aims at: '... short-circuiting efforts to bring about conservative change, eliminating reforms within the embattled administration, and forcing the defenders to adopt policies of intransigence.'[190] This second view thus appears to be tough-minded compared with the model of change built on the rational exchange of ideas, in which members of the dominant class might come to realize the necessity of a new egalitarian social structure. The danger with the second view is that it too is liable to succumb to a romantic corruption. Violence as a revolutionary tactic has always appealed to those impatient with the process of politics.[191] This strategy is almost invariably rationalized on the ground that violence is just another form of politics. In fact, it is the substitute for genuine political activity.[192] Some critical legal writing has hovered on the edge of this fallacy. It is therefore difficult to accede to the critical legal reassurance that a progressive transformation, because it is already immanent within our established patterns of thought, will be a result of eminently rational discussion and empathy and not a real struggle for power in which fundamental human interests might be harmed in the realization of a new community.

Conclusion

Critical legal writers have faced a political dilemma: should they lend legitimacy to the existing political structures by participating through them in the continuing tasks of government (and thereby invite the disillusionments of gradualism), or should they abandon the process as fatally infected by liberal lies and disingenuous apologies? Escaping from this dilemma has involved moving the locus of political action to a level of theory, analysis, and commentary. The discursive role of the radical critic has predominantly involved the imaginative interpretation of legal texts to illuminate the hidden implications for progressive social change. To this extent, the critical legal writer has been content to practise visionary or prophetic politics, to assume the role of a diviner or inspired commentator whose research agenda is to describe the ideal conditions of political and personal life. That project stops short of any engagement, attachment, or commitment to a particular scheme of political organization.

It may perhaps be premature to claim that there has been an irreversible retreat from the agitational form of 1960s radicalism to the academic form represented by critical legal studies, or that the latter is a mutation of the former.[193] One of the most interesting topics for critical legal writers that remains to be investigated is the place of the movement within the twentieth-century history of leftist political activity in the West, particularly in the United States. The conditions of contemporary radical practice in view of the types of repression and backsliding that have affected the radical cause would prove a fascinating subject.[194] The sources which begin to sum up the dynamics of the intellectual left would provide a starting point for radical critics to reflect upon the efficacy and aspirations of their own enterprise.[195]

The critical legal attempt to address the shortcomings of liberal institutions has not led to a campaign for collective mobilization. Instead, there are only adjurations that, owing to the artifactual nature of society and the plasticity of political arrangements, we are free to reshape our existing institutions into whatever we as a group determine are the forms most conducive to our flourishing as independent, yet mutually vulnerable, persons. This confinement of the scope of politics to describing the institutional outline that will empower and promote such creative activities leaves large political issues untouched.

In the continuation of their radical project, critical legal writers must begin to spell out the practical political ramifications of their ideals. The relevant questions are both prudential and institutional. The strategies these scholars commend or follow, the leadership styles they exhibit, the compromises they are willing to entertain, will all reveal the substance of the proposals. Credible political action requires some stake in the outcome of the process critical legal writers envision.[196]

At the end of this discussion the question remains whether significant social change, to be achieved in the direction that the radical critique prefers, does not require forms of political practice that go beyond writing in professional journals, teaching what is arguably an élite audience, or holding forth in academic conferences.[197] The critical legal focus on doctrine as providing the materials for novel insights into the plasticity of social structures fits poorly with a conception of political study based on grasping an understanding of the whole context in which laws are formed. Doctrinal sources frequently cannot penetrate to this level of understanding.[198]

The most urgent question facing critical legal writers, from the point of view of communitarian ideals, is how they are to accommodate their interest in sweeping social change with acceptance within the main community of legal academics. Various strategies might be proposed. In one, the task of the movement should be to place its members in strategic spots within existing hierarchies, where they could practise 'sly, collective tactics ... to confront, outflank, sabotage or manipulate the bad guys and build the possibility of something better.'[199] In another, the movement might set itself up as a claustral community on the fringe of events, biding its time until the proper conjunctural circumstances provide an opportunity to move to the centre of the political stage. These are political issues, to be debated as practical initiatives with vast implications for the message being sent out to the citizens who would be invited to join a collective reconstruction of prevailing institutions.[200]

The paradox of engagement is a blemish on the current situation of critical legal studies. So long as radical critics continue to defer the task of bringing their communitarian vision into line with the central questions of political philosophy, and fail to commit themselves to any particular scheme of values, their claims about the inescapably political nature of law add up to an apolitical quiescence. The paradox of postponement similarly rigs the terms of political debate. It allows the critical legal side of the argument to avoid dealing with the nature of the structures that should serve chosen values. Readers of the radical literature should be given the chance to compare the principles espoused by critical legal studies with the actual forms of social and political life to which those principles are supposed to lead. Where what is at stake involves how we teach, how we practice, and how we explain, turnabout on these issues is only fair play.[201]

6

Epilogue

Major things are wind, evil, a good fighting horse, prepositions, inexhaustible
love, the way people choose their king. Minor things include dirt, the names of
schools of philosophy, mood and not mood, the correct time.

Anne Carson, *Plainwater*

In setting down my thoughts in this book, I have girded myself in
anticipation of the different types of responses it will arouse. First among
these will be complaints about the topicality of the subject matter. Why
choose to write about the formative period of a movement that, according to more than a few of my academic colleagues, is played out and has
been virtually demolished?[1] What a quaint project. But is the task of
assessing the contributions of early critical legal writers to central jurisprudential debates really no more interesting or useful than flogging a
dead horse? Does the major value of the critical legal movement lie
solely in its foreshadowing of subsequent, and what now appear to be
trendier, intellectual developments in the law, such as post-modernism
or the various critiques made from the perspectives of race, gender,
sexuality, or cultural studies?[2] Has the 1970s version of radical legal
critique in North America become an outmoded fashion, just as the art
of David Salle, which made him seem so avant-garde and interesting in
the 1980s – a regular Andy Warhol – has since been discredited by
influential taste makers?[3]

These judgments on the vitality and currency of critical legal studies
might be true, if one were to treat jurisprudential ideas as no more
significant or durable than trends in wide ties and narrow lapels. They
are also shaped by invidious comparisons to the rate of increase in the

acquisition of scientific knowledge. Developments in medicine and the biological sciences have accelerated to a dizzying pace, making obsolete publications not just from twenty-five years before, but even those dating from five years earlier. Why should the speed of evolution in legal theory lag behind? Critical legal studies is now out of fashion and making it the subject of a sustained analysis is similarly unfashionable. This is, of course, a lamentably shallow view. Legal ideas are not so ephemeral and revisiting them for the purpose of weighing them up, regardless of the era in which they first appeared, is never a dated exercise. In the last two decades, as shown in the new and revised works by William Twining, Laura Kalman, John Henry Schlegel, and William Wiecek, our understanding of legal realism has been enlarged and to some extent altered, as we grasp better its theoretical underpinnings, its rivals, and its influence on legal scholarship.[4]

A second complaint that will no doubt surface is that critical legal literature extends beyond the contributions made to jurisprudential debates by the founders of the Conference on Critical Legal Studies. That is true. To offer a comprehensive retrospective analysis of the achievements of critical legal work, my discussion would have to assess a substantially broader range of scholarship, including a vast array of academic articles on specific doctrinal subjects; it would have to delineate carefully the fractures and shifts within different strands of the movement; and it would have to distill the self-perceptions of members who continue to find sustenance in the movement's original promise.

On the first of these points, let it be said that the task envisioned would require work of an encyclopaedic magnitude. Nobody knows this better, for I have tried to organize and provide a basic taxonomy and summary of pertinent themes arising from the wealth of literature published in or about critical legal studies to the mid-1990s.[5] Nearly every subject area in the law school curriculum and every doctrinal field has been subject to a revaluation from a critical legal perspective. Even orthodox law teachers otherwise averse to the radical political agenda of critical legal theorists would find it useful to consult (to name only a few examples) the thoughtful analyses of Morton Horwitz in legal history, William Simon on the legal profession, Elizabeth Schneider on criminal law, Joseph William Singer in property law, David Kairys in constitutional law, and Karl Klare on the development of modern labour law regimes. The three editions so far published of Kairys's anthology of critical perspectives carefully select the most astute critical literature in relation to individual legal fields.[6] There is, however, no clear demarcation between critical legal work that arises out of consideration of specific legal issues and that animated by theoretical concerns. Any enduring value to the 'critique' offered derives from the fundamental rethinking of the ordinary or 'normal' terms that shape the debate over specific issues. I have tried to show that much of what passes for theoretical argument in critical legal writing is interstitial. It is raised as part of the necessary background in so-called doctrinal contributions or in historical reconstructions. On this score, critical legal writing is 'drenched in theory,' to use a phrase coined in another context.[7] I have not ignored this doctrinal dimension of critical legal writing over the past quarter-century. Instead, I have paid especially close attention to the very terms in which doctrinal critique has been framed, and have avoided treating them as mere scaffolding that could be removed without affecting the structure.

Another characterization, at cross-purposes to the one just mentioned, might arguably apply to early critical legal work. I have been tempted to call this the harmlessly mischievous function of critical legal studies. If that characterization were true, it would exonerate to some extent the authors in question. If the ideas offered in the first wave of critical legal studies were not intended as serious attempts at engaging in legal or political theorizing, some latitude or charity should be shown and the work should not be appraised using benchmarks derived from professional philosophy. On this view, the gravamen of critical legal arguments was merely to stir things up, to plough up and aerate well-trod ground. It would be unfortunate, and a waste of energy, to examine too rigorously, literature intended only to spice up what had become bland fare to generations of law students. This defence of critical legal work, which is ultimately self-depreciating, cuts away much of the ground underlying the point of early critical legal studies. Had that literature not promised theoretical insights and innovations into the foundations of legal reasoning and legal practices, it would have had no future and little impact. In my opinion, the harmless mischief defence arrives too late and is inconsistent with the express claims of early critical legal authors. I believe that those authors saw themselves as full participants in the great cavalcade of U.S. legal philosophy, not simply as spectators in the crowd diverting those around them with deflationary comments, tossing off aperçus designed to startle (rather in the spirit of Oliver Wendell Holmes, Jr), but not intended to form the basis for a coherent philosophy of law.

A footnote attaches to my comments on the mischievous function of the movement. Have not some of the leading lights of early critical legal studies subsequently elaborated on and improved their theories? Duncan

Kennedy, for example, continues to publish dense tracts, an indication perhaps that critical legal theory has continued to evolve since the mid-1980s. Kennedy himself, in his most recent book, concedes that critical legal studies as a collective 'movement' that tried to create elbow room for broader ideological challenges to mainstream institutions has run its course – in his phrase, it has 'come apart.'[8] That does not mean, however, that critical legal work has disappeared or become extinct. In Kennedy's characterization, critical legal studies survives as a 'school of thought' or theory; it has resulted in a 'canon' of literature or ideas that can usefully be drawn on or criticized.[9] This fits with my own project of attempting to define what those early ideas amounted to, where they were provocative and inspirational, and where they were flawed. Pulling together his newest ideas, Kennedy expressly calls for a re-examination of critical legal theory, in order to identify precisely where early critical legal ideas went wrong. Does Kennedy's discussion, deploying techniques derived from phenomenology, itself represent a striking new departure for critical legal studies? The answer is no. He has brought into play new arguments and fresh metaphors. He has also chosen to joust with contemporary legal theorists to a markedly greater degree than he did in his work classifying different states of consciousness. Overall, however, Kennedy still aims to vindicate his long-standing theory about law, including its typical forms of reasoning, the behaviour and justification of its agents, and the various approaches taken to unpacking and applying legal texts. In his view, mainstream theory remains embarrassed by ideological critiques. Faith in rights analysis and the skill of the courts to wield rights in the process of legal reasoning continue to obscure and deflect fundamental issues that only politics can resolve. The theoretical commitments that prompted Kennedy to help found critical legal studies in the first place are not altered.

Some readers may question my choice to omit from this book a portrait of the radical ways of thinking about the law – apart from critical legal studies – that proliferated in the 1990s. This decision will disappoint readers seeking guidance on the relationship between the critical legal movement and other perspectives out of the mainstream, such as feminism, post-structuralism, or post-modernism.[10] Each of these might or might not be in competition with a critical legal point of view. Conceivably, there are sufficient points of contact that a self-identified postmodernist or feminist could claim to be a current rather than former member of the heterogeneous critical legal movement. Can a postmodernist understanding of law, then, be plausibly explained as an outgrowth or evolutionary change in direction of critical legal studies?[11] Or is it more accurately viewed as a successor perspective that arose once many critical legal writers grasped the importance of identity or positionality? To the extent that both critical legal authors and post-modernists are occupied with criticizing the latent presuppositions of modern law, often through a close examination of the language used to frame key issues, one might be inclined to view post-modern approaches as a type of critical legal writing that has been corrected or updated to reflect greater sensitivity to the range of ineluctable differences, both among individuals and among cultures. However, radical critics in the 1990s, while focusing on some of the same stalking horses that occupied critical legal writers a decade or more before, took something of a different tack.

At the heart of my discussion lies something valuable to the pathologists, the mourners, and the celebrants, respectively, who linger after critical legal studies' so-called demise. My curiosity has never been satisfied by any of the attempted answers to the question of why critical legal writing is now supposedly passé. The claim that it has metamorphosed into a more complex series of critiques (built to reflect especially salient social differences and intractable identities) does not explain why critical legal studies was not the prelude to an intellectual revolution – or any other type of revolution for that matter. Such responses have only generated more questions in return. What flaws proved to be the undoing of critical legal studies? Where did the radical critique go wrong? Do any parts of the body of critical legal theory retain value? What lessons can be learned from the ambitious if failed attempt to revise dominant conceptions of basic legal ideas?

This book is the result of my dissatisfaction with almost everything I have ever read on the subject, both from inside and outside the critical legal movement. It is an essay in sympathetic understanding and grounded critique. Avoiding sweeping gestures has been particularly difficult in this context, for opinions have hardened since critical legal literature first appeared. Some readers might also lament the lack of information or discussion about the personal dynamics and jockeying for leadership and influence within the movement. In response, all I can say is that my analysis deals with jurisprudence, not journalism. It is concerned with the theoretical ideas espoused by critical legal writers. I am in no position, located as I am in the hinterland of North American law schools, to draw a profile of those authors' personal characteristics, their interpersonal relations, or their institutional milieu. One colleague, intending I am sure to be helpful, went so far to suggest that I examine the rise of critical legal studies for evidence that it was an attempt by the U.S. government to flush out threateningly leftist radicals who would otherwise have stayed under cover. In other words, I ought to trace any parallels with the creation and use of *Encounter* magazine as a 'front' in the 1950s and 60s by U.S. counter-espionage officials.[12] On this hypothesis, bringing critical legal writing into prominence was a useful way to discover who might be tempted to disloyalty. At venturing into this twilight zone of paranoia and suspicion, I draw the line.

Notes

1 Introduction

1 On the impact of critical legal studies on Harvard in particular, see Calvin Trillin, 'A Reporter at Large: Harvard Law,' *New Yorker* (26 March 1984), 53; Jennifer A. Kingson, 'Harvard Tenure Battle Puts "Critical Legal Studies" on Trial,' *New York Times* (30 August 1987), E6; and Eleanor Kerlow, *Poisoned Ivy: How Egos, Ideology, and Power Politics Almost Ruined Harvard Law School* (New York: St Martin's Press, 1994). A more detailed list of the numerous reports of faculty divisions at Harvard is contained in Neil Duxbury, *Patterns of American Jurisprudence* (Oxford: Clarendon Press, 1995), at 495 n.421.

2 See Anthony Chase, 'What Should a Law Teacher Believe?' *Nova Law Journal* 10 (1986), 403; Jay M. Feinman and Marc Feldman, 'Pedagogy and Politics,' *Georgetown Law Journal* 73 (1985), 875; and Robert W. Gordon, 'Critical Legal Studies as a Teaching Method, Against the Background of the Intellectual Politics of Modern Legal Education in the United States,' *Legal Education Review* 1 (1989), 59.

3 In references to the Conference on Critical Legal Studies, I capitalize the name of this group, though this is not meant to imply any remarkable degree of cohesion or bureaucratic formality within it. Elsewhere in my discussion (and this is my preponderant usage), I have used the terms 'critical legal studies,' 'radical critique,' or, in adjectival contexts, 'critical legal.' My usage is on analogy with other terms used frequently throughout this book, including 'liberalism' and 'realism.'

4 A representative anthology of critical legal work, David Kairys, ed., *The Politics of Law: A Progressive Critique* (New York: Pantheon, 1982), revised and enlarged editions of which appeared in 1990 and 1998, resulted from a

joint project of the Conference on Critical Legal Studies and the Theoretical Studies Committee of the National Lawyers Guild.

5 The process of coalescence is sketched in John Henry Schlegel, 'Notes toward an Intimate, Opinionated, and Affectionate History of the Conference on Critical Legal Studies,' *Stanford Law Review* 36 (1984), 391 and in Duxbury, *Patterns of American Jurisprudence.*

6 Schlegel's article, *supra,* note 5, suggests some of the major influences on the origins of critical legal ideas. This topic is also covered in Allan C. Hutchinson and Patrick Monahan, 'Law, Politics, and the Critical Legal Scholars: The Unfolding Drama of American Social Thought,' *Stanford Law Review* 36 (1984), 199.

7 See Malcolm Gladwell, *The Tipping Point: How Little Things Can Make a Big Difference* (Boston: Little, Brown, 2000).

8 Though one should note that in 1987 Duncan Kennedy provided as a 'generous estimate' that there 'might be 120 law teachers in the country who have a strong identification with the Crit network': see 'Are Lawyers Really Necessary? *Barrister* Interview with Duncan Kennedy,' *Barrister* 14 (Fall, 1987), 10 at 17.

9 For the United Kingdom, see Peter Fitzpatrick and Alan Hunt, eds., *Critical Legal Studies* (Oxford: Basil Blackwell, 1987) and Peter Goodrich, 'Critical Legal Studies in England: Prospective Histories,' *Oxford Journal of Legal Studies* 12 (1992), 195. For a sample of Australian critical legal work see Stephen Bottomley, Neil Gunningham, and Stephen Parker, *Law in Context* (Leichhardt, NSW: Federation Press, 1991). In Canada, one author frequently identified in this vein is Allan C. Hutchinson: see his *Dwelling on the Threshold: Critical Essays in Modern Legal Thought* (Scarborough, ON: Carswell, 1988).

10 See Duncan Kennedy and Karl Klare, 'A Bibliography of Critical Legal Studies,' *Yale Law Journal* 94 (1984), 461; Alan Hunt, 'Critical Legal Studies: A Bibliography,' *Modern Law Review* 47 (1984), 369; and Richard W. Bauman, *Critical Legal Studies: A Guide to the Literature* (Boulder, CO: Westview Press, 1996). This last source is a substantially augmented version of the unpublished work cited in Mark Tushnet, 'Critical Legal Studies: A Political History,' *Yale Law Journal* 100 (1991), 1515 at 1516 n.3 and David Kairys, 'Conservative Legal Theory Revisited,' *Columbia Law Review* 91 (1991), 1847 at 1859 n.54.

11 The multifarious uses of the footnote are entertainingly and learnedly explored in Anthony Grafton, *The Footnote: A Curious History* (Cambridge: Harvard University Press, 1997). For the studied omission, see ibid. at 9–10.

12 For a response to the wholesale version of this assessment, see Richard

Michael Fischl, 'The Question That Killed Critical Legal Studies,' *Law and Social Inquiry* 17 (1992), 779 (Fischl does not himself believe that critical legal studies is dead). For a retail version of a common critique, see the summing up in Duxbury, *Patterns of American Jurisprudence* at 423–8.

13 See, for example, Adrien Katherine Wing, ed., *Critical Race Feminism: A Reader* (New York: New York University Press, 1997).

14 For a discussion of what constitutes genuinely radical legal or political theory, see the contrasting views offered by Richard T. De George, Wade Robison, Patricia Smith, and Joseph Ellin in Stephen M. Griffin and Robert C.L. Moffat, eds., *Radical Critiques of the Law* (Lawrence: University Press of Kansas, 1997).

15 An example of such denunciation, inviting critical legal teachers to depart faculties of law and look for shelter in other disciplines, is Paul Carrington, 'Of Law and the River,' *Journal of Legal Education* 34 (1984), 222. Among the responses and rejoinders to Carrington's piece are Ted Finman, 'Critical Legal Studies, Professionalism, and Academic Freedom: Exploring the Tributaries of Carrington's River,' *Journal of Legal Education* 35 (1985), 180; Sanford Levinson, 'Professing Law: Commitment of Faith or Detached Analysis?' *St. Louis University Law Journal* 31 (1986), 3; and Gary Minda, 'Of Law, the River and Legal Education,' *Nova Law Journal* 10 (1986), 705. To the extent that some opponents, especially in the United States, charge critical legal adherents with professing profound cynicism or scepticism about the law – of demonstrating a loss of faith or at least the embrace of heresy – it is instructive to recall the progressive advances that have been made throughout U.S. history by legal dissenters, from anti-slavery advocates to suffragettes: see David Ray Papke, *Heretics in the Temple: Americans Who Reject the Nation's Legal Faith* (New York: New York University Press, 1998).

16 In an accessible and perspicuous discussion, Andrew Altman, *Critical Legal Studies: A Liberal Critique* (Princeton: Princeton University Press, 1990), defends liberalism by appealing to certain aspects of the rule of law. By contrast, a virtually impenetrable account of several key critical legal abstractions is contained in Matthew H. Kramer, *Legal Theory, Political Theory, and Deconstruction: Against Rhadamanthus* (Bloomington: Indiana University Press, 1991), at 205–69. The mysteries are compounded in Matthew H. Kramer, *Critical Legal Theory and the Challenge of Feminism: A Philosophical Reconception* (Lanham, MD: Rowman and Littlefield, 1995), where Kramer continues breathlessly to exploit, with Nietzschean delight, paradoxes that allegedly emerge from some generalized themes in feminism and critical legal studies. For an antidote, consult Luc Ferry and Alain Renaut, eds.,

Why We Are Not Nietzscheans, trans. Robert de Loaiza (Chicago: University of Chicago Press, 1997).

17 For a discussion of the intersections among pragmatism, postmodernism, and the later versions of critical legal studies, see Alan Hunt, 'The Big Fear: Law Confronts Postmodernism,' *McGill Law Journal* 35 (1990), 507 at 533–40 and Gary Minda, *Postmodern Legal Movements* (New York: New York University Press, 1995), at 189–207. On one view, modernity is so closely identified with liberalism that the demise of one is supposed to spell the end of the other. Yet, understood as the ambitious attempt to use reason to design a total arrangement of human actions in their social setting, modernity can be assimilated to communism. On this latter account, the dream of modernity has died with the collapse of East European totalitarianism, while liberal values endure: see Zygmunt Bauman, *Intimations of Postmodernity* (London: Routledge, 1992), at 178.

18 Hanna Fenichel Pitkin, *The Attack of the Blob: Hannah Arendt's Concept of the Social* (Chicago: University of Chicago Press, 1998).

2 Writing on a Slant: The Construction and Critique of Liberalism

1 See, for example, Bruce Ackerman, *The Future of Liberal Revolution* (New Haven: Yale University Press, 1992). Liberalism also seems to have been reborn elsewhere in continental Europe, to judge by the contributions in Mark Lilla, ed., *New French Thought: Political Philosophy* (Princeton: Princeton University Press, 1994).

2 See Nancy L. Rosenblum, *Another Liberalism: Romanticism and the Reconstruction of Liberal Thought* (Cambridge: Harvard University Press, 1987).

3 A reflective analysis that cautions against the wholesale embrace of liberal-oriented institutions in the new central Europe is offered in Ronald Beiner, *What's the Matter with Liberalism?* (Berkeley: University of California Press, 1992).

4 For a discussion of different strands of anti-liberalism, beginning with Joseph de Maistre and brought up to the present with critical assessments of Alasdair MacIntyre and Roberto Unger, see Stephen Holmes, *The Anatomy of Antiliberalism* (Cambridge: Harvard University Press, 1993). Holmes's treatment of each of the major thinkers in question is polemical and dismissive. His approach to his subjects does not probe as deeply into their intellectual environment as does, say, the work of Isaiah Berlin. See Berlin's 'Joseph de Maistre and the Origins of Fascism,' in *The Crooked Timber of Humanity*, ed. Henry Hardy (London: Fontana Books, 1991) 91–174.

5 Resemblances and connections between legal realism and critical legal studies form a subject unto itself. Critical legal writing may simply be an anachronistic reflorescence of legal realism, suggested as a possibility by Ronald Dworkin in *Law's Empire* (Cambridge: Harvard University Press, 1986), at 272. There are good reasons, however, for viewing critical legal studies as something distinct and novel which, although its heyday might have passed, is nevertheless worth studying as an important contribution to modern legal theory. In support of the latter view, see Neil Duxbury, *Patterns of American Jurisprudence* (Oxford: Clarendon Press, 1995), at 427.

6 See, for example, James Boyle, 'The Politics of Reason: Critical Legal Theory and Local Social Thought,' *University of Pennsylvania Law Review* 133 (1985), 685 at 705–8. Boyle's discussion should be read cautiously as he treats some types of post-realist jurisprudence (for example, process-oriented theory) as simply a later species of realism rather than as a response to it.

7 For a description of the chief characteristics of the realist approach, and their influence on the curriculum at Yale and Columbia law schools in particular, see Laura Kalman, *Legal Realism at Yale, 1927–1960* (Chapel Hill: University of North Carolina Press, 1986).

8 It is consistent with the radical critique of realist predecessors to view the creation of a large administrative apparatus in the New Deal as part of a design to stifle political militancy and serious redistributive conflicts. This perspective underlies the historical account offered in Peter Irons, *The New Deal Lawyers* (Princeton: Princeton University Press, 1982), especially at 290–300.

9 See Roberto Mangabeira Unger, *Knowledge and Politics* (New York: Free Press, 1975), esp. at 3 where he discusses the so-called prison-house of a general theory that enthrals modern thinking. He views liberalism as a powerful system of ideas which, while they recur throughout all social disciplines, have not been adequately treated in their entirety.

10 See Thomas C. Heller, 'The Importance of Normative Decision-Making: The Limitations of Legal Economics as a Basis for a Liberal Jurisprudence – As Illustrated by the Regulation of Vacation Home Development,' *Wisconsin Law Review* [1976], 385 at 473.

11 Karl Klare, 'Judicial Deradicalization of the Wagner Act and the Origins of Modern Legal Consciousness, 1937–1941,' *Minnesota Law Review* 62 (1978), 265 at 275–6.

12 Ibid. at 277 n.38.

13 Klare continues this critique in other articles, including 'Labor Law as Ideology: Toward a New Historiography of Collective Bargaining Law,'

Industrial Relations Law Journal 4 (1981), 450; 'Labor Law and the Liberal Political Imagination,' *Socialist Review* 62 (1982), 45; 'Traditional Labor Law Scholarship and the Crisis of Collective Bargaining Law: A Reply to Professor Finkin,' *Maryland Law Review* 44 (1985), 731; and 'Critical Theory and Labor Relations Law,' in David Kairys, ed., *The Politics of Law: A Progressive Critique*, 3rd ed. (New York: Basic Books, 1998), 539–68.

14 See Duncan Kennedy, 'Form and Substance in Private Law Adjudication,' *Harvard Law Review* 89 (1976), 1685 at 1767; Mark Tushnet, 'Legal Scholarship: Its Causes and Cure,' *Yale Law Journal* 90 (1981), 1205 at 1206–7; and James Boyle, 'Thomas Hobbes and the Invented Tradition of Positivism: Reflections on Language, Power, and Essentialism,' *University of Pennsylvania Law Review* 135 (1987), 383.

15 Kennedy sees these two types of attitudes as 'radically contradictory' and incapable of resolution by such means as 'balancing': see 'Form and Substance in Private Law Adjudication,' at 1774–5.

16 Ibid., at 1768.

17 Ibid., at 1776.

18 Peter Gabel, 'Review of Ronald Dworkin, *Taking Rights Seriously*,' *Harvard Law Review* 91 (1977), 302.

19 Ibid., at 314–15. See William H. Simon, 'Homo Psychologicus: Notes on a New Legal Formalism,' *Stanford Law Review* 32 (1980), 487, at 549–50 for a critique of lawyering that 'legitimates the prevailing modes of practice' and 'devalues the social world.'

20 See *supra*, note 9. *Knowledge and Politics* has been called 'perhaps *the* seminal early CLS work' by Mark Kelman, *A Guide to Critical Legal Studies* (Cambridge: Harvard University Press, 1987), at 55 (emphasis in the original).

21 For example, in Note [Debra Livingston], ''Round and 'Round the Bramble Bush: From Legal Realism to Critical Legal Scholarship,' *Harvard Law Review* 95 (1982), 1669 at 1679 n.70 and 1680 n.74, Unger's 'critique of liberalism' is mentioned without any clarification of how his work relates to other critical scholarship. Other work footnotes Unger but makes no effort to explore the themes of *Knowledge and Politics* in any depth: see, for example, Alan Hyde, 'Is Liberalism Possible?' *New York University Law Review* 57 (1982), 1031 at 1037 n.31, 1029 n.36, and 1048 n.75. It is surprising how many of the references to Unger within critical legal scholarship are brief footnotes; genuine attempts to evaluate Unger's work are owed to authors outside the critical legal studies movement. For relevant references to this literature, see Richard W. Bauman, *Critical Legal Studies: A Guide to the Literature* (Boulder, CO: Westview Press, 1996) in chap. 3.

22 See *Knowledge and Politics*, at 31–6, 51–7, 88–100, and 133–7. Indeed, the

persuasiveness of Unger's scheme on this score has been doubted: see Kelman, *Guide to Critical Legal Studies*, at 65.

23 The practical details are contained in Unger's three-volume treatise on liberal social theory and liberal institutions transformed: see Roberto Mangabeira Unger, *Politics: A Work in Constructive Social Theory* (Cambridge: Cambridge University Press, 1987) discussed *infra*, Chapter 5. Unger continues striving to this day to articulate a successor to what he has called 'pretended liberalism' and to inspire a movement that will create the conditions for 'a fuller realization of liberal claims': Roberto Mangabeira Unger, *What Should Legal Analysis Become?* (London: Verso, 1996), at 141.

24 Unger, *Knowledge and Politics*, at 63.

25 Ibid., at 68–9.

26 Ibid., at 70.

27 By 'autonomy' in this context Unger understands that liberals mean simply freedom from restraint to make choices. It is thus a negative attribute and should not be confused with the Kantian notion of autonomy by which (a) a rational being, in the process of ethical reasoning and action, needs no external authority to understand morality, and (b) an individual can effectively impose obligations on herself: see Immanuel Kant, *Groundwork of the Metaphysic of Morals*, trans. H.J. Paton (New York: Harper and Row, 1964), at 84–9 and J.B. Schneewind, 'Autonomy, Obligation, and Virtue: An Overview of Kant's Moral Philosophy,' in Paul Guyer, ed., *The Cambridge Companion to Kant* (Cambridge: Cambridge University Press, 1992), 309–41.

28 This perception of subjectivism as a root principle of liberalism permeates critical legal writing: see, for example, William Forbath, 'Taking Lefts Seriously,' *Yale Law Journal* 92 (1983), 1041 at 1042–3 and Heller, 'The Importance of Normative Decision-Taking,' at 475.

29 So, for example, Charles Taylor has written of 'political atomism' as the background for theories in favour of the primacy of individual rights. This kind of atomism is taken as linked (directly or indirectly) to issues of ontological priority. Thus Taylor speaks of Hobbes's nominalism: see Charles Taylor, 'Atomism,' in *Philosophy and the Human Sciences*, 2 vols. (Cambridge: Cambridge University Press, 1985), II: 187–210 at 201. An even clearer example of this characterization is found in Andrew Levine, *Liberal Democracy: A Critique of the Theory* (New York: Columbia University Press, 1981), at 45: 'I shall call the form of individualism pertinent here atomic individualism because its character is best brought out by analogy with early atomistic theories of matter ... Like atoms in an enclosed space, individuals in society do come into contact with one another. But this contact is in no way constitutive of the individual's nature. Society no more constitutes individuals

than space constitutes atoms.' The conflictual perspective of so-called liberal atomism in the social sphere is also described in Benjamin R. Barber, *Strong Democracy: Participatory Politics for a New Age* (Berkeley: University of California Press, 1984), at 5 and 32–7.

30 See Kenneth Casebeer, 'Escape from Liberalism: Fact and Value in Karl Llewellyn,' *Duke Law Journal* [1977], 671 at 685 n.56. Cf. Ellen M. Wood, *Mind and Politics: An Approach to the Meaning of Liberal and Socialist Individualism* (Berkeley: University of California Press, 1972), at 47–73 and Marshall Berman, *The Politics of Authenticity: Radical Individualism and the Emergence of Modern Society* (London: Allen and Unwin, 1971), at xiii–xxii.

31 See Thomas Hobbes, *Leviathan*, ed. Richard Tuck (Cambridge: Cambridge University Press, 1991), Pt I, Ch. 13, at 86–90.

32 See also Mark Tushnet, 'A Note on the Revival of Textualism in Constitutional Theory,' *Southern California Law Review* 58 (1985), 683.

33 That liberals are not univocal about the need for a social contract to explain political association and obligation, in either an historical or a hypothetical sense, is clear from the contributions in David Boucher and Paul Kelly, eds., *The Social Contract from Hobbes to Rawls* (London: Routledge, 1994).

34 See Hobbes, *Leviathan*, at 91–100. For another use of the idea of a social contract, which may not neatly fit the alleged liberal basis for such an agreement, see Jean-Jacques Rousseau, 'Of the Social Contract,' in *The Social Contract and Other Later Political Writings*, trans. Victor Gourevitch (Cambridge: Cambridge University Press, 1997), at 48–53.

35 See Thomas Hobbes, *De Cive*, ed. and trans. Howard Warrender (Oxford: Clarendon Press, 1983) Ch. I, s. 7, at 47. On the notion of a 'common prudence,' see David Gauthier, *The Logic of Leviathan* (Oxford: Clarendon Press, 1969), at 89–99.

36 Must the processes of political association or assimilation amount to a contract among the population? Various forms of consent theory have been offered that do not depend on a contract analogy: see Don Herzog, *Happy Slaves: A Critique of Consent Theory* (Chicago: University of Chicago Press, 1989). Of course, we should pay attention to precisely which subjects are counted free and equal and thus entitled to give their consent, for these may not include important categories of persons such as women, slaves, and children. See Carole Pateman, *The Sexual Contract* (Stanford: Stanford University Press, 1988).

37 And 'equilibrium' becomes, in Robinson's delightful account, a 'blessed state': see Joan Robinson, *Economic Philosophy* (Harmondsworth: Penguin, 1962), at 86. Markets could have a radically redistributive impact if, for

example, the goal of 'efficiency' were consistently pursued: see Morton Horwitz, 'Law and Economics: Science or Politics?' *Hofstra Law Review* 8 (1981), 905 at 910–11.

38 See John Locke, 'Second Treatise of Government,' in *Two Treatises of Government,* ed. Peter Laslett (Cambridge: Cambridge University Press, 1960, repr. 1988), at 285–302, where Locke describes individuals as having different degrees of industry and through 'appropriation' acquiring different amounts of wealth under the law of nature. For discussion of the context in which Locke adopted these views, see James Tully, *A Discourse on Property: John Locke and His Adversaries* (Cambridge: Cambridge University Press, 1980), at 115ff. and Ian Shapiro, *The Evolution of Rights in Liberal Theory* (Cambridge: Cambridge University Press, 1986), at 89–100.

39 C.B. Macpherson, *The Political Theory of Possessive Individualism: Hobbes to Locke* (Oxford: Clarendon Press, 1962). For an example of the use of Macpherson's perspective, see Stephen B. Presser, 'Some Realism about Orphism or the Critical Legal Studies Movement and the New Chain of Being: An English Legal Academic's Guide to the Current State of American Law,' *Northwestern University Law Review* 79 (1984–85), 869 at 881. In critical legal writing on the Lockean understanding of rights rather less attention is paid to the work of those political historians, such as John Dunn or J.G.A. Pocock, who disagree with some of Macpherson's main themes. See, for example, John Dunn, *Political Obligation in Its Historical Context: Essays in Political Theory* (Cambridge: Cambridge University Press, 1980), at 29–52 and J.G.A. Pocock, 'The Myth of John Locke and the Obsession with Liberalism,' in J.G.A. Pocock and Richard Ashcraft, *John Locke* (Los Angeles: University of California [Clark Memorial Library], 1980), 3–24.

40 For another critical legal account of the importance of the concept of liberty to liberal theory, see Joseph William Singer, 'The Legal Rights Debate in Analytical Jurisprudence from Bentham to Hohfeld,' *Wisconsin Law Review* [1982], 975 at 995–9.

41 This dichotomy, which numerous critical legal writers view as distinctively liberal, is discussed at greater length in, for instance, Karl Klare, 'The Public-Private Distinction in Labor Law,' *University of Pennsylvania Law Review* 130 (1982), 1358.

42 This term occurs frequently in modern political theory – for several alternative contemporary conceptions, see Benjamin R. Barber, *A Place for Us: How to Make Society Civil and Democracy Strong* (New York: Hill and Wang, 1998), at 12–37 – but it has been especially common in Marxist-inspired accounts of the struggles by democratic opposition against totalitarian

governments. For a critical overview of the various theories of civil society that have emerged since Hegel at the start of the eighteenth century, see Jean L. Cohen and Andrew Arato, *Civil Society and Political Theory* (Cambridge: MIT Press, 1992). Cohen and Arato contend that the institutions of civil society can be reinvigorated according to the democratic, egalitarian model spelled out in their book. Among the institutions typically subsumed under civil society are the family, voluntary associations (such as trade unions or sports clubs), the professions, religious groups, various forms of media, and generally any small-scale institutions for preserving autonomy and solidarity in the face of the modern economy as well as the state.

43 See, for example, Frances Olsen, 'The Family and the Market: A Study of Ideology and Legal Reform,' *Harvard Law Review* 96 (1983), 1497 at 1502 and 1560–6.

44 This ideology reached its extreme form in a book originally published in 1870, Herbert Spencer's *The Man versus the State* (Indianapolis: Liberty Classics, 1980), at 31–70. For his description of 'Economic Man' as a distillation of human nature that arguably was in the ascendent until the 1930s, see Simon, 'Homo Psychologicus,' at 491–4.

45 See Peter Gabel, 'Intention and Structure in Contractual Conditions: Outline of a Method for Critical Legal Theory,' *Minnesota Law Review* 61 (1977), 601 at 617 and 620. On corporatism, see Roberto Mangabeira Unger, *Law in Modern Society: Toward a Criticism of Social Theory* (New York: Free Press, 1976) at 200–3 and *What Should Legal Analysis Become?* at 99–104.

46 See Mark Tushnet, 'Darkness on the Edge of Town: The Contributions of John Hart Ely to Constitutional Theory,' *Yale Law Journal* 89 (1980), 1037 at 1060; Gary Peller, 'The Metaphysics of American Law,' *California Law Review* 73 (1985), 1152 *passim*; and Howard Lesnick, 'The Consciousness of Work and the Value of American Labor Law,' *Buffalo Law Review* 32 (1983), 832 at 840–1.

47 See David Sugarman, 'The Legal Boundaries of Liberty: Dicey, Liberalism and Legal Science,' *Modern Law Review* 46 (1983), 102; Robert W. Gordon, 'Holmes' Common Law as Legal and Social Science,' *Hofstra Law Review* 10 (1982), 719; and Robert W. Gordon, Book Review, *Vanderbilt Law Review* 36 (1983), 431.

48 See Duncan Kennedy, 'Legal Education as Training for Hierarchy,' in David Kairys, ed., *The Politics of Law: A Progressive Critique*, 2nd ed. (New York: Pantheon Books, 1990), 38–58 at 45 (the two full paragraphs on this page have been excised from the third edition of Kairys's anthology: see *supra*, note 13, 54–75 at 61) and William H. Simon, 'The Ideology of Advocacy:

Procedural Justice and Professional Ethics,' *Wisconsin Law Review* [1978], 29.

49 See Alan Hyde, 'Economic Labor Law v. Political Labor Relations: Dilemmas for Liberal Legalism,' *Texas Law Review* 60 (1981), 1 at 33.

50 For accounts of this circumscribed role, see Lionel Robbins, *An Essay on the Nature and Significance of Economic Science*, 2nd rev. ed. (London: Macmillan, 1935), at 72–103 and Robinson, *Economic Philosophy*, at 25–8.

51 Examples of critical discussion of the rule of law include Morton J. Horwitz, 'The Rule of Law: An Unqualified Human Good?' *Yale Law Journal* 86 (1977), 561 at 566 (where the 'dark side' of the ideal is emphasized); Mark Tushnet, 'The Dilemmas of Liberal Constitutionalism,' *Ohio State Law Journal* 42 (1981), 411 at 415; Jerold S. Auerbach, 'The Quest for Justice under the Rule of Law,' *Suffolk Law Review* 19 (1985), 560; and Klare, 'Judicial Deradicalization of the Wagner Act,' at 338.

52 See John Austin, *The Province of Jurisprudence Determined*, ed. H.L.A. Hart (New York: Humanities Press, 1965).

53 See Allan Hutchinson and Patrick Monahan, 'Democracy and the Rule of Law,' in Allan Hutchinson and Patrick Monahan, eds., *The Rule of Law: Ideal or Ideology* (Scarborough, ON: Carswell, 1987), 97–123 at 101.

54 To some degree, then, critical legal theorists have followed a path parallel to that adopted by other communitarian critiques of liberalism, including Michael J. Sandel, *Liberalism and the Limits of Justice*, 2nd ed. (Cambridge: Cambridge University Press, 1998), chap. 4; Alasdair MacIntyre, *After Virtue: A Study in Moral Theory*, 2nd ed. (London: Duckworth, 1981), at 137–53; and Charles Taylor, *Hegel and Modern Society* (Cambridge: Cambridge University Press, 1979), at 89–95. The different approaches of these contemporary thinkers are usefully distinguished and compared in Stephen Mulhall and Adam Swift, *Liberals and Communitarians*, 2nd ed. (Oxford: Blackwell, 1996).

55 Allan C. Hutchinson, *Waiting for Coraf: A Critique of Law and Rights* (Toronto: University of Toronto Press, 1995), at 8.

56 See Alan D. Freeman, 'Legitimizing Racial Discrimination Through Antidiscrimination Law: A Critical Review of Supreme Court Doctrine,' *Minnesota Law Review* 62 (1978), 1049 at 1119.

57 For the 'perpetrator perspective,' see Freeman, 'Legitimizing Racial Discrimination,' at 1054; Derrick Bell, 'A Hurdle Too High: Class-Based Roadblocks to Racial Remediation,' *Buffalo Law Review* 33 (1984), 1 at 12; and Mark Tushnet, 'Truth, Justice and the American Way: An Interpretation of Public Law Scholarship in the Seventies,' *Texas Law Review* 57 (1979), 1307 at 1352.

58 See Mark Tushnet, *The American Way of Slavery, 1810–1860: Considerations of Humanity and Interest* (Princeton: Princeton University Press, 1981); Sidney Wilhelm, 'The Supreme Court: A Citadel for White Supremacy,' *Michigan Law Review* 79 (1981), 847 at 852–3; and Aviam Soifer, 'Complacency and Constitutional Law,' *Ohio State Law Journal* 42 (1981), 383 at 404.

59 See Derrick A. Bell, *Race, Racism and American Law*, 2nd ed. (Boston: Little, Brown, 1980). For an attempt to describe basic conditions necessary for substantive equality, see, for example, C. Edwin Baker, 'Neutrality, Process, and Rationality: Flawed Interpretations of Equal Protection,' *Texas Law Review* 58 (1980), 1029 at 1032–4 and C. Edwin Baker, 'Outcome Equality or Equality of Respect: The Substantive Content of Equal Protection,' *University of Pennsylvania Law Review* 131 (1983), 933 at 959–60.

60 See Nadine Taub and Elizabeth M. Schneider, 'Women's Subordination and the Role of Law,' in Kairys, ed., *The Politics of Law*, 3rd ed., 328–55.

61 Thus social security schemes have humanitarian as well as redistributive purposes, though according to Simon, both of these types of purposes have played only a supplementary role, and 'the primary role would continue to be that of the private market': William H. Simon, 'Rights and Redistribution in the Welfare System,' *Stanford Law Review* 38 (1986), 1431 at 1440.

62 See William H. Simon, 'The Invention and Reinvention of Welfare Rights,' *Maryland Law Review* 44 (1985), 1, at 29–34.

63 See Gerald Frug, 'The Ideology of Bureaucracy in American Law,' *Harvard Law Review* 97 (1984), 1276 and William H. Simon, 'Legality, Bureaucracy, and Class in the Welfare System,' *Yale Law Journal* 92 (1983), 1198.

64 See Anthony Arblaster, *The Rise and Decline of Western Liberalism* (Oxford: Blackwell, 1984), at 264–83 for a summary of this tendency, and also Morton Horwitz, 'The Legacy of 1776 in Legal and Economic Thought,' *Journal of Law and Economics* 19 (1976), 621 at 622.

65 See John Rawls, *A Theory of Justice*, rev. ed. (Cambridge: Harvard University Press, 1999); John Rawls, 'Kantian Constructivism in Moral Theory,' *Journal of Philosophy* 77 (1980), 515 at 534; John Rawls, 'Justice as Fairness: Political not Metaphysical,' *Philosophy and Public Affairs* 14 (1985), 223 at 232; and Mulhall and Swift, *Liberals and Communitarians*, chap. 5.

66 See, for example, Mari J. Matsuda, 'Liberal Jurisprudence and Abstracted Visions of Human Nature: A Feminist Critique of Rawls' Theory of Justice,' *New Mexico Law Review* 16 (1986), 613.

67 Rawls, 'Justice as Fairness: Political not Metaphysical,' at 230. See also his *Political Liberalism* (New York: Columbia University Press, 1993), at 10.

68 See Holmes, *Anatomy of Antiliberalism*, at 149 for a discussion of the pervasiveness of this generalization in the anti-liberal tradition.

69 See John Rawls, 'The Idea of an Overlapping Consensus,' *Oxford Journal of Legal Studies* 7 (1987), 1. One illustration he gives of a 'familiar intuitive idea,' shared within modern constitutional democracies, is that citizens, regardless of their specific ideological differences, agree that their society should be 'a system of fair social cooperation between free and equal persons': see Rawls, 'Justice as Fairness: Political not Metaphysical,' at 229 and Rawls, *Political Liberalism*, at 15–22.

70 Rawls, 'The Idea of an Overlapping Consensus,' at 2 n.1.

71 See Charles E. Larmore, *Patterns of Moral Complexity* (Cambridge: Cambridge University Press, 1987), at 25.

72 See ibid. at 34–5.

73 For a brief and lucid overview of liberalism's reaction against elements of the 'old order,' see L.T. Hobhouse, *Liberalism* (Oxford: Oxford University Press, 1911, repr. 1964), at 16–29.

74 Modern liberalism's development out of a civil situation in which freedom of conscience and religious profession were of primary concern is described in Quentin Skinner, *The Foundations of Modern Political Thought*, 2 vols. (Cambridge: Cambridge University Press, 1978), II: 3–108. On the scope for a liberal understanding of the importance of cultural membership, see Will Kymlicka, *Liberalism, Community and Culture* (Oxford: Clarendon Press, 1991).

75 For a description of the recrudescence of nationalism and the violence it has engendered, see Michael Ignatieff, *Blood and Belonging: Journeys into the New Nationalism* (New York: Viking, 1993).

76 See ibid. at 108–34 for the prospect of Quebec leaving Canada to become its own sovereign state.

77 See Ronald Dworkin, *Taking Rights Seriously*, rev. ed. (Cambridge: Harvard University Press, 1978), at 206–22.

78 Rawls, 'Justice as Fairness: Political not Metaphysical,' at 245 and Rawls, *Political Liberalism*, at 77–81, 174–6, and 220–2.

79 See the synopsis of Marx's perfectionism in Will Kymlicka, *Contemporary Political Philosophy: An Introduction* (Oxford: Clarendon Press, 1990), at 186–9.

80 See ibid. at 191. For an example of Engels's refusal to let the state establish a model of interpersonal relations, as distinct from economic or property relations, see Friedrich Engels, *The Origin of the Family, Private Property and the State* (Harmondsworth: Penguin, 1985), at 113–14.

81 Joseph Raz, *The Morality of Freedom* (Oxford: Clarendon Press, 1986), at 133.

82 See William A. Galston, *Liberal Purposes: Goods, Virtues and Diversity in the Liberal State* (Cambridge: Cambridge University Press, 1991).

83 Raz, *Morality of Freedom*, at 426.
84 See Robert W. Gordon, 'Historicism in Legal Scholarship,' *Yale Law Journal* 90 (1981), 1017; Robert W. Gordon, 'New Developments in Legal Theory,' in Kairys, ed., *The Politics of Law*, 3rd ed., 641–61; and Robert W. Gordon, 'Critical Legal Histories,' *Stanford Law Review* 36 (1984), 57 at 60–71.
85 See Elizabeth Mensch, 'The History of Mainstream Legal Thought,' in Kairys, ed., *The Politics of Law*, 3rd ed., 23–53.
86 See Duncan Kennedy, 'The Structure of Blackstone's Commentaries,' *Buffalo Law Review* 28 (1979), 205.
87 See the description of analogous goals in relation to social anthropology in John Sturrock, *Structuralism* (London: Grafton Books, 1986), at 46. For further examples of structuralist approaches in critical legal writing, see Al Katz, 'Studies in Boundary Theory: Three Essays in Adjudication and Politics,' *Buffalo Law Review* 28 (1979), 383 and Thomas C. Heller, 'Structuralism and Critique,' *Stanford Law Review* 36 (1984), 127.
88 See Peter Gabel and Duncan Kennedy, 'Roll Over Beethoven,' *Stanford Law Review* 36 (1984), 1.
89 See Duncan Kennedy, 'Freedom and Constraint in Adjudication: A Critical Phenomenology,' *Journal of Legal Education* 36 (1986), 518; Duncan Kennedy, 'The Semiotics of Legal Argument,' *Syracuse Law Review* 42 (1991), 75; and Duncan Kennedy, *A Critique of Adjudication: Fin de siècle* (Cambridge: Harvard University Press, 1997).
90 Hobbes's quasi-geometric method has been summarized in both Andrzej Rapaczynski, *Nature and Politics: Liberalism in the Philosophies of Hobbes, Locke, and Rousseau* (Ithaca: Cornell University Press, 1987), at 36–51 and Gregory S. Kavka, *Hobbesian Moral and Political Theory* (Princeton: Princeton University Press, 1986), 4–18.
91 On Locke's method, see James Tully, *An Approach to Political Philosophy: Locke in Context* (Cambridge: Cambridge University Press, 1993).
92 Isaiah Berlin, *Four Essays on Liberty* (Oxford: Oxford University Press, 1969), at 107.
93 Unger, *Knowledge and Politics*, at 52.
94 Rawls, *A Theory of Justice*, at 53 for a list of basic liberties and at 266 for Rawls's final statement of his principles of justice.
95 See Hutchinson, *Waiting for Coraf*, at 9.
96 Larmore, *Patterns of Moral Complexity*, at 44.
97 Not all liberals agree on the best terminology in this context. While Larmore prefers the language of 'neutrality,' Rawls objects to it as unfortunate and uses it reluctantly: see John Rawls, 'The Priority of Right and Ideas of the Good,' *Philosophy and Public Affairs* 17 (1988), 251 at 260 and Rawls, *Political Liberalism*, at 191.

98 Rawls, 'The Priority of Right and Ideas of the Good,' at 263 and Rawls, *Political Liberalism*, at 194–5.

99 David Hume, *A Treatise of Human Nature*, ed. L.A. Selby-Brigge, 2nd ed. rev. P.H. Nidditch (Oxford: Clarendon Press, 1978), at 415 and 457.

100 See Holmes, *Anatomy of Antiliberalism*, at 56 and Alan S. Kahan, *Aristocratic Liberalism: The Social and Political Thought of Jacob Burckhardt, John Stuart Mill and Alexis de Tocqueville* (New York: Oxford University Press, 1992). A contemporary expression of this idea is found in Rawls, *Political Liberalism*, at 196: 'But given their capacity to assume responsibility for their ends, we do not view citizens as passive carriers of desires. That capacity is part of the moral power to form, to revise, and rationally to pursue a conception of the good ...'

101 See Rawls, *Political Liberalism*, at 15 and 62–3.

102 See Larmore, *Patterns of Moral Complexity*, at 149–50.

103 Unger, *Knowledge and Politics*, at 78.

104 Ronald Dworkin, 'Liberalism,' in *A Matter of Principle* (Cambridge: Harvard University Press, 1985), 181–204 at 183 and Ronald Dworkin, *Sovereign Virtue: The Theory and Practice of Equality* (Cambridge: Harvard University Press, 2000), at 237.

105 Dworkin, 'Liberalism,' at 191.

106 Rawls, *Political Liberalism*, at 6–7.

107 Amy Gutmann, *Liberal Equality* (Cambridge: Cambridge University Press, 1980).

108 See ibid. at 173–217.

3 A Simple Matter of Conviction: Legal Consciousness and Critical Theory

1 For various meanings of the notion of critique that have evolved in the history of philosophy, see John B. Thompson, *Studies in the Theory of Ideology* (Cambridge: Cambridge University Press, 1984), at 230 and Seyla Benhabib, *Critique, Norm, and Utopia: A Study of the Foundations of Critical Theory* (New York: Columbia University Press, 1986), at 19–20.

2 See Karl Klare, 'Contracts Jurisprudence and the First-Year Casebook,' *New York University Law Review* 54 (1979), 876 at 887–8.

3 The dominant trend in the United States has been to treat critical legal studies as largely inspired by indigenously American forerunners, such as the progressive historiography and legal realism of the 1920s and 1930s: see, for example, Mark Tushnet, 'Critical Legal Studies: An Introduction to Its Origins and Underpinnings,' *Journal of Legal Education* 36 (1986), 505. Tushnet suggests, without expounding on it further, some connection

between radical legal critiques, European critiques of social theory (ibid. at 510 n.15), and French post-structuralism (ibid. at 513 n.24). Other commentators on critical legal studies detected stronger echoes, especially as the 1980s wore on, of the work of Nietzsche, Foucault, and Derrida: see Christopher Norris, 'Law, Deconstruction, and the Resistance to Theory,' *Journal of Law and Society* 15 (1988), 166 at 167. For express reliance on the work of Habermas, see Christine A. Desan Husson, 'Expanding the Legal Vocabulary: The Challenge Posed by the Deconstruction and Defense of Law,' *Yale Law Journal* 95 (1986), 969 at 974–81. In the United Kingdom, critical legal writing has been, it is claimed, 'less eclectic' in terms of its influences: see the editors' 'Introduction' in Peter Fitzpatrick and Alan Hunt, eds., *Critical Legal Studies* (Oxford: Blackwell, 1987), 1–3 at 2.

4 Fitzpatrick and Hunt specifically mention the formative influence (with respect to British legal critiques) of 'Marxism, feminism and critical social theory of the Frankfurt variety': see *Critical Legal Studies* and also Alan Hunt, 'The Theory of Critical Legal Studies,' *Oxford Journal of Legal Studies* 6 (1986), 1 at 3 n.7 (rep. in Alan Hunt, *Explorations in Law and Society: Toward a Constitutive Theory of Law* [London: Routledge, 1993], 139–81 at 140 n.5). A very selective sampling of work from the United States that shows similar influences includes Drucilla Cornell, 'Two Lectures on the Normative Dimensions of Community in the Law,' *Tennessee Law Review* 54 (1987), 327 at 330–4 (invoking Hegel's notion of morality or *Sittlichkeit* to illuminate legal interpretation); Mark Tushnet, 'A Marxist Analysis of American Law,' *Marxist Perspectives* 1 (1978), 96; and Drucilla Cornell, 'Toward a Modern/Postmodern Reconstruction of Ethics,' *University of Pennsylvania Law Review* 133 (1985), 291 at 308–11 (comparing Frankfurt School critical theory on the issue of subjectivity with the philosophical views of Roberto Unger and Alasdair MacIntyre). Direct acknowledgment of the relevance of Frankfurt School theory is made in J.M. Balkin, 'Deconstructive Practice and Legal Theory,' *Yale Law Journal* 96 (1987), 743 at 765.

5 Much critical legal writing, including the work by Duncan Kennedy on contradictions, to be studied later in this chapter, contains echoes of dialectical structures, à la Hegel: see Michael Rosen, *Hegel's Dialectic and Its Criticism* (Cambridge: Cambridge University Press, 1982). Marxist ideas that foreshadow some aspects of critical legal analysis can be found in, for example, Karl Marx, 'On the Jewish Question,' in Quintin Hoare, ed., *Karl Marx: Early Writings*, trans. Rodney Livingstone and Gregor Benton (New York: Vintage Books, 1975), 211–41; Karl Marx, 'A Contribution to the Critique of Hegel's Philosophy of Right: Introduction,' in ibid., 243–57;

Karl Marx, 'Economic and Philosophical Manuscripts,' in ibid., 279–400; Karl Marx, 'The German Ideology: Part I,' in Robert C. Tucker, ed., *The Marx-Engels Reader* (New York: W.W. Norton, 1972), 110–64; and Karl Marx, 'Preface to *A Critique of Political Economy*,' in David McLellan, ed., *Karl Marx: Selected Writings* (Oxford: Oxford University Press, 1977), 388–92.

6 Of course, how Marx's use of ideology should be interpreted is itself far from settled. For a general review of the common characteristics of ideology as used in Marx's framework see Bertell Ollman, *Alienation: Marx's Conception of Man in Capitalist Society*, 2nd ed. (Cambridge: Cambridge University Press, 1976), at 232–3: 'Bourgeois ideology takes many other forms, but it is always partial, it is always unscientific (limited to appearances), it is always class biased, it always loses sight of the real history and actual potential of its subject and it always confuses – generally turning in an opposite sense – the real relations between its elements.' Writers remain divided over at least two conflicting conceptions of ideology derivable from Marx's work. The first of these is 'global' and merely descriptive, in the sense that it labels as ideology all human beliefs, values, and ideas. The second is a pejorative use of the term 'ideological,' in the name of which, for example, liberalism is condemned. For a discussion of such possible ambiguity and its consequences, see R.G. Peffer, *Marxism, Morality, and Social Justice* (Princeton: Princeton University Press, 1990), at 236–67. Other relevant sources include Richard W. Miller, *Analyzing Marx: Morality, Power and History* (Princeton: Princeton University Press, 1984), at 45–50 (emphasizing the sense of ideology as false consciousness); Steven Lukes, *Marxism and Morality* (Oxford: Oxford University Press, 1985), at 3 (identifying the paradox created by treating all moral thinking as ideological illusion); and Jon Elster, *Making Sense of Marx* (Cambridge: Cambridge University Press, 1985), at 459–510 (attempting a rational reconstruction of this part of Marxism by re-examining the foundations of ideology as distorted belief formation).

7 The concept of legal consciousness has been described as 'the central tenet of the critical legal studies creed': see David Trubek, 'Where the Action Is: Critical Legal Studies and Empiricism,' *Stanford Law Review* 36 (1984), 575 at 592.

8 See Thomas Heller, 'Structuralism and Critique,' *Stanford Law Review* 36 (1984), 127 at 131. For a description of a so-called liberal conception of consciousness as a matter largely of individual attitude, shaped independently of social history, see Patricia Ewick and Susan Sibley, 'Conformity, Contestation, and Resistance: An Account of Legal Consciousness,' *New England Law Review* 26 (1992), 731 at 738–9.

9 See Willard Van Orman Quine, 'Two Dogmas of Empiricism,' in *From a Logical Point of View: Nine Logico-Philosophical Essays*, 2nd rev. ed. (Cambridge: Harvard University Press, 1961), 20–46 at 42–4.

10 See Ewick and Sibley, 'Conformity, Contestation, and Resistance,' at 739–41 for a description of legal consciousness in the epiphenomenal sense, according to which consciousness is a 'by-product of the operations of social structures.'

11 It is controversial, of course, whether psychoanalysis, with its model of psychological structures or its use of dialogic therapy, can serve as the basis for social or political theory. Various affinities between psychoanalysis and critical theory are noted in Thomas McCarthy, *The Critical Theory of Jürgen Habermas* (Cambridge: Polity Press, 1984), at 193–213 and in David Held, *Introduction to Critical Theory: Horkheimer to Habermas* (Berkeley: University of California Press, 1980), at 111–47. For some objections to such use, see Jürgen Habermas, *Theory and Practice*, trans. John Viertel (Boston: Beacon Press, 1973), at 16. Notwithstanding the cautions raised by Habermas, some critical legal writers have analogized their critical practice to psychoanalytic techniques aimed at the 'possibility of emancipation from customary ways of thinking': see Balkin, 'Deconstructive Practice and Legal Theory,' at 765.

12 See David Couzens Hoy and Thomas McCarthy, *Critical Theory* (Oxford: Blackwell, 1994), at 77. On Gadamer's presentation of hermeneutical tasks, '[i]t is the tyranny of hidden prejudices that makes us deaf to the language that speaks to us in tradition': Hans-Georg Gadamer, *Truth and Method*, 2nd rev. ed., trans. John Cumming (London: Sheed and Ward, 1979), at 239. Gadamer uses another trope when he claims that hermeneutical '[r]eflection on a given preunderstanding brings before me something that otherwise happens *behind my back*': Hans-Georg Gadamer, 'On the Scope and Function of Hermeneutical Reflection,' in *Philosophical Hermeneutics*, trans. and ed. David E. Linge (Berkeley: University of California Press, 1976), 18–43 at 38 (emphasis in the original). As with psychoanalysis, the use of hermeneutics to buttress political or social critique is problematic: witness the debate between Habermas and Gadamer. Among the issues joined were the relative power of reflection alone to achieve political insight; the relationship between language and any 'reality' that allegedly lies behind it; the plausibility of the notion of 'legitimate prejudices'; and whether anyone can justifiably claim to have insight into another person's delusion. For an outline of the terms of the debate, see Jack Mendelson, 'The Habermas-Gadamer Debate,' *New German Critique* 18 (1979), 44.

13 See Max Horkheimer, *Critical Theory*, trans. Matthew J. O'Connell (New York: Continuum, 1972), at 22.

14 The thesis that social control is maintained by creating dominant forms of consciousness, so that ruling groups do not have to resort to overt means of domination, is to be found in literature discussing cultural formations generally (including education, art, sports, the media, and so forth). See Raymond Williams, *Marxism and Literature* (Oxford: Oxford University Press, 1977), at 95–114; Michael J. Cormack, *Ideology* (Ann Arbor: University of Michigan Press, 1992); and John B. Thompson, *Ideology and Modern Culture: Critical Social Theory in the Era of Mass Communication* (Cambridge: Polity Press, 1990).

15 Klare, 'Contracts Jurisprudence,' at 876 n.2.

16 Along the way, Kennedy has repudiated his own original contributions to critical legal thinking in the 1970s. In a dialogue with Peter Gabel which, because of its element of playfulness, has been notoriously difficult to interpret, Kennedy stated: 'First of all, I renounce the fundamental contradiction. I recant it, and I also recant the whole idea of individualism and altruism and the idea of legal consciousness, very much for the reasons you just said. I mean these things are absolutely classic examples of "philosophical" abstractions which you can manipulate into little structures.' See Peter Gabel and Duncan Kennedy, 'Roll Over Beethoven,' *Stanford Law Review* 36 (1984), 1 at 15–16. Although it is not entirely transparent, Kennedy's objection to these key elements of early critical legal literature appeared to be that other writers have used those phrases to achieve in their work 'some surface plausibility' as radical critics (see ibid. at 16). Kennedy indicated that he was abandoning the practice of 'philosophy' (the term he uses in the dialogue to disparage Gabel's efforts to construct a legal and social theory) in favour of 'small-scale, microphenomenological evocation of real experiences in complex contextualized ways in which one makes it into doing it' (ibid. at 3). Something like that latter process is found in Duncan Kennedy, 'Freedom and Constraint in Adjudication: A Critical Phenomenology,' *Journal of Legal Education* 36 (1986), 518. In that article Kennedy does not deal with a 'real' experience (as promised in the above prescription), but he does imaginatively develop what might be the experience of a judge in adjudicating a hypothetical case. In particular, Kennedy's account emphasizes the radically contingent and manipulable nature of legal argument, a characterization that Kennedy claims runs counter to all traditional legal theory. Despite Kennedy's protests in 'Roll Over Beethoven' that investigations of legal consciousness are at a dead end, his subsequent efforts to understand adjudication use many of the methods that mark his earlier work. For example, he continues to pursue the idea that participants in legal reasoning are subject to the pull of normative factors, and he still organizes the imagined judge's analysis around bipolar nodes. In Kennedy's

hypothetical scenario, the judge is torn between what the law seems to require and how he wants it to 'come out.' Viewed in light of his subsequent work, Kennedy's earlier renunciation should not be accepted at face value. After all, as he states elsewhere in the dialogue with Gabel: 'I want paradox and unconsciousness' ('Roll Over Beethoven,' at 23).

17 This is pre-eminently illustrated in Duncan Kennedy, 'The Structure of Blackstone's Commentaries,' *Buffalo Law Review* 28 (1979), 205.

18 Duncan Kennedy, 'Toward an Historical Understanding of Legal Consciousness: The Case of Classical Legal Thought in America, 1850–1940,' in Stephen Spitzer, ed., *Research in Law and Sociology*, vol. 3 (Greenwich, CT: JAI Press, 1980), 3–24 at 23.

19 Ibid. at 6.

20 Ibid. at 21.

21 Ibid. at 5.

22 Ibid. at 21.

23 See Thomas S. Kuhn, *The Structure of Scientific Revolutions*, 2nd ed. (Chicago: University of Chicago Press, 1970) and T.S. Kuhn, 'A Function for Thought Experiments,' in Ian Hacking, ed., *Scientific Revolutions* (Oxford: Oxford University Press, 1981), 6–27.

24 For background on the purpose of such accounts as well as the doubts, applications, and criticisms they have engendered in fields other than natural science, see Richard J. Bernstein, *The Restructuring of Social and Political Theory* (Oxford: Blackwell, 1976); Barry Barnes, *T.S. Kuhn and Social Science* (London: Macmillan, 1982); and Richard J. Bernstein, *Beyond Objectivism and Relativism: Science, Hermeneutics, and Praxis* (Oxford: Blackwell, 1983).

25 See Richard Rorty, *Consequences of Pragmatism* (Minneapolis: University of Minnesota Press, 1982), at 221 and 227.

26 See, for example, Kennedy, 'Toward an Historical Understanding,' at 7, where he claims that by carefully delineating the transformations in consciousness 'we will find a way to understand the mass of seemingly self-contradictory or plainly mistaken verbiage that makes up the greater part of our legal tradition.'

27 The Whig interpretation is 'the tendency in many historians to write on the side of Protestants and Whigs, to praise revolutions provided they have been successful, to emphasize certain principles of progress in the last and to produce a story which is the ratification if not the glorification of the present': Herbert Butterfield, *The Whig Interpretation of History* (Harmondsworth: Penguin, 1973), at 9. It is ironic that lawyers have been credited with

inventing this form of historical scholarship: see G.R. Elton, *F.W. Maitland* (London: Weidenfeld & Nicolson, 1985), at 107 n.27.

28 See Robert W. Gordon, 'Some Critical Theories of Law and Their Critics,' in David Kairys, ed., *The Politics of Law: A Progressive Critique*, 3rd ed. (New York: Basic Books, 1998), 641–61 and Robert W. Gordon, 'Critical Legal Histories,' *Stanford Law Review* 36 (1984), 57.

29 Roberto Mangabeira Unger, *The Critical Legal Studies Movement* (Cambridge: Harvard University Press, 1986), at 23.

30 Roberto Mangabeira Unger, *Social Theory: Its Situation and Its Task* (Cambridge: Cambridge University Press, 1987), at 88–9.

31 Roberto Mangabeira Unger, *False Necessity: Anti-Necessitarian Social Theory in the Service of Radical Democracy* (Cambridge: Cambridge University Press, 1987), at 4.

32 Unger, *Social Theory*, at 89.

33 Unger, *Critical Legal Studies Movement*, at 26.

34 Ibid. at 111.

35 Unger, *False Necessity*, at 556–60.

36 Unger, *Critical Legal Studies Movement*, at 4.

37 Ibid. at 116.

38 Alan Hunt has also commented on these two different uses of the concept within critical legal literature: see Hunt, 'Theory of Critical Legal Studies,' at 13–14 (and at 151–2 in the reprinted version of his essay).

39 See Douglas Hay, 'Property, Authority and the Criminal Law,' in Douglas Hay, Peter Linebaugh, John Rule, E.P. Thompson, and Cal Winslow, *Albion's Fatal Tree: Crime and Society in Eighteenth-Century England* (London: Allen Lane, 1975), 17–63.

40 Trubek, 'Where the Action Is,' at 592.

41 Ewick and Sibley, 'Comformity, Contestation, and Resistance,' at 731.

42 See also Eugene D. Genovese, *Roll, Jordan, Roll: The World the Slaves Made* (New York: Random House, 1976), at 25–49.

43 For textured accounts of the application of employment law, see Craig Becker, 'Property in the Workplace: Labor, Capital, and Crime in the Eighteenth-Century British Woolen and Worsted Industry,' *Virginia Law Review* 69 (1983), 1487; James Atleson, 'Obscenities in the Workplace: A Comment on Fair and Foul Expression and Status Relationships,' *Buffalo Law Review* 34 (1985), 693; and Christopher L. Tomlins, *The State and the Unions: Law, Labor Relations Policy and the Organized Labor Movement in the United States, 1880–1960* (New York: Cambridge University Press, 1985). On legal services for the poor, see Anthony V. Alfieri, 'Reconstructive Poverty

Law Practice: Learning Lessons of Client Narrative,' *Yale Law Journal* 100 (1991), 2107–47; Carrie Menkel-Meadow, 'Legal Aid in the United States: The Professionalization and Politicization of Legal Services in the 1980's,' *Osgoode Hall Law Journal* 22 (1984), 29; and Paul R. Tremblay, 'Rebellious Lawyering, Regnant Lawyering, and Street-Level Bureaucracy,' *Hastings Law Journal* 43 (1992), 947. The possibility of socially progressive corporate decision making is discussed in Robert W. Gordon, 'Corporate Law Practice as a Public Calling,' *Maryland Law Review* 49 (1990), 255. The legal matrix of entitlements and benefits form the background for the analyses in Austin Sarat, '". . . The Law Is All Over": Power, Resistance and the Legal Consciousness of the Welfare Poor,' *Yale Journal of Law and the Humanities* 2 (1990), 343; Lucie E. White, 'No Exit: Rethinking "Welfare Dependency" from a Different Ground,' *Georgetown Law Journal* 81 (1993), 1961; and Joel F. Handler, '"Constructing the Social Spectacle": The Interpretation of Entitlements, Legalization, and Obligations in Social Welfare History,' *Brooklyn Law Review* 56 (1990), 899.

44 See James Boyle, 'The Politics of Reason: Critical Legal Theory and Local Social Thought,' *University of Pennsylvania Law Review* 133 (1985), 685 at 769–83.

45 Ibid. at 750.

46 See Richard Abel, 'Law Books and Books about Law,' *Stanford Law Review* 26 (1973), 175.

47 An excellent example of the use of this kind of material can be found in Robert W. Gordon, 'The Ideal and the Actual in the Law: Fantasies and Practices of New York City Lawyers, 1870–1910,' in Gerard W. Gawalt, ed., *The New High Priests: Lawyers in Post-Civil War America* (Westport, CT: Greenwood Press, 1984), 51–74.

48 See, for example, John Henry Schlegel, 'American Legal Realism and Empirical Social Science: From the Yale Experience,' *Buffalo Law Review* 28 (1979), 459.

49 See Mark Tushnet, 'Post-Realist Legal Scholarship,' *Journal of the Society of Public Teachers of Law* 15 (1979), 20 and Mark Tushnet, 'Legal Scholarship: Its Causes and Cure,' *Yale Law Journal* 90 (1981), 1205 at 1211–12.

50 See Jürgen Habermas, *Knowledge and Human Interests*, trans. Jeremy J. Shapiro (Boston: Beacon Press, 1971), at 61–2 and Held, *Introduction to Critical Theory*, at 269–70.

51 Trubek, 'Where the Action Is,' at 612.

52 At least one critical legal writer, sensing the problem identified here, sought to conflate the two kinds of analysis, so that a 'study of doctrine is itself an empirical study': see Peter Gabel, 'The Phenomenology of Rights-

Consciousness and the Pact of the Withdrawn Selves,' *Texas Law Review* 62 (1984), 1563 at 1595 n.39.

53 Trubek, 'Where the Action Is,' at 612.

54 See Stewart Macaulay, 'Non-Contractual Relations in Business: A Preliminary Study,' *American Sociological Review* 28 (1963), 55 and Stewart Macaulay, 'Elegant Models, Empirical Pictures, and the Complexities of Contract,' *Law and Society Review* 11 (1977), 507.

55 Kennedy, 'Toward an Historical Understanding,' at 7. See also Elizabeth Mensch, 'The History of Mainstream Legal Thought,' in Kairys, ed., *Politics of Law*, 23–53 at 28–32 for a description of jurists' 'Classical Legal Consciousness.'

56 Kennedy, 'Toward an Historical Understanding,' at 21.

57 Ibid.

58 Ibid. at 8.

59 See Gabel and Kennedy, 'Roll Over Beethoven,' at 44, where Kennedy admits: 'When I first started doing historical research, I sort of imagined that people in the late nineteenth century *had* classical legal consciousness. Now, I used to say to myself that was a dangerous way to think about it. But there was some real tendency on my part to think about it that way. So I was working it out as though I had a scalpel and I was opening up their heads and analyzing the classical legal consciousness there was in their heads.'

60 In this respect, Kennedy's account differs from that offered by Morton Horwitz. In his book, *The Transformation of American Law, 1780–1860* (Cambridge: Harvard University Press, 1977), Horwitz painstakingly described the extent to which judges were fully conscious of economic considerations in their fashioning of, or changing, the common law. This does not mean that, on Horwitz's analysis, economics is determinative of legal development: judges did not abruptly alter the law to suit the interests of dominant economic classes. Rather, the process was gradual, and overall, on the basis of the numerous judicial opinions surveyed by Horwitz, one could conclude that the evolution of legal doctrine worked to redistribute an increasing proportion of wealth to entrepreneurial and commercial groups in U.S. society. In the sequel to his earlier book, Horwitz has acknowledged a direct debt to Kennedy's formulation of late-nineteenth-century 'Classical Legal Thought.' Horwitz adopts especially the notions of law as an apolitical science; the penchant for categorization; and legal reasoning as dependent on a series of dichotomies. See Morton J. Horwitz, *The Transformation of American Law, 1870–1960: The Crisis of Legal Orthodoxy* (New York: Oxford University Press, 1992), at 10–16 and 273 n.1.

61 There are no references to the possible resonance, within U.S. legal theory

of the mid-nineteenth century, of the ideas of Savigny or von Jhering. For example, something might have been made of the romanticized conception of lawyers or judges as agents of popular consciousness in advanced societies: see Friedrich Karl von Savigny, *Of the Vocation of Our Age for Legislation and Jurisprudence*, trans. Abraham Hayward (New York: Arno Press, 1975, repr. of 1831 ed.). Also, claims on behalf of legal science and law as the primary social instruments to harmonize individual and group interests were advanced in Rudolf von Jhering, *Law as a Means to an End*, trans. Isaac Husik (New York: A.M. Kelley, 1968, repr. of 1913 ed.).

62 Neil Duxbury, *Patterns of American Jurisprudence* (Oxford: Clarendon Press, 1995), at 10–11.

63 Duncan Kennedy, 'Legal Formality,' *Journal of Legal Studies* 2 (1973), 370 at 385.

64 See *supra*, note 58, and accompanying text.

65 See Duncan Kennedy, 'Form and Substance in Private Law Adjudication,' *Harvard Law Review* 89 (1976), 1685 at 1713–22.

66 Jay Feinman, 'Critical Approaches to Contract Law,' *U.C.L.A. Law Review* 30 (1983), 829 at 845ff.

67 A common pairing in critical legal literature: for a good illustration of how the concepts are manipulated, see Frances Olsen, 'The Family and the Market: A Study of Ideology and Legal Reform,' *Harvard Law Review* 96 (1983), 1497.

68 See Paul Brest, 'The Fundamental Rights Controversy: The Essential Contradictions of Normative Constitutional Scholarship,' *Yale Law Journal* 90 (1981), 1063 at 1108–9 and Jennifer Jaff, 'Radical Pluralism: A Proposed Theoretical Framework for the Conference on Critical Legal Studies,' *Georgetown Law Journal* 72 (1984), 1143 at 1145.

69 See Elizabeth Mensch, 'Freedom of Contract as Ideology,' *Stanford Law Review* 33 (1981), 753 at 759–60 and Allan Hutchinson and Patrick Monahan, 'The "Rights" Stuff: Roberto Unger and Beyond,' *Texas Law Review* 62 (1984), 1477 at 1483.

70 Kennedy, 'Form and Substance,' *passim.*

71 See Feinman, 'Critical Approaches to Contract Law,' at 833 n.44: '[b]alancing may be the single most distinguishing feature of modern law.'

72 See Mark Kelman, 'Trashing,' *Stanford Law Review* 36 (1984), 293 at 296–7.

73 See Clare Dalton, 'An Essay in the Deconstruction of Contract Doctrine,' *Yale Law Journal* 94 (1985), 997 at 1007–8.

74 Kennedy, 'Form and Substance,' at 1712 (emphasis in the original).

75 See Gabel.

76 Ibid. at 1568.

77 Ibid. at 1570.
78 See Roberto M. Unger, *Knowledge and Politics* (New York: Free Press, 1975), at 31–6, 51–5, and 88–100.
79 See ibid. at 49–55.
80 See Kennedy, 'The Structure of Blackstone's Commentaries,' at 211.
81 Ibid. at 213.
82 Ibid. at 216–17.
83 Ibid. at 221.
84 This is not the same argument as that used by, for example, Rousseau, whose theory of the general will attempted to affirm the compatibility of individual freedom with the constraints imposed on behalf of the common interest. On Rousseau's theory, we end up with the unsatisfying (and counterintuitive) result that social coercion can force an individual to be free: see Jean-Jacques Rousseau, 'Of the Social Contract,' in *The Social Contract and Other Later Political Writings*, trans. Victor Gourevitch (Cambridge: Cambridge University Press, 1997), at 51–3.
85 This tack is followed in Denise Meyerson, 'Fundamental Contradictions in Critical Legal Studies,' *Oxford Journal of Legal Studies* 11 (1991), 439 at 444–5.
86 This view is summarized in Allan C. Hutchinson and Patrick J. Monahan, 'Law, Politics and the Critical Legal Scholars: The Unfolding Drama of American Legal Thought,' *Stanford Law Review* 36 (1984), 199 at 211: '. . . every doctrinal dispute is reducible to the contradictory claims of communal security and individual freedom. Any particular resolution of that conflict is simply an arbitrary choice.'
87 Note the words of Lord Wright in *Sedleigh-Denfield v. O'Callaghan*, [1940] A.C. 880 at 903: 'A balance has to be maintained between the rights of the occupier to do what he likes with his own, and the rights of his neighbour not to be interfered with.'
88 Thus the neighbour can bring an action in the tort of nuisance for protection against both physical and non-physical forms of interference. Complaints in respect of the latter category could include such things as unduly excessive noise or noxious smells. The degree of interference necessary to ground an action in nuisance will be disputed in the circumstances of each case. For a summary of modern doctrines, see Gerry Cross, 'Does Only the Careless Polluter Pay? A Fresh Examination of the Nature of Private Nuisance,' *Law Quarterly Review* 111 (1995), 445.
89 Technically, the particular circumstances involving the bringing onto the land of something which, if it escapes, would harm the neighbour's property is covered by the non-natural use requirement of the doctrine estab-

lished in *Rylands v. Fletcher* (1866) L.R. 1 Ex. 265, aff'd (1868) L.R. 3 H.L. 330.

90　The discussion in this section should not be read as implying that all critical legal writers share Kennedy's orientation towards 'irrationalism': see Clare Dalton, 'Review of David Kairys, ed., *The Politics of Law: A Progressive Critique,' Harvard Women's Law Journal* 6 (1983), 229 and Boyle, 'Politics of Reason,' at 715–18 and 764–5.

91　See Gordon, 'Some Critical Theories of Law and Their Critics,' at 649.

92　Clifford Geertz, *The Interpretation of Cultures* (New York: Basic Books, 1973), at 217.

93　They are corroborated in this point of view by works such as Richard Rorty, *Philosophy and the Mirror of Nature* (Oxford: Basil Blackwell, 1980), esp. chaps. 3–6.

94　See, for example, Alan D. Freeman, 'Antidiscrimination Law: The View from 1989,' in David Kairys, ed., *The Politics of Law: A Progressive Critique*, 2nd rev. ed (New York: Pantheon, 1990), 121–50 at 122.

95　As noted *supra*, note 6, tensions exist within Marxism about the place of ideology in critical analysis. The orthodox or 'pejorative' view is recounted in John Plamenatz, *Ideology* (London: Macmillan, 1970), at 23–7. By contrast, in the Althusserian view all thought is inherently ideological. Ideology in this latter scheme is not a distorted representation of real material conditions, but rather the relation through which all of us operate in the world. Althusser specifically includes the legal system in his enumeration of 'ideological state apparatuses': see Louis Althusser, *Lenin and Philosophy and Other Essays*, trans. Ben Brewster (London: New Left Books, 1971), at 137 and 141. See also Nicos Poulantzas, *Political Power and Social Classes*, trans. Timothy O'Hagan (London: New Left Books, 1973), at 205–21 and Alex Callinicos, *Marxism and Philosophy* (Oxford: Oxford University Press, 1983), at 89–95.

96　See Raymond Geuss, *The Idea of a Critical Theory: Habermas and the Frankfurt School* (Cambridge: Cambridge University Press, 1981), at 75–88. By reference to Geuss's analysis, Rorty has commented on the 'uselessness' of the notion of ideology: see Richard Rorty, *Contingency, Irony, and Solidarity* (Cambridge: Cambridge University Press, 1989), at 59 n.15.

97　See Geuss, *Idea of a Critical Theory*, at 57.

98　Wythe Holt, 'Morton Horwitz and the Transformation of American Legal History,' *William and Mary Law Review* 23 (1982), 663 at 703. See also Kenneth Casebeer, 'Toward a Critical Jurisprudence – A First Step by Way of the Public-Private Distinction in Constitutional Law,' *University of Miami Law Review* 37 (1983), 379 at 382–3.

99 This criticism turns back the problems of epistemological realism or relativism on the radical critique itself, arguing that critical legal writing has been committed to two incompatible propositions: in other words, critical legal writers have not exhibited the 'circumspection' that Foucault, for one, thinks is necessary in handling any theory of ideology: see Michel Foucault, *Power/Knowledge: Selected Interviews and Other Writings, 1972–1977*, ed. Colin Gordon (New York: Pantheon Books, 1980), at 118.

100 Feminist debates since the 1980s have brought into sharp focus the serious problems created by generalizing about the concept of 'woman,' women's nature, the essential characteristics of women, or the similar experiences of all women. For a discussion of the rise of new forms of feminism that stress, as against biological or cultural feminisms, not only the differences between men and women but also the differences among women, see Linda Alcoff, 'Cultural Feminism versus Post-Structuralism: The Identity Crisis in Feminist Theory,' *Signs: Journal of Women in Culture and Society* 13 (1988), 405. A relatively early diagnosis of the paradoxes created by defining progressive goals in terms of adjusting the system so that women would have the rights traditionally associated with men is contained in Wendy Williams, 'The Equality Crisis: Some Reflections on Culture, Courts, and Feminism,' *Women's Rights Law Reporter* 7 (1982), 175. One way of escaping the apparent conundrums identified by Alcoff is to see women as a collective involved in a fluid process, so that they are not subsumed under a single concept that attributes to them common characteristics or a common identity: see Iris Marion Young, 'Gender as Seriality: Thinking about Women as a Social Collective,' *Signs: Journal of Women in Culture and Society* 19 (1994), 713.

101 Some feminists have also objected to legal scholarship, whether written by traditional or critical legal authors, that attempts to develop a 'grand theory' of the law: see Martha L.A. Fineman, 'Feminist Legal Scholarship and Women's Gendered Lives,' in Maureen Cain and Christine B. Harrington, eds., *Lawyers in a Postmodern World: Translation and Transgression* (New York: New York University Press, 1994), 229–46 at 230. For a defence of such theorizing, in the cause of understanding women's oppression, see Frances Olsen, 'Feminist Theory in Grand Style,' *Columbia Law Review* 89 (1989), 1147.

102 A summary of feminist criticisms of the critical legal concept of a pervasive legal consciousness is provided in Phyllis Goldfarb, 'From the Worlds of "Others": Minority and Feminist Responses to Critical Legal Studies,' *New England Law Review* 26 (1992), 683.

103 One of the most influential attempts to describe the distinctive moral

consciousness and development of women is found in Carol Gilligan, *In a Different Voice: Psychological Thinking and Women's Development* (Cambridge: Harvard University Press, 1982). Gilligan's theory valorized women as nurturers who prize the values of responsibility, connection, and selfless caring. When faced with difficult moral dilemmas, women were viewed by Gilligan as tending to engage in contextual thinking, in contrast with men, who practise abstract thinking that idealizes separation, autonomy, and hierarchy. Among legal feminists, Robin West has explored the ramifications of such emphasis on connection and intimacy: see Robin West, 'Jurisprudence and Gender,' *University of Chicago Law Review* 55 (1988), 1. For a critique of Gilligan, especially the dangers created by the domestic imagery in her theory, see Joan C. Williams, 'Deconstructing Gender,' in Leslie Friedman Goldstein, ed., *Feminist Jurisprudence: The Difference Debate* (Lanham, MD: Rowman and Littlefield, 1992), 41–98. The potentially conservative uses of Gilligan's theory are criticized in Mary Joe Frug, *Postmodern Legal Feminism* (New York: Routledge, 1992), at 30–49. Lest the impression is created that feminism presents irresolvable antagonisms, it should also be mentioned that defences have been offered of a 'universalist specification of impartiality' that is expanded to include 'consideration of care': see Seyla Benhabib, *Situating the Self: Gender, Community, and Postmodernism in Contemporary Ethics* (Cambridge: Polity Press, 1992), at 178–202.

104 See Williams, 'Deconstructing Gender,' at 71, where she notes that ideology continues to create false forms of consciousness. Men are occluded from acknowledging the importance of certain needs, while women have denied their own competitiveness. For analyses of how women's consciousness is formed, see Catharine A. MacKinnon, *Toward a Feminist Theory of the State* (Cambridge: Harvard University Press, 1989), at 83–105 and Gerda Lerner, *The Creation of Feminist Consciousness: From the Middle Ages to Eighteen-seventy* (New York: Oxford University Press, 1993). The difficulty of explaining consciousness-formation and consciousness-raising in a society where male domination is supposed to be pervasive and all-powerful is dealt with in Ruth Colker, 'Feminist Consciousness and the State: A Basis for Cautious Optimism,' *Columbia Law Review* 90 (1990), 1146 at 1150–9.

105 See Kimberlé Williams Crenshaw, 'Race, Reform and Retrenchment: Transformation and Legitimation in Antidiscrimination Law,' *Harvard Law Review* 101 (1988), 1331 at 1356–87.

106 See Richard Delgado, 'The Ethereal Scholar: Does Critical Legal Studies Have What Minorities Want?' *Harvard Civil Rights–Civil Liberties Law Review*

22 (1987), 301 at 305 and 315 and Patricia J. Williams, *The Alchemy of Race and Rights* (Cambridge: Harvard University Press, 1991), at 150–2.

107 See Ernesto Laclau and Chantal Mouffe, *Hegemony and Socialist Strategy: Towards a Radical Democracy* (London: Verso, 1985), at 2. This view is challenged in Ellen Meiksins Wood, *The Retreat From Class: A New 'True' Socialism* (London: Verso, 1986).

108 It has already been noted that, from the outset, critical legal writers were uncomfortable with the traditional economist model of orthodox Marxism for explaining legal phenomena. While Feinman, 'Critical Approaches to Contract Law,' at 849 described Horwitz's work along traditional lines, Horwitz himself rejected the 'simplistic slogans' of Marxism: see Morton Horwitz, 'The Rule of Law: An Unqualified Human Good?' *Yale Law Journal* 86 (1977), 561 at 563. The so-called relative autonomy thesis has similarly been found wanting by a number of critical legal writers: for an invocation of this theory, see Isaac Balbus, 'Commodity Form and Legal Form: An Essay on "Relative Autonomy" of the Law,' *Law and Society Review* 11 (1977), 571. The drawbacks to the theory of relative autonomy are brought together in Hugh Collins, *Marxism and Law* (Oxford: Oxford University Press, 1982), at 124–46. In conjunction with the theory of legal consciousness, some critical legal writers sketched out what they have called a constitutive theory of law: see Jay M. Feinman and Peter Gabel, 'Contract Law as Ideology,' *Politics of Law*, 3rd ed. in Kairys, ed., 497–510 at 506; Karl Klare, 'Law-Making as Praxis,' *Telos* 40 (1979), 123 at 125–8; Gordon, 'Some Critical Theories of Law and Their Critics,' at 647–50; and Andrew Fraser, 'The Legal Theory We Need Now,' *Socialist Review* 8 (1978), 147 at 149–50. The most refined version of this theory can be found in Hunt, *Explorations in Law and Society*, at 147–8, 173–8, 202–10, and 301–33 where he elaborates his notion of legal relations as constituting the framework within which economic, social, and political activities take place: the legal form is important. At the same time, Hunt conceives of these realms as interpenetrative or 'imbricative.' This is not to give up on finding a causal mode of explanation: Hunt claims that a constitutive understanding of law still investigates causal factors, but not in the 'unidirectional' manner associated with instrumentalist Marxism. Seeds of this approach were already present in Weber: see Max Weber, *On Law in Economy and Society*, ed. Max Rheinstein, trans. Edward Shils (Cambridge: Harvard University Press, 1954), at 98–9, 131 and 304. Proponents of a leftist constitutive theory of law have to overcome the kinds of arguments raised in G.A. Cohen, *Karl Marx's Theory of History: A Defence* (Oxford: Oxford

University Press, 1978), at 217–37, that property relations, for example, can be described solely in non-legal, economic terms.

109 For expressions of this point see, for example, Alan D. Freeman, 'Race and Class: The Dilemma of Liberal Reform,' *Yale Law Journal* 90 (1981), 1880 at 1894; Regina Austin, 'The Problem of the Legitimacy of the Welfare State,' *University of Pennsylvania Law Review* 130 (1982), 1510 at 1511–12; Hutchinson and Monahan, 'The "Rights" Stuff,' at 1486; and Karl Klare, 'The Public-Private Distinction in Labor Law,' *University of Pennsylvania Law Review* 130 (1982), 1358 at 1358.

110 Legal doctrine, such as the law of confessions, is replete with cases in which one of the parties claims that her capacity to make a rational choice was undermined and that, therefore, she should not be held responsible for the ordinary legal effects of her act. On such unjustifiable forms of coercion, see Alan Wertheimer, *Coercion* (Princeton: Princeton University Press, 1987). Wertheimer specifically refrains from discussing situations in which the issue is whether the state's use of coercive measures is justified.

111 See Weber, *On Law in Economy and Society*, at 336–7.

112 See Gregory S. Alexander, 'History as Ideology in the Basic Property Course,' *Journal of Legal Education* 36 (1986), 381; Elizabeth Mensch, 'The Colonial Origins of Liberal Property Rights,' *Buffalo Law Review* 31 (1982), 635; and Joseph William Singer, 'Re-reading Property,' *New England Law Review* 26 (1992), 711.

113 Boyle, 'Politics of Reason,' at 712.

114 Ibid. Note that it is difficult to pin down the sense in which, for Boyle, politics is supposed to be something material, while law is not.

115 See Judith Jarvis Thomson, *The Realm of Rights* (Cambridge: Harvard University Press, 1990), for a discussion of the complex ways in which rights are claimed, ascribed, and justified.

116 See Michael Mann, 'The Social Cohesion of Liberal Democracy,' *American Sociological Review* 35 (1970), 423. Note also the deployment of a notion of 'fragmented consciousness' as described in Thompson, *Studies in the Theory of Ideology*, at 300–1 and derived from Habermas.

117 See Ewick and Sibley, 'Conformity, Contestation, and Resistance,' at 742 where the authors, while generally sympathetic to the utility of the concept of legal consciousness, advise against using it to 'totalize' popular understanding, and would prefer instead that it be used in the sense of 'something local, contextual, pluralistic, filled with conflict and contradiction.'

118 See Unger, *Critical Legal Studies Movement*, at 15–22.

119 See Gordon, 'Some Critical Theories of Law and Their Critics,' at 656.

120 See Paul Connerton, *The Tragedy of Enlightenment* (Cambridge: Cambridge University Press, 1980), at 113–14.

121 Although Gramsci's concept of hegemony was occasionally mentioned in early critical legal literature, there have been surprisingly few attempts to explore its meaning in the development of a distinctively legal consciousness. This gap is due perhaps to the difficulty of deriving a coherent position from all the contexts in which Gramsci related hegemony (especially in the domain of civil society) to the residual Marxist notion of ideology. See Antonio Gramsci, *Selections from the Prison Notebooks*, ed. and trans. Quintin Hoare and Geoffrey Nowell Smith (New York: International Publishers, 1971) and Michèle Barrett, *The Politics of Truth: From Marx to Foucault* (Stanford: Stanford University Press, 1991), at 54–5.

122 See Geuss, *The Idea of a Critical Theory*, at 74–5.

123 A recognition of the germ of such doubts can be found in Trubek, 'Where the Action Is,' at 599.

124 See Mark Tushnet, 'Following the Rules Laid Down: A Critique of Interpretivism and Neutral Principles,' *Harvard Law Review* 96 (1983), 781 at 825–6.

125 This is one way of interpreting Habermas's final statement in his *Tanner Lectures*: 'There can be no autonomous law without the realization of democracy.' See Jürgen Habermas, 'Law and Morality: Two Lectures,' in Sterling M. McMurrin, ed., *The Tanner Lectures VIII* (Salt Lake City: University of Utah Press, 1987), 217–79 at 279. This interpretation is prompted by the discussion in David M. Rasmussen, *Reading Habermas* (Oxford: Basil Blackwell, 1990), at 75–93.

126 See, for example, Niklas Luhmann, *The Differentiation of Society*, trans. Stephen Holmes and Charles Larmore (New York: Columbia University Press, 1982).

127 See Thomas McCarthy, *Ideals and Illusions: On Reconstruction and Deconstruction in Contemporary Critical Theory* (Cambridge: MIT Press, 1991), at 152–80. Even Habermas, who pointedly criticized systems analysis in the earlier part of his career, has attempted to connect his theory of communicative action with systems analysis: for his earlier views, see Jürgen Habermas, *Legitimation Crisis*, trans. Thomas McCarthy (Boston: Beacon Press, 1975), at 2–8 and 117–30; for his current position, see Jürgen Habermas, *The Theory of Communicative Action*, Vol. 2, *Lifeworld and System*, trans. Thomas McCarthy (Boston: Beacon Press, 1987), at 129, 185–6, and 267–94 and Jürgen Habermas, *The Philosophical Discourse of Modernity*, trans. Frederick G. Lawrence (Cambridge: MIT Press, 1987), at 368–85. See also Robert C. Holub, *Jürgen Habermas: Critic in the Public Sphere* (London:

Routledge, 1991), at 106–32. It would also be fertile to investigate how the systems approach resembles or differs from the constitutive theory outlined *supra*, note 108.

128 For an assessment of the tensions between critical legal studies and contemporary sociological methods, see David Trubek and John Esser, '"Critical Empiricism" in American Legal Studies: Paradox, Program, or Pandora's Box,' *Law and Social Inquiry* 14 (1989), 3 at 45–6.

4 Renovating through Counterpoint: Critical Contract Law

1 Mark Kelman, *A Guide to Critical Legal Studies* (Cambridge: Harvard University Press, 1987), at 258.

2 The aims and methods of this aggressive side of the radical critique are summarized and illustrated in Mark Kelman, 'Trashing,' *Stanford Law Review* 36 (1984), 293 and Kelman, *Guide to Critical Legal Studies*, at 3–6. Owing to the vigour of many critical legal authors in dismissing conventional or mainstream views, a popular image has been created, according to one commentator, in which radical criticism is supposed to be accompanied by bad manners: see William W. Bratton, Jr, 'Manners, Metaprinciples, Metapolitics and Kennedy's *Form and Substance*,' *Cardozo Law Review* 6 (1985), 871 at 880.

3 See Andrew Altman, *Critical Legal Studies: A Liberal Critique* (Princeton: Princeton University Press, 1990), at 132–9 for a terse discussion of the extent to which contract law manifests contradictions and at 123–6 for a similar treatment of contrasting orientations in tort law.

4 On legal consciousness, see *supra*, Chapter 3. In critical legal writing, doctrine is used sweepingly to include not only the more precise sense in which lawyers use it (for example, the doctrine of consideration), but also such propositional forms as rules, principles, and definitions. These different forms need not be distinguished in this context, though in other situations legal theorists have judged it important to do so: see Brian Simpson, 'The Common Law and Legal Theory,' in William Twining, ed., *Legal Theory and Common Law* (Oxford: Basil Blackwell, 1986), 8–25 at 9.

5 The far-reaching influence of the contract casebook is emphasized in Mary Joe Frug, *Postmodern Legal Feminism* (New York: Routledge, 1992), at 55–6.

6 Samuel Williston, *A Treatise on the Law of Contracts*, 4th ed., ed. Richard A. Lord, 5 vols. (Rochester, NY: Lawyers Cooperative Publishing, 1990). The three previous editions were published in 1920, 1936, and 1957.

7 C.C. Langdell, ed., *A Selection of Cases on the Law of Contracts* (Boston: Little, Brown, 1871).

8 See Robert Stevens, *Law School: Legal Education From the 1850s to the 1980s* (Chapel Hill: University of North Carolina Press, 1983), at 51–5.

9 American Law Institute, *Restatement of the Law: Contracts* (St Paul, MN: American Law Institute Publishers, 1932).

10 William Blackstone, *Commentaries on the Laws of England*, 4 vols. (Chicago: University of Chicago Press, 1979, facsimile of first ed., published 1765–9).

11 That the radical critics generally restrict the ambit of their discussion to U.S. materials is rarely qualified or justified explicitly in their analyses. Instead, their arguments proceed as if contract law in other jurisdictions emulated what has occurred in the United States. This is problematic to the extent that contract treatises in the United Kingdom, Canada, or other common law countries have not shared the ambitious scope that marks their counterparts in the United States. So, for instance, it is possible to argue that late-twentieth-century contract texts and casebooks published outside the United States still exhibit traces of classical contract theory. In the Canadian context, such a standard source as Christine Boyle and David Percy, eds., *Contracts: Cases and Commentaries*, 6th ed. (Scarborough, ON: Carswell, 1999) bears affinities, in terms of its traditional structure and topics, with British models, like the earlier editions of J.C. Smith and J.A.C. Thomas, eds., *A Casebook on Contract*, 10th ed. (London: Sweet and Maxwell, 1996), and many fewer points of similarity with the distinctly post-realist approach adopted in leading U.S. compilations, such as Friedrich Kessler, Grant Gilmore, and Anthony T. Kronman, eds., *Contracts: Cases and Materials*, 3rd ed. (Boston: Little, Brown, 1986).

12 This thesis of a transition from status to contract is most commonly associated with Henry Maine, *Ancient Law: Its Connection with the Early History of Society and Its Relation to Modern Ideas*, 10th ed. (London: John Murray, 1930). Although the critical legal account resembles Maine's essential point, one should not infer that this commits critical legal writers to the whole of Maine's argument over the passage from archaic to classical law. The illicit comparison between the ancient situation and that pertaining in eighteenth-century England or the United States is roundly criticized in Manfred Rehbinder, 'Status, Contract, and the Welfare State,' *Stanford Law Review* 23 (1971), 941. See also Max Radin, 'Contract Obligation and the Human Will,' *Columbia Law Review* 43 (1943), 575 at 576: 'There never was a time in Western communities so far as our records go, when all social and economic functions were determined by status.'

13 Jay M. Feinman, 'Critical Approaches to Contract Law,' *U.C.L.A. Law Review* 30 (1983), 829 at 831.

14 See Jay M. Feinman and Peter Gabel, 'Contract Law as Ideology,' in David Kairys, ed., *The Politics of Law: A Progressive Critique*, 3rd ed. (New York: Basic Books, 1998), 497–510 at 499–500.

15 See Morton J. Horwitz, *The Transformation of American Law, 1780–1860* (Cambridge: Harvard University Press, 1977), at 161–73 and P.S. Atiyah, *The Rise and Fall of Freedom of Contract* (Oxford: Clarendon Press, 1979), at 60–7.

16 See Elizabeth Mensch, 'Freedom of Contract as Ideology,' *Stanford Law Review* 33 (1981), 753 at 756; Charles M. Gray, 'The Ages of Classical Law,' *Yale Law Journal* 90 (1980), 216 at 221; and Horwitz, *Transformation of American Law*, at 173–7.

17 See Atiyah, *Rise and Fall of Freedom of Contract*, at 216.

18 See Radin, 'Contract Obligation,' at 575.

19 See Morris R. Cohen, 'The Basis of Contract,' *Harvard Law Review* 46 (1932), 553 at 575 and E. Allan Farnsworth, *Contracts*, 3rd ed. (New York: Aspen Law and Business, 1999), at 943–5.

20 See Samuel Williston, 'Freedom of Contract,' *Cornell Law Quarterly* 6 (1921), 365 at 368.

21 The perception of what is 'classical' in traditional contract theory varies somewhat, depending on the vantage point of the cataloguer. Llewellyn, for example, distinguished the older Langdellian theory from the later orthodox view represented by Williston and the first *Restatement*: see Karl N. Llewellyn, 'Our Case-Law of Contract: Offer and Acceptance, Part II,' *Yale Law Journal* 48 (1938), 779 at 780. This says no more, perhaps, than that one person's early classicism is another person's late baroque.

22 See Grant Gilmore, *The Death of Contract* (Columbus: Ohio State University Press, 1974), which gives a particularly illuminating, if controversial, account of the relationship between Holmes and Williston.

23 See Melvin Eisenberg, 'The Bargain Principle and Its Limits,' *Harvard Law Review* 95 (1982), 741 at 751.

24 Feinman, 'Critical Approaches to Contract Law,' at 831.

25 See Williston, 'Freedom of Contract,' at 367 and Roscoe Pound, 'Liberty of Contract,' *Yale Law Journal* 18 (1909), 454 at 457.

26 Lon L. Fuller, 'Consideration and Form,' *Columbia Law Review* 41 (1941), 799 at 806.

27 See the extended discussion of the implications of the doctrine of mistake for the objective theory of contractual liability in Richard Bronaugh, 'Agreement, Mistake, and Objectivity in the Bargain Theory of Contract,'

William and Mary Law Review 18 (1976), 213 and in William Howarth, 'The Meaning of Objectivity in Contract,' *Law Quarterly Review* 100 (1984), 265.

28 See Cohen, 'Basis of Contract,' at 570.

29 See, for example, Peter Gabel, 'Intention and Structure in Contractual Conditions: Outline for a Method of Critical Legal Theory,' *Minnesota Law Review* 61 (1977), 601 at 608–9.

30 See Horwitz, *Transformation of American Law*, at 101–8.

31 See Edwin Patterson, 'An Apology for Consideration,' *Columbia Law Review* 58 (1958), 929 at 942.

32 See ibid. at 945–6. Judicial recognition of this link can be found in the opinion of Cardozo, C.J. in *Allegheny College* v. *National Chautauqua County Bank*, 246 N.Y. 369, 159 N.E. 173 (1927).

33 For an extensive discussion of the range of such a background, see Atiyah, *Rise and Fall of Freedom of Contract*, at 602–59.

34 *Lochner v. New York*, 198 U.S. 45 (1904). See Pound, 'Liberty of Contract.' note 25.

35 See Gray, 'The Ages of Classical Law,' at 218.

36 The classic expression of this thesis is in Max Weber, *On Law in Economy and Society*, ed. Max Rheinstein, trans. Edward Shils (Cambridge: Harvard University Press, 1954), at 181–9.

37 See Karl Klare, 'Contracts Jurisprudence and the First-Year Casebook,' *New York University Law Review* 54 (1979), 876 at 877. On formalism generally, as well as the respects in which the classical contract theorists were emulated in other doctrinal areas, see Duncan Kennedy, 'Legal Formality,' *Journal of Legal Studies* 2 (1973), 351. This technique has also been called the 'strict law approach': see Lawrence Friedman and Stewart Macaulay, 'Contract Law and Contract Teaching: Past, Present, and Future,' *Wisconsin Law Review* [1967], 805 at 805. One has to be careful to ascertain the precise meaning of such epithets in the context of U.S. intellectual history over the past century. Holmes was, in Klare's terms, the prototypical formalist, while for other purposes, Holmes is seen as rebelling against formalism: see Morton G. White, *Social Thought in America: The Revolt Against Formalism* (New York: Oxford University Press, 1976), at 59–75.

38 This development has been well-served by historians who have investigated the factual and legal circumstances surrounding the leading decision in *Hadley v. Baxendale* (1854) 9 Exch. 341, 156 E.R. 145. See Richard Danzig, '*Hadley v. Baxendale*: A Study in the Industrialization of the Law,' *Journal of Legal Studies* 4 (1975), 249; A.W.B. Simpson, 'Innovation in Nineteenth Century Contract Law,' *Law Quarterly Review* 91 (1975), 247 at 274–7; and

J.L. Barton, 'Contractual Damages and the Rise of Industry,' *Oxford Journal of Legal Studies* 7 (1987), 40.

39 Danzig, '*Hadley v. Baxendale*,' at 273–8.

40 See Williston, 'Freedom of Contract,' at 371.

41 Ibid. at 369.

42 See Williston, *Treatise on the Law of Contract,* at § 1:1.

43 See Lon L. Fuller, 'Williston on Contracts,' *North Carolina Law Review* 18 (1939), 1 at 9.

44 See Atiyah, *Rise and Fall of Freedom of Contract,* at 146.

45 Compare this approach with the remarkably similar attitude towards the purposes of contract in the common law as described in Richard Posner, *Economic Analysis of the Law,* 5th ed. (New York: Aspen Law and Business, 1998), at 90–6.

46 See *The Port Caledonia and The Anna,* [1903] P. 184. During a gale in an English harbour, when the master of one vessel discovered that, despite its anchors, it was being dragged dangerously towards another ship taking shelter in the harbour, he hailed a tug for assistance. He offered the tug master £100. The latter agreed to tow the ship to a safe berth, but insisted on a price of '£1000 or no rope.' The ship's master gave in to this demand. Afterwards, the ship's owner refused to pay the £1000. At trial, the judge chastised the tug master for his 'most reprehensible conduct' and labelled him a coward (see ibid. at 189). Holding that the demand for £1000 was 'extortionate,' the court awarded damages in the amount of £200 (ibid. at 190).

47 64 F. 2d 344 (1933). In *Baird,* the defendant sent out offers for the supply of linoleum to numerous contractors who were likely to bid on the construction of a public building. When the defendant realized that its bid underestimated by about half the total amount of linoleum required, it communicated its withdrawal of the original offer and substituted a new one. By the time this communication reached the plaintiff contractor, the plaintiff had already lodged a lump sum bid with the public authorities and that bid had been accepted. Despite receiving the letter of withdrawal, the plaintiff formally accepted the defendant's original offer. The defendant refused to recognize the existence of a contract and declined to provide the linoleum. As Hand, J. notes in his judgment at 346: 'The contractors had a ready escape from their difficulty by insisting upon a contract before they used the figures; and in commercial transactions it does not in the end promote justice to seek strained interpretations in aid of those who do not protect themselves.'

48 See Williston, 'Preface to the First Edition,' *Treatise on the Law of Contracts,* at xiii.

49 Radin, 'Contract Obligation,' at 585.

50 Friedrich Kessler, 'Contracts of Adhesion: Some Thoughts About Freedom of Contract,' *Columbia Law Review* 43 (1943), 629 at 637.

51 See Lon L. Fuller and William R. Perdue, Jr, 'The Reliance Interest in Contract Damages,' *Yale Law Journal* 46 (1936), 52 and *Yale Law Journal* 46 (1937), 373, and Mensch, at 760.

52 See Robert L. Hale, 'Bargaining, Duress and Economic Liberty,' *Columbia Law Review* 43 (1943), 603 at 628 and, for an analysis that attempts to build systematically on Hale's insights, Duncan Kennedy and Frank Michelman, 'Are Property and Contract Efficient?' *Hofstra Law Review* 8 (1980), 711.

53 See Feinman, 'Critical Approaches to Contract Law,' at 840–2.

54 On the notion of such 'socialization,' see Gilmore, *The Death of Contract*, at 87–103 and the preceding edition of Kessler et al., *Contracts: Cases and Materials*, which was Friedrich Kessler and Grant Gilmore, eds., *Contracts: Cases and Materials* (Boston: Little, Brown, 1970), chaps. 17–19. Part II of these earlier materials was eliminated as a separate heading and its contents, in abbreviated form, were redistributed throughout other sections of the third edition.

55 Arthur A. Leff, 'Unconscionability and the Code: The Emperor's New Clause,' *University of Pennsylvania Law Review* 115 (1967), 485 at 505. See also Feinman, 'Critical Approaches to Contract Law,' at 836.

56 See Gabel, 'Intention and Structure,' at 617. This of course is not a thesis confined to theorists inclined to follow, for example, Paul Baran and Paul M. Sweezy, *Monopoly Capital* (New York: Monthly Review Press, 1974). It will also appeal to Galbraithians: see John Kenneth Galbraith, *The New Industrial State*, 4th ed. (Boston: Houghton Mifflin, 1985). See also Kessler, 'Contracts of Adhesion,' 640.

57 See Clyde W. Summers, 'Collective Agreements and the Law of Contracts,' *Yale Law Journal* 78 (1969), 525 at 534.

58 Ibid. at 547, 562–3, and 565.

59 Franklin Schultz, 'The Firm Offer Puzzle: A Study of Business Practice in the Construction Industry,' *University of Chicago Law Review* 19 (1952), 237.

60 See Stewart Macaulay, 'Non-contractual Relations in Business: A Preliminary Inquiry,' *American Sociological Review* 28 (1963), 55.

61 See Hugh Beale and Tony Dugdale, 'Contracts between Businessmen: Planning and the Use of Contractual Remedies,' *British Journal of Law and Society* 2 (1975), 45 and Richard Lewis, 'Contracts between Businessmen: Reform of the Law of Firm Offers and an Empirical Study of Tendering Practices in the Building Industry,' *Journal of Law and Society* 9 (1982), 153.

62 Stewart Macaulay, 'Elegant Models, Empirical Pictures, and the Complexi-

ties of Contract,' *Law and Society Review* 11 (1977), 507 at 509 (emphasis in the original).

63 Arthur L. Corbin, 'Recent Developments in the Law of Contracts,' *Harvard Law Review* 50 (1937), 449 at 449.

64 Karl N. Llewellyn, 'Our Case-Law of Contract: Offer and Acceptance,' Part I *Yale Law Journal* 48 (1938), 1 at 19 n.38.

65 Ibid. at 32 (emphasis in the original).

66 See, for example, Klare, 'Contracts Jurisprudence,' at 889 (contract doctrine's 'remoteness from the lived social relationships they purported to govern') and Stanley D. Henderson, 'Promises Grounded in the Past: The Idea of Unjust Enrichment and the Law of Contracts,' *Virginia Law Review* 57 (1971), 1115 at 1156 (the importance of designing contract law to accord with the 'realities of daily life, social or economic').

67 Charles Fried, *Contract as Promise: A Theory of Contractual Obligation* (Cambridge: Harvard University Press, 1981).

68 Ibid. at 24–5.

69 Ibid. at 59–61 and 69.

70 See, for example, P.S. Atiyah, 'Review of Fried, *Contract as Promise,*' *Harvard Law Review* 95 (1981), 509.

71 See Eugene Mooney, 'Old Kontract Principles and Karl's New Kode: An Essay on the Jurisprudence of Our New Commercial Law,' *Villanova Law Review* 11 (1966), 213.

72 See Friedman and Macaulay, 'Contract Law and Contract Teaching,' at 808–9.

73 See Fuller and Perdue, 'Reliance Interest in Conract Damages,' at 54 for a definition of the expectation interest, namely, the plaintiff's desire to be put in 'as good a position as he would have occupied had the defendant performed his promise.'

74 Ibid. at 70.

75 Ibid. at 383 where Fuller and Perdue suggest the case of the employer who, by selling the business, makes impossible the further performance of a contract with an employee. Instead of having to choose between measuring damages by the employee's full expectation interest or nothing at all, the court could award reliance damages based on what the employee actually incurred in relying on the reasonable assumption that he would be with the employer's business for the whole term of the contract.

76 Ibid. at 386. See also Lon L. Fuller, 'American Legal Realism,' *University of Pennsylvania Law Review* 82 (1934), 429 at 431–8.

77 A similar exception to the expectation principle is the doctrine of mitigation, under which the innocent party has a duty to take reasonable steps to

minimize losses due to the breach. This could take the form of hiring someone to perform the work which the party in breach originally contracted for. In practice, this means that 'the damages which the breaching party pays will not be what he has promised to pay': P.S. Atiyah, *Essays on Contract*, rev. ed. (Oxford: Clarendon Press, 1990), at 125.

78 See *supra*, note 47.

80 Malcolm P. Sharp, 'Promises, Mistakes and Reciprocity,' *University of Chicago Law Review* 19 (1952), 286 at 289.

80 51 Cal. 2d 409, 333 P. 2d 757 (1958). In *Drennan*, the bid by a subcontractor for paving work at a new school was $7,000, which turned out to be a serious underestimate. The plaintiff relied on this figure in submitting its bid on the general contract. After the latter bid was opened and the plaintiff was awarded the general construction contract, the defendant claimed that it could not do the work for less than $15,000. Eventually, the plaintiff hired another firm to do the paving work for $11,000.

81 For the law in England see *Combe v. Combe*, [1951] 2 K.B. 215 (C.A.) and Lord Denning, *The Discipline of Law* (London: Butterworths, 1979), at 214ff. A departure from the orthodox interpretation of this case, which sees it as reconcilable with older cases, is suggested in Atiyah, *Essays on Contract*, at 232–3. The Canadian position is exemplified in *Gilbert Steel Ltd. v. University Construction Ltd.* (1976), 67 D.L.R. (3d) 606 (Ont. C.A.).

82 See Stanley D. Henderson, 'Promissory Estoppel and Traditional Contract Doctrine,' *Yale Law Journal* 78 (1969), 343. For a survey and analysis of the case law decided under this head after 1969, see Jay M. Feinman, 'Promissory Estoppel and Judicial Method,' *Harvard Law Review* 97 (1984), 678.

83 Henderson, 'Promissory Estoppel,' at 348.

84 Ibid. at 381.

85 Ibid. at 378.

86 See Leff, 'Unconscionality and the Code.'

87 See Arthur A. Leff, 'Unconscionability and the Crowd: Consumers and the Common Law Tradition,' *University of Pittsburgh Law Review* 31 (1970), 349 at 350. It should be noted that Leff was extremely sceptical about the good that can be achieved by litigation in the context of unconscionable bargains reached through the use of adhesion contracts.

88 Richard A. Epstein, 'Unconscionability: A Critical Reappraisal,' *Journal of Law and Economics* 18 (1975), 293 at 294.

89 See Leff, 'Unconscionality and the Crowd,' at 357–8.

90 See, for example, John Dalzell, 'Duress by Economic Pressure,' *North Carolina Law Review* 20 (1942), 237 and 341 and John P. Dawson, 'Economic Duress: An Essay in Perspective,' *Michigan Law Review* 45 (1947), 253.

91 See Dalzell, 'Duress by Economic Pressure,' at 240.

92 See Dawson, 'Economic Duress,' at 287–8.

93 The range of restitutionary cases will not be discussed here; a good survey of the emerging authority and its potential scope, particularly under s. 89A of the *Restatement (Second)*, is Henderson, 'Promises Grounded in the Past.' He notes at 1147 that in cases he studied the actions in quasi-contract are often indistinguishable from those brought on a contract in which reliance is alleged as the basis of liability.

94 See Epstein, 'Unconscionability,' at 297–8.

95 George Gardner, 'An Inquiry into the Principles of Contracts,' *Harvard Law Review* 46 (1932), 1 at 21–2.

96 Karl N. Llewellyn, 'What Price Contract: An Essay in Perspective,' *Yale Law Journal* 40 (1931), 704 at 733 n.63.

97 See Fuller, 'Consideration and Form,' at 823–4.

98 See Ian R. Macneil, 'Whither Contracts?' *Journal of Legal Studies* 21 (1969), 403.

99 For a complete explication of the importance of the 'social matrix' in learning about the different types of contracts, see Ian R. Macneil, 'The Many Futures of Contracts,' *Southern California Law Review* 47 (1974), 691; Ian R. Macneil, *The New Social Contract: An Inquiry into Modern Contractual Relations* (New Haven: Yale University Press, 1980); and Ian R. Macneil, 'Exchange Revisited: Individual Utility and Social Solidarity,' *Ethics* 96 (1985–6), 567. An assessment of Macneil's contribution and its meaning for critical legal analyses of contract doctrine is sketched in Robert W. Gordon, 'Macaulay, Macneil, and the Discovery of Solidarity and Power in Contract Law,' *Wisconsin Law Review* [1985], 565.

100 See Ian R. Macneil, 'Contracts: Adjustment of Long-Term Relationships,' *Northwestern University Law Review* 72 (1978), 854 at 900. It should be noted that a principle can operate at a covert level for years without contract theorists deigning to take notice of it: see Fuller, 'Consideration and Form,' at 811 n.18.

101 See, for example, Cohen, 'The Basis of Contract,' at 585.

102 See Karl N. Llewellyn, *The Common Law Tradition: Deciding Appeals* (Boston: Little, Brown, 1960), at 362–71, where he laments the lack of regulative techniques for overcoming the classical approach even to dealings that involve standard form agreements.

103 See Charles Fried, Review of Atiyah, *The Rise and Fall of Freedom of Contract*, *Harvard Law Review* 93 (1980), 1858 at 1867.

104 See Klare, 'Contracts Jurisprudence,' at 892.

105 Kessler, 'Contracts of Adhesion,' at 633.

106 See Patterson, 'An Apology for Consideration,' at 945.

107 For the historical details, see S.F.C. Milsom, 'A Pageant in Modern Dress,' *Yale Law Journal* 84 (1975), 1585 at 1586.

108 See Klare, 'Contracts Jurisprudence,' at 881.

109 See Feinman, 'Critical Approaches to Contract Law,' at 845–50.

110 Some critical legal writers, such as Feinman and Gabel, accept that modern contract doctrine is explained by capitalist class domination, while others, such as Duncan Kennedy, reject this. See Feinman and Gabel, 'Contract Law as Ideology,' at 500–1 and Duncan Kennedy, 'Form and Substance in Private Law Adjudication,' *Harvard Law Review* 89 (1976), 1685 at 1721–2.

111 Feinman, 'Critical Approaches to Contract Law,' at 837.

112 Ibid. at 845–6.

113 Ibid. at 851.

114 A good example of the desire to reinvent the single, general model of contract is to be found in W. David Slawson, 'The New Meaning of Contract: The Transformation of Contracts Law by Standard Forms,' *University of Pittsburgh Law Review* 46 (1984), 21.

115 Duncan Kennedy, 'Distributive and Paternalist Motives in Contract and Tort Law, with Special Reference to Compulsory Terms and Unequal Bargaining Power,' *Maryland Law Review* 41 (1982), 563 at 581.

116 Jay M. Feinman, 'The Significance of Contract Theory,' *University of Cincinnati Law Review* 58 (1990), 283 at 1285.

117 See Macaulay, 'Elegant Models,' at 511–23 and Robert W. Gordon, 'Review of Gilmore, *The Death of Contract*,' *Wisconsin Law Review* [1974], 1216.

118 See Mensch, 'Freedom of Contract as Ideology,' at 769. In the words of Frank, J.: '[i]n part at least, advocacy of the "objective" standard in contracts appears to have represented a desire for legal symmetry, legal uniformity, a desire seemingly prompted by aesthetic impulses': *Ricketts v. Pennsylvania R.R.*, 153 F.2d 757 (1946), at 761.

119 Kennedy, 'Form and Substance,' at 1724.

120 See Duncan Kennedy, 'The Structure of *Blackstone's Commentaries*,' *Buffalo Law Review* 28 (1979), 205.

121 See Duncan Kennedy and Peter Gabel, 'Roll Over Beethoven,' *Stanford Law Review* 36 (1984), 1 and *supra*, Chapter 3, at note 16.

122 Kennedy, 'Form and Substance,' at 1713.

123 Ibid. at 1717. Though I do not explore this point further, it might be questioned whether altruism, rather than standing in opposition to individualism, does not assume an individualist background. An altruist action acquires its character because the agent would ordinarily be ex-

pected to engage in egocentric behaviour. Owing to a motive such as generosity, pity, or philanthropy, the agent makes a caring gesture based on recognition of another individual's desires and interests. But this action by itself does not undermine the altruist's general disposition to live in a way that is primarily guided by considerations of self-interest. Perhaps Kennedy's scheme needs the specification of a more solidaristic principle to countervail individualism.

124 Ibid. at 1775–6.
125 Ibid. at 1771–2.
126 Ibid. at 1777.
127 Ibid. at 1688.
128 Ibid. at 1767.
129 See *supra*, Chapter 2 at note 69, and accompanying text.
130 Kennedy, 'Form and Substance,' at 1775.
131 For other examples of rule-based reasoning aimed at altruistic, rather than individualistic goals, see Bratton, 'Manners, Metaprinciples,' at 896–7; Kelman, 'Trashing,' at 56–9; and Altman, *Critical Legal Studies*, at 112–13. Added to this is the argument that the oppositional pairing of rules and standards is an error, for in order to have legal force, each standard has to be incorporated as a rule: see Neil MacCormick, 'Reconstruction after Deconstruction,' *Oxford Journal of Legal Studies* 10 (1990), 539 at 545.
132 Klare, 'Contracts Jurisprudence,' at 895.
133 See Karl Klare, 'Law-Making as Praxis,' *Telos* 40 (1979), 123.
134 Roberto M. Unger, *The Critical Legal Studies Movement* (Cambridge: Harvard University Press, 1986), at 19.
135 Ibid. at 16–17.
136 Ibid. at 59.
137 Ibid. at 61.
138 Ibid. at 81.
139 Ibid. at 78–80.
140 John Finnis goes further than this and criticizes Unger for his 'oversight' of areas of law outside contract, such as tort and restitution, as well as for his failure to see that, like familial relationships and friendships, the realm of commerce as envisaged in contract law is one in which 'mutual obligations are not only controlled by the side-constraints of fairness but are actually grounded on fairness and on the common benefits made available by respect for undertakings': J.M. Finnis, 'On "The Critical Legal Studies Movement,"' *American Journal of Jurisprudence* 30 (1985), 21 at 31 and 36.
141 Clare Dalton, 'An Essay in the Deconstruction of Contract Doctrine,' *Yale Law Journal* 94 (1985), 997.

142 Ibid. at 1010–11.

143 Ibid. at 1014.

144 American Law Institute, *Restatement (Second) of the Law: Contracts* (St Paul, MN: American Law Institute Publishers, 1981). The *Restatement (Second)* was actually officially adopted in 1979.

145 Dalton, 'Essay in the Deconstruction of Contract Doctrine,' at 1090.

146 See *Hertzog v. Hertzog*, 29 Pa. 465 (1857), discussed in ibid. at 1015–19, and *Balfour v. Balfour*, [1919] 2 K.B. (C.A.).

147 See Dalton, 'Essay in the Deconstruction of Contract Doctrine,' at 1106–13.

148 See Donald F. Brosnan, 'Serious But Not Critical,' *Southern California Law Review* 60 (1987), 262 at 384–9 for criticism along this line.

149 See A.W.B. Simpson, 'The Horwitz Thesis and the History of Contracts,' *University of Chicago Law Review* 46 (1979), 533 at 536. See also ibid. at 542: 'many of the doctrines that he identifies as characteristic of the transformation were common in the eighteenth century.'

150 See Atiyah, *Essays on Contract*, at 330–1.

151 Feinman, 'Promissory Estoppel,' at 682 n.21.

152 Kelman, *Guide to Critical Legal Studies*, at 233.

153 Duncan Kennedy, 'Legal Formality,' *Journal of Legal Studies* 2 (1973), 351 at 359 (emphasis in the original).

154 Lawrence B. Solum, 'On the Indeterminacy Crisis: Critiquing Critical Dogma,' *University of Chicago Law Review* 54 (1987), 462 at 475.

155 See ibid. at 496.

156 See James R. Gordley, 'Review of Gilmore, *The Death of Contract*,' *Harvard Law Review* 89 (1975), 452 at 453–4. On the necessity of consent and promise for some medieval jurists' conception of a binding agreement, see James Gordley, *The Philosophical Origins of Modern Contract Doctrine* (Oxford: Clarendon Press, 1991), at 73–5. The idea that each party to a contract gives up something in order to obtain some advantage was certainly present in Hobbes and Locke: see ibid. at 116. Note also the following comment in A.W.B. Simpson, *A History of the Common Law of Contract: The Rise of the Action of Assumpsit* (Oxford: Clarendon Press, 1975), at 324: 'Such contractual theories as these [liability based on promisor's unjust enrichment, for example] will be found lurking in modern case law as they are to be found in old cases, there being in this field nothing new under the sun.'

157 See, for example, Frederick Pollock and F.W. Maitland, *The History of English Law before the Time of Edward I*, 2 vols., 2nd ed., ed. S.F.C. Milsom (Cambridge: Cambridge University Press, 1968) II: 184–5 where it is asserted in respect of contract law: 'Ideas assumed as fundamental by this

branch of law in modern times and so familiar to modern lawyers as apparently to need no explanation had perished in the general breaking up of the Roman system, and had to be painfully reconstructed in the middle ages.'

158 See, for example, Dalton, 'An Essay in the Deconstruction of Contract Doctrine,' at 1000 and Feinman, 'Promissory Estoppel,' 681.

159 This is the 'strong' version of indeterminacy propounded by some, but not all, critical legal authors: see Solum, 'On the Indeterminacy Crisis,' at 470–1.

160 Ronald Dworkin has offered an elaborate portrait of how judges fashioning the common law (and, in particular for his purposes, the law of accidents) 'impose whatever order they can ... on a historically haphazard process': Ronald Dworkin, *Law's Empire* (Cambridge: Harvard University Press, 1986), at 409. But he goes further than this and claims, with respect to his concept of law as pure integrity, that the law could be reorganized by his ideal judge, Hercules, to eliminate inconsistencies in the principles of different doctrinal areas (ibid. at 405–6). This has been interpreted as committing Dworkin to the view that judges should indeed be licensed to purify the law and insist on uniform principles: see Altman, *Critical Legal Studies*, at 146–7. Against Altman's interpretation, I think it more reasonable, after situating Dworkin's comments in context with his conception of 'inclusive integrity,' to grant that he is perfectly aware of the institutional constraints that make this pursuit of complete coherence politically unacceptable.

161 *Cf.* Dworkin, *Law's Empire*, at 404: 'Law as integrity not only permits but fosters different forms of substantive conflict or tension within the overall best interpretation of law.'

162 John Eekelaar, 'What Is "Critical" Family Law?' *Law Quarterly Review* 105 (1989), 244 at 248.

163 A major source of excitement in teaching derives from the presence of competing models at the foundation of each doctrinal subject. This is illustrated in contemporary corporate law theory, which in the past two decades has been awakened from its normative slumber by debates about whether a contractual model best captures the structure and status of the corporate business form, and about what this implies for the relationship between firms and the state. See Richard W. Bauman, 'Liberalism and Canadian Corporate Law' in Richard F. Devlin, ed., *Canadian Perspectives on Legal Theory* (Toronto: Emond Montgomery, 1991), 75–97.

164 See Charles M. Yablon, 'The Indeterminacy of the Law: Critical Legal Studies and the Problem of Legal Explanation,' *Cardozo Law Review* 6 (1985), 917 at 934.

165 Kelman, *Guide to Critical Legal Studies*, at 76–8 and 103–9.
166 See Anthony T. Kronman, 'Contract Law and Distributive Justice,' *Yale Law Journal* 89 (1980), 472 for an attempted justification of designing contract law so that judges are enabled expressly to achieve redistributive effects. The contrary point of view is articulated in W.N.R. Lucy, 'Contract as a Mechanism of Distributive Justice,' *Oxford Journal of Legal Studies* 9 (1989), 132.
167 See Hugh Collins, 'Contract and Legal Theory,' in Twining, ed., *Legal Theory and Common Law*, 136–54.
168 See Fried, *Contract as Promise.*
169 See Atiyah, *Rise and Fall of Freedom of Contract*, at 778–9.
170 See Randy E. Barnett, 'Contract Scholarship and the Reemergence of Legal Philosophy,' *Harvard Law Review* 97 (1984), 1223 and his 'A Consent Theory of Contract,' *Columbia Law Review* 86 (1986), 269.
171 Dalton, 'An Essay in the Deconstruction of Contract Doctrine,' at 1084.
172 Ibid. at 1087.
173 It is partly on this basis that Dworkin objects to Hart's concept of a rule of recognition: see Ronald Dworkin, *Taking Rights Seriously*, rev. ed. (Cambridge: Harvard University Press, 1978), at 40–5.
174 See S.L. Hurley, *Natural Reasons: Personality and Polity* (Oxford: Oxford University Press, 1989), at 211–19. The paradigm Hurley uses to support her discussion is slightly different from the one I use in the discussion below, but the differences are not material.
175 Ibid. at 213–16.
176 In *Drennan, supra*, note 80, at 758, it was made clear that a relevant factor in the case was evidence about whether it was customary in that geographic area for general contractors to receive bids from subcontractors and immediately rely on them in calculating and submitting their own bids.
177 Hurley, *Natural Reasons*, at 216. That is, reasons arising under contracts adjudication provide authority for action or guidance in both the case decided and in future contract planning and cases: see Robert S. Summers, 'Statutes and Contracts as Founts of Formal Reasoning,' in Peter Cane and Jane Stapleton, eds., *Essays for Patrick Atiyah* (Oxford: Clarendon Press, 1990), 71–85.
178 For his discussion of how law strives for coherence, see Neil MacCormick, *Legal Reasoning and Legal Theory* (Oxford: Clarendon Press, 1978), at 152–94.
179 MacCormick finds this metaphor problematic: see ibid. at 155–6 and 194.
180 For an extensive discussion of these recent trends that favour non-classical

virtues such as paternalism, trust, fairness, and cooperation, see Hugh
Collins, *The Law of Contract*, 2nd ed. (London: Butterworths, 1993), chaps.
8–10. This is not to say that contract law has been fundamentally rea-
ligned. Rather, there continue to be different strands in doctrine, some of
which are designed for the greater protection of consumers, some for the
paternalistic protection of 'weaker parties.' For a discussion of British
contract law in these terms, see Roger Brownsword, 'The Philosophy of
Welfarism and its Emergence in Modern English Contract Law,' in Roger
Brownsword, Geraint Howells, and Thomas Wilhelmsson, eds., *Welfarism in
Contract Law* (Aldershot, Hants: Dartmouth, 1994), 21–62. Examples of
the critical legal use of reliance concepts outside of contract doctrine, on
analogy with what has been discussed above, are contained in Joseph
William Singer, 'The Reliance Interest in Property,' *Stanford Law Review* 40
(1988), 611.

181 Collins has been criticized from within critical legal studies for both his
choice of values and their sources. Feinman faults Collins for selecting
values solely from within established contract doctrine, rather than resorting to some external source. In Feinman's view, this would not require
looking to values outside legal doctrine altogether. They could be drawn
from, for example, tort law (Feinman has long been keen to abolish the
boundaries between contractual and tortious obligation). See Jay M. Feinman, 'Contract after the Fall,' *Stanford Law Review* 39 (1987), 1537 at
1548–9.

182 But see Girardeau A. Spann, 'A Critical Legal Studies Perspective on
Contract Law and Practice,' *Annual Survey of American Law* 1 [1988], 223
at 257: 'Legal decisions are guided by the invisible hand of our complex
cultural values, operating through their embodiment in our social decision makers. Nevertheless, by paying undue attention to doctrine we risk
interference with proper decision making through diversion of the invisible hand from its appointed course. As a result, the most significant thing
about legal doctrine is its insignificance.'

183 See Hugh Collins, 'The Transformation Thesis and the Ascription of
Contractual Responsibility,' in Thomas Wilhelmsson, ed., *Perspectives of
Critical Contract Law* (Aldershot, Hants: Dartmouth, 1993), 293–310 at 295.

184 Feinman, 'Critical Approaches to Contract Law,' at 860.

185 See Finnis, 'On "The Critical Legal Studies Movement,"' at 39.

5 Darn That Dream: The Communitarian Vision of Critical Legal Studies

1 See Bonnie Honig, *Political Theory and the Displacement of Politics* (Ithaca:
Cornell University Press, 1993). The paradox of postponement could be

viewed as the obverse of what Honig calls the 'dream of displacement,' which she attributes, despite their other theoretical differences, to both John Rawls and Michael Sandel. Honig claims that they both believe that adopting the right laws will free a society's members from the responsibility and burden of politics (ibid. at 210–11). By the paradox of postponement, I am referring to the critical legal view that, until a society's politics can be perfected, its members are freed from the responsibility and burden of projecting a legal regime.

2 The literature that treats of community from political, historical, and sociological perspectives is vast. The ways of looking at the relationship of individuals to a community, and of one community to another, are manifold and therefore immune to any short, facile summary. The theme of antagonisms between the need for group life and the importance of personal values is ancient: see, for instance, Sophocles, *Antigone*, trans. Richard Emil Braun (Oxford: Oxford University Press, 1974), 11: 806–943 and the interpretations in George Steiner, *Antigones* (Oxford: Clarendon Press, 1984), at 277–83 and Jean Bethke Elshtain, 'Antigone's Daughters,' *Democracy* 2 (1982), 46. The historical resonance of the theme in the United States is surveyed in Wilson Carey McWilliams, *The Idea of Fraternity in America* (Berkeley: University of California Press, 1973). Sociology as a discipline has generally been fascinated with the distinction between community and society: see, for example, Robert A. Nisbet, *The Quest for Community* (New York: Oxford University Press, 1969); Robert N. Bellah, Richard Madsen, William M. Sullivan, Ann Swidler, and Stephen M. Tipton, *Habits of the Heart: Individualism and Commitment in American Life* (Berkeley: University of California Press, 1985); and Robert N. Bellah, Richard Madsen, William M. Sullivan, Ann Swidler, and Stephen M. Tipton, *The Good Life* (New York: Random House, 1991). Critical legal writing occasionally taps into one or more of these streams of inquiry and discussion, but there is no specific reliance on one conception of community as the key by which to understand post-liberal social arrangements. Consequently, in this chapter I am more interested in pursuing the particular discussions of the critical legal writers on this and allied topics: I will mention only cursorily the way in which a critical legal point is clarified by reference to outside sources and debates. Although there are numerous invocations of the values of, and gestures towards, 'community,' 'solidarity,' and 'intersubjectivity,' in critical legal discussions, the abstract concepts are not the subject of this chapter. Rather, I concentrate on the uses and nuances of those terms as they bear some meaning for actual and projected political structures.

3 Two examples of the historical and sociological treatment of proposed and actual attempts at building utopian communities, both of which provide a

detailed portrait of the integration of legal structures or alternatives to law into the whole vision, are Rosabeth Moss Kanter, *Commitment and Community: Commune and Utopia in Sociological Perspective* (Cambridge: Harvard University Press, 1972) and Seymour R. Kesten, *Utopian Episodes: Daily Life in Experimental Colonies Dedicated to Changing the World* (Syracuse, NY: Syracuse University Press, 1993).

4 Roberto Mangabeira Unger, *Knowledge and Politics* (New York: Free Press, 1975). See *infra*, notes 96–113 and accompanying text.

5 This deficiency has not gone unnoticed in the critical legal literature: see, for instance, the comments of David Fraser, 'Truth and Hierarchy: Will the Circle Be Unbroken?' *Buffalo Law Review* 33 (1984), 729 at 755.

6 Paul Brest, 'The Fundamental Rights Controversy: The Essential Contradictions of Normative Constitutional Scholarship,' *Yale Law Journal* 90 (1981), 1063 at 1109.

7 Jennifer Jaff, 'Radical Pluralism: A Proposed Theoretical Framework for the Conference on Critical Legal Studies,' *Georgetown Law Journal* 72 (1984), 1143 at 1147.

8 Anthony Arblaster, *Democracy* (Minneapolis: University of Minnesota Press, 1987), at 86.

9 Andrew Levine, *Liberal Democracy: A Critique of the Theory* (New York: Columbia University Press, 1981), at 142. See also Nancy L. Schwartz, *The Blue Guitar: Political Representation and Community* (Chicago: University of Chicago Press, 1988), at 28–37.

10 See Brest, 'Fundamental Rights Controversy,' at 1107.

11 See Levine, *Liberal Democracy*, at 145. For similar critiques, also outside critical legal studies, see the evidence and arguments contained in the following works: Josh Cohen and Joel Rogers, *On Democracy: Toward a Transformation of American Society* (New York: Penguin, 1983); Benjamin R. Barber, *Strong Democracy: Participatory Politics for a New Age* (Berkeley: University of California Press, 1984); Ronald Mason, *Participatory and Workplace Democracy* (Carbondale: Southern Illinois University Press, 1982); and Carol C. Gould, *Rethinking Democracy: Freedom and Social Cooperation in Politics, Economy, and Society* (Cambridge: Cambridge University Press, 1988).

12 See Mark Tushnet, 'Darkness on the Edge of Town: The Contributions of John Hart Ely to Constitutional Theory,' *Yale Law Journal* 89 (1980), 1037 at 1047–8; Michael J. Sandel, 'The Procedural Republic and the Unencumbered Self,' *Political Theory* 12 (1984), 81; and Michael J. Sandel, *Democracy's Discontent: America in Search of a Public Philosophy* (Cambridge: Harvard University Press, 1996), at 5–6.

13 See Gerald Frug, 'The Ideology of Bureaucracy in American Law,' *Harvard Law Review* 97 (1984), 1276 and Michael Mandel, *The Charter of Rights and the Legalization of Politics in Canada,* 2nd ed. (Toronto: Thompson Educational Publishing, 1994).

14 A claim frequently associated by critical legal writers with Dworkin's jurisprudence: see Ronald Dworkin, *Taking Rights Seriously,* rev. ed. (Cambridge: Harvard University Press, 1978) and his *A Matter of Principle* (Cambridge: Harvard University Press, 1986).

15 See the comment by James Boyle, 'The Politics of Reason: Critical Legal Theory and Local Social Thought,' *University of Pennsylvania Law Review* 133 (1985), 685 at 703. For a comparison of the different root principles that separate Dworkin from his critical legal detractors, see Andrew Altman, 'Legal Realism, Critical Legal Studies, and Dworkin,' *Philosophy and Public Affairs* 15 (1986), 205 and Andrew Altman, *Critical Legal Studies: A Liberal Critique* (Princeton: Princeton University Press, 1990), at 22–56 and 123–6.

16 See Brest, 'Fundamental Rights Controversy,' at 1106.

17 This is one of the consequences of the critical legal view of individualism, discussed *supra,* Chapter 2. The critical view incorporates several different meanings of 'individualism,' drawn from different contexts. On the variety possible, see Philip Pettit, *Judging Justice* (London: Routledge & Kegan Paul, 1980), at 65–8; Steven Lukes, *Individualism* (Oxford: Basil Blackwell, 1973); and Charles Taylor, 'Cross-Purposes: The Liberal-Communitarian Debate,' in Nancy Rosenblum, ed., *Liberalism and the Moral Life* (Cambridge: Harvard University Press, 1992), 159–82.

18 Morton J. Horwitz, 'The History of the Public-Private Distinction,' *University of Pennsylvania Law Review* 130 (1982), 1423 at 1427. Although the present chapter does not tackle the question whether liberal theory and liberal politics should be conflated for the purposes of a critique, it is a useful exercise to contrast Horwitz's denunciation of liberal politics with the analysis of 'neutrality' as a liberal desideratum in Thomas Morawetz, 'Persons without History: Liberal Theory and Human Experience,' *Boston University Law Review* 66 (1986), 1013.

19 Mark Tushnet, 'An Essay on Rights,' *Texas Law Review* 62 (1984), 1363 at 1382. The revolt against the 'abstract,,' in contradistinction to tropes invoking the 'concrete,' is a recurrent rhetorical theme of critical legal writing. For an example of the critique of a project of abstraction, see Mari J. Matsuda, 'Liberal Jurisprudence and Abstracted Visions of Human Nature: A Feminist Critique of Rawls' Theory of Justice,' *New Mexico Law Review* 16 (1986), 613. Critical legal writing has itself been criticized for

adopting 'a characteristically modern tendency toward abstraction': see Suzanna Sherry, 'Civic Virtue and the Feminine Voice in Constitutional Adjudication,' *Virginia Law Review* 72 (1986), 543 at 569.

20 See Tushnet, 'Essay on Rights,' at 1392 and Joseph William Singer, 'The Player and the Cards: Nihilism and Legal Theory,' *Yale Law Journal* 94 (1984), 1 at 69.

21 See Karl Klare, 'The Public-Private Distinction in Labor Law,' *University of Pennsylvania Law Review* 130 (1982), 1358 and Frances Olsen, 'The Family and the Market: A Study of Ideology and Legal Reform,' *Harvard Law Review* 96 (1983), 1497.

22 See Andrew Fraser, 'The Legal Theory We Need Now,' *Socialist Review* 40 (1978), 147 at 167.

23 See Kenneth Casebeer, 'Toward a Critical Jurisprudence – A First Step by Way of the Public-Private Distinction in Constitutional Law,' *University of Miami Law Review* 37 (1983), 379.

24 Peter Gabel, 'Review of Dworkin, *Taking Rights Seriously,*' *Harvard Law Review* 91 (1977), 302 at 313 n.18. See also Alan D. Freeman, 'Truth and Mystification in Legal Scholarship,' *Yale Law Journal* 90 (1981), 1229 at 1235.

25 See Mark Tushnet, 'Truth, Justice and the American Way: An Interpretation of Public Law Scholarship in the Seventies,' *Texas Law Review* 57 (1979), 1307 at 1350 and Stephen B. Presser, 'Subjects of Bargaining Under the NLRA and the Limits of Liberal Political Imagination,' *Harvard Law Review* 97 (1983), 475 at 493.

26 See Michael Taylor, *Community, Anarchy and Liberty* (Cambridge: Cambridge University Press, 1982), at 53–8; David Miller, *Anarchism* (London: Dent, 1984), at 49–50; and George Crowder, *Classical Anarchism: The Political Thought of Proudhon, Bakunin, and Kropotkin* (Oxford: Clarendon Press, 1991). For a critical legal intimation of this approach to the question of how capitalist legality dissolves cultural traditions and values, 'leaving the individual isolated and exposed in what appears to be an objectively meaningless world,' see Fraser, 'The Legal Theory We Need Now,' at 173.

27 See Karl Marx, 'Economic and Philosophical Manuscripts,' in Quintin Hoare, ed., *Karl Marx: Early Writings*, trans. Rodney Livingstone and Gregor Benton (New York: Vintage Books, 1975), 211–41; Bertell Ollmann, *Alienation: Marx's Conception of Man in Capitalist Society*, 2nd ed. (Cambridge: Cambridge University Press, 1976); and Steven Lukes, 'Alienation and Anomie,' in Peter Laslett and W.G. Runciman, eds., *Philosophy, Politics and Society, Third Series* (Oxford: Basil Blackwell, 1967), 134–56.

28 David Trubek, 'Complexity and Contradiction in the Legal Order: Balbus

and the Challenge of Critical Social Thought about Law,' *Law and Society Review* 11 (1977), 529 at 543. A good source of insight into the complexity of state-sponsored forms of legality is the fortunes and operations of informal dispute processing: see Boaventura de Sousa Santos, 'Law and Community: The Changing Nature of State Power in Late Capitalism,' *International Journal of the Sociology of Law* 8 (1980), 379; Richard L. Abel, ed., *The Politics of Informal Justice*, 2 vols. (New York: Academic Press, 1982); and Christine B. Harrington, *Shadow Justice: The Ideology and Institutionalization of Alternatives to Court* (Westport, CT: Greenwood Press, 1985).

29 See Sheldon S. Wolin, *Politics and Vision: Continuity and Innovation in Western Political Thought* (London: Allen and Unwin, 1961), at 17–19.

30 Duncan Kennedy, 'Form and Substance in Private Law Adjudication,' *Harvard Law Review* 89 (1976), 1685 at 1685.

31 See Mark Tushnet, 'Truth, Justice and the American Way: An Interpretation of Public Law Scholarship in the Seventies,' *Texas Law Review* 57 (1979), 1307 at 1322 and 1372–3.

32 See Jaff, 'Radical Pluralism,' at 1145.

33 See Wolin, *Politics and Vision* at 31–2.

34 The process of reification is inescapably associated with ideology: see John B. Thompson, *Studies in the Theory of Ideology* (Cambridge: Cambridge University Press, 1984), at 130.

35 See Charles Taylor, *Hegel* (Cambridge: Cambridge University Press, 1975), at 428–61.

36 See Tushnet, 'Essay on Rights,' at 1400.

37 For an expression of these goals, which one might say formed an essential part of the vision of the New Deal in the United States, see John Dewey, *Individualism Old and New* (London: George Allen and Unwin, 1931), at 79–83.

38 See Mark Kelman, 'Trashing,' *Stanford Law Review* 36 (1984), 293 at 306 and Robin West, 'Authority, Autonomy, and Choice: The Role of Consent in the Moral and Political Visions of Franz Kafka and Richard Posner,' *Harvard Law Review* 99 (1985), 384.

39 See the remarks on 'edifying discourse' (a concept borrowed from Richard Rorty) in Singer, 'The Player and the Cards,' at 8. Rorty's reputation among leftist intellectuals is mixed: see Rebecca Comay, 'Interrupting the Conversation: Notes on Rorty,' *Telos* 69 (1986), 119 at 123: 'Rorty depoliticizes philosophy to the same degree, and by the same logic, as he aestheticizes politics.' Rorty's embrace of liberal institutions and practices, or at least a poeticized version of liberal culture, has been criticized from the left: see Richard Rorty, *Contingency, Irony, and Solidarity* (Cambridge: Cambridge

University Press, 1989), at 44–69; Richard Rorty, *Achieving Our Country: Leftist Thought in Twentieth-Century America* (Cambridge: Harvard University Press, 1998); Nancy Fraser, *Unruly Practices: Power, Discourse and Gender in Contemporary Social Theory* (Minneapolis: University of Minnesota Press, 1989), at 93–110; and Allan Hutchinson, 'The Three R's: Reading/Rorty/ Radically,' *Harvard Law Review* 103 (1989), 555.

40 For a discussion of this purpose, see Fraser, 'The Legal Theory We Need Now,' at 183.

41 See, for example, Jennifer Jaff, 'An Open Letter to Critical Legal Studies,' in *CLS: Newsletter of the Conference on Critical Legal Studies* (May, 1987), at 9–10.

42 David Trubek, 'Where the Action Is: Critical Legal Studies and Empiricism,' *Stanford Law Review* 36 (1984), 575 at 581.

43 It has been argued that critical legal writers, or at least one branch among them, have misconstrued the point of philosophically sophisticated versions of pragmatism: see John Stick, 'Can Nihilism Be Pragmatic?' *Harvard Law Review* 100 (1986), 332.

44 See, for example, Donald F. Brosnan, 'Serious but Not Critical,' *Southern California Law Review* 60 (1987), 259 at 271–332. For an instance of critical legal objections to some modern types of Marxist analysis, see Fraser, 'The Legal Theory We Need Now,' at 160–1.

45 See, for example, Andrew Levine, *The General Will: Rousseau, Marx, Communism* (Cambridge: Cambridge University Press, 1993).

46 See *supra*, Chapter 3.

47 On the other hand, there are no grounds for inferring that critical legal writers during the 1970s and 1980s felt, like Castoriadis, that 'socialism,' as a convenient label for the emancipatory program of the left, must be abandoned: see Cornelius Castoriadis, 'Socialism and Autonomous Society,' *Telos* 43 (1980), 91.

48 See Gabel, 'Review of Dworkin,' at 315. Abel also notes various forms of experimentation in worker control of productive enterprises in various political cultures: see Richard L. Abel, 'A Socialist Approach to Risk,' *Maryland Law Review* 51 (1982), 695, but he acknowledges that no extant society realizes a socialist ideal throughout.

49 Mark Tushnet, 'Dia-Tribe,' *Michigan Law Review* 78 (1980), 694 at 697.

50 Tushnet, 'Truth, Justice, and the American Way,' at 1347. Socialist principles 'are usually treated as utopian and marginal in American public discourse': William H. Simon, 'Social-Republican Property,' *U.C.L.A. Law Review* 38 (1991), 1335 at 1337.

51 See, for example, Karl Klare, 'The Quest for Industrial Democracy and the

Struggle against Racism: Perspectives from Labor Law and Civil Rights Law,' *Oregon Law Review* 61 (1982), 157 at 163.

52 For an expression of reasons against such intervention, see Olsen, 'The Family and the Market,' at 1528. An example of the use of history to recover some sense of how social ordering can be achieved on a local scale without a fully developed legal apparatus is Jerold S. Auerbach, *Justice without Law?* (New York: Oxford University Press, 1983). The history and forms of work-related enterprises that offer some pattern for promoting a sense of common purpose are surveyed in Simon, 'Social-Republican Property,' at 1368–86.

53 Freeman, 'Truth and Mystification,' at 1236. The historical and ideological background to the liberal reluctance to decentralize power is given in Gerald E. Frug, 'The City as a Legal Concept,' *Harvard Law Review* 93 (1980), 1059.

54 Tushnet, 'Essay on Rights,' at 1383–4.

55 See Tushnet, 'Dia-Tribe,' at 706.

56 See Lester Mazor, 'The Crisis of Liberal Legalism,' *Yale Law Journal* 81 (1972), 1032 at 1046–7 for a discussion of the rise and meaning of 'veto-communities.'

57 If large-scale deliberative and administrative institutions are retained, they should be subject to democratic direction and control, according to various models canvassed in April Carter, 'Industrial Democracy and the Capitalist State,' in Graeme Duncan, ed., *Democracy and the Capitalist State* (Cambridge: Cambridge University Press, 1989), 277–93.

58 See Carole Pateman, *Participation and Democratic Theory* (Cambridge: Cambridge University Press, 1970), at 34 and 42. On the relationship between the level of participation and the size of the political system, see Robert A. Dahl and Edward R. Tufte, *Size and Democracy* (Stanford: Stanford University Press, 1974), at 41–65.

59 See Boyle, 'The Politics of Reason,' at 739.

60 On strategies that are 'restorative' rather than 'revolutionary,' see Chalmers Johnson, *Revolutionary Change*, 2nd ed. (London: Longman, 1982), at 123–5.

61 This reflects a general movement away from some of the formerly dominant depictions of pre-revolutionary America as essentially guided by Lockean ideas in political conceptions. The older tradition is represented best by Louis Hartz, *The Liberal Tradition in America* (New York: Harcourt, 1955).

62 See Simon, 'Social-Republican Property,' at 1340 and Richard D. Parker, 'The Past of Constitutional History – And Its Future,' *Ohio State Law Journal*

42 (1981), 223 at 258 n.146. See also Richard D. Parker, 'Here, the People Rule': A Constitutional Populist Manifesto (Cambridge: Harvard University Press, 1994).

63 See in particular J.G.A. Pocock, The Machiavellian Moment: Florentine Political Thought and the Atlantic Republican Tradition (Princeton: Princeton University Press, 1975); Quentin Skinner, The Foundations of Modern Political Thought, 2 vols. (Cambridge: Cambridge University Press, 1978); Wolin, Politics and Vision; J.G.A. Pocock, 'The Machiavellian Moment Revisited: A Study in History and Ideology,' Journal of Modern History 53 (1981), 49. For critical assessments of the work of Pocock in this context, see Isaac Kramnick, Republicanism and Bourgeois Radicalism (Ithaca: Cornell University Press, 1990) and Joyce O. Appleby, Liberalism and Republicanism in the Historical Imagination (Cambridge: Harvard University Press, 1992). For a critical legal description of the elements of Hobbesian political theory (and the background of liberalism) see Mark Tushnet, 'Anti-Formalism in Recent Constitutional Theory,' Michigan Law Review 83 (1985), 1502 at 1539. It should also be noted that Machiavelli's examples and figures were drawn largely from Rome, not Greece: see Terence Ball, Reappraising Political Theory (New York: Oxford University Press, 1995), at 76.

64 See Aristotle, The Politics, trans. Ernest Barker (Oxford: Oxford University Press, 1958), at 1323a14–1331b23 and Bernard Yack, The Problems of a Political Animal: Community, Justice, and Conflict in Aristotelian Political Thought (Berkeley: University of California Press, 1993). On the use of the polis as an ideal in Renaissance Florence, by which 'virtue was not politicized,' see Pocock, Machiavellian Moment, at 74–5. A contemporary lament over the loss of agreement about what is good and virtuous that was present in the ancient polis can be found in Alasdair MacIntyre, After Virtue, 2nd ed. (London: Duckworth, 1981), at 146.

65 On Dante, see Judith Koffler, 'Capital in Hell: Dante's Lesson on Usury,' Rutgers Law Review 32 (1979), 608 at 618. On the use of the image of the polis by Herder, Schiller, and Hegel, see Raymond Plant, Community and Ideology: An Essay in Applied Social Philosophy (London: Routledge & Kegan Paul, 1974), at 16.

66 A caution should be registered here that republicanism does not have to be interpreted as necessarily connected to Aristotle's conception of the healthy public life. Republicanism can be more modestly conceived as a way of picturing political liberty that stresses civic virtue, but which is not committed to the idea that human liberty is only realized when certain determinate purposes are acted on: see Quentin Skinner, 'The Republican Ideal of Political Liberty,' in Gisela Bock, Quentin Skinner, and Russell L.

Hanson, eds., *Machiavelli and Republicanism* (Cambridge: Cambridge University Press, 1993), 293–309.

67 See Paul Brest, 'Who Decides?' *Southern California Law Review* 58 (1985), 661 at 670 and Frug, 'The Ideology of Bureaucracy,' at 1295. An extensive attempt to demonstrate how a certain 'republican tradition' animated lawyers in the nineteenth century and then died in the face of modern U.S. religious ideas and capitalist social relations has been made in Andrew Fraser, 'Legal Amnesia: Modernism Versus the Republican Tradition in American Legal Thought,' *Telos* 60 (1984), 15. But even Fraser's discussion fails to overcome the problems of vagueness, as is illustrated in the following passage: '[O]ur moral identity is rooted in patterns of practical intersubjectivity which cannot be reduced to the autonomous and instrumental logic of a system of socialized value production without threatening the very foundation of that identity. It may be said, therefore, that the hope of emancipation lies in our willingness to confront anew the problem of regenerating stable, well-ordered and virtuous republican polities within the corrupt and decaying body of Anglo-American civilization.' Ibid. at 52. This expression of anti-modernist rhetoric fits neatly into its own tradition: see Marshall Berman, *All That Is Solid Melts into Air: The Experience of Modernity* (New York: Simon and Schuster, 1982). It lacks, however, or at least it fails to communicate, a positive vision of much substance. An alternative to the nostalgic strategy employed by Fraser is evident in Zygmunt Bauman, 'The Left as the Counter-Culture of Modernity,' *Telos* 70 (1986–7), 81 and Claus Offe, 'The Utopia of Zero-Option – Modernity and Modernization as Normative Political Criteria,' *Praxis International* 7 (1987), 1. To be fair, Fraser has in subsequent writings tried to show the relevance of rejuvenated republicanism to specific constitutional contexts, including Australia and Canada. See Andrew Fraser, *The Spirit of the Laws: Republicanism and the Unfinished Project of Modernity* (Toronto: University of Toronto Press, 1990) and Andrew Fraser, 'Beyond the Charter Debate: Republicanism, Rights and Civic Virtue in the Civil Constitution of Canadian Society,' *Review of Constitutional Studies* 1 (1993), 27.

68 For an appraisal of Pocock's success in conveying a sense of the shifting language and implicit paradigms of politics, see J.H. Hexter, *On Historians* (Cambridge: Harvard University Press, 1979), 255–303.

69 See Pocock, *Machiavellian Moment*, at 269.

70 Ibid. at 486.

71 Ibid. at 507.

72 The history of this gradual abandonment of the austere republican vision is recounted at length in Gordon S. Wood, *The Creation of the American Repub-*

lic, 1776–1787 (New York: Norton, 1969) and Gordon S. Wood, *The Radical-ism of the American Revolution* (New York: Knopf, 1992).

73 See Pocock, *Machiavellian Moment,* at 521, where he cites Madison's discus-sion of political factions in the tenth issue of *The Federalist* as expressing a sea change in the fortunes of classical republicanism. For example, note these assertions by Madison:

> So strong is this propensity of mankind to fall into mutual animosities that where no substantial occasion presents itself the most frivolous and fanciful distinctions have been sufficient to kindle their un-friendly passions and excite their most violent conflicts.
>
> The inference to which we are brought is that the *causes* of faction cannot be removed and that relief is only to be sought in the means of controlling its *effects.*
>
> A republic, by which I mean a government in which the scheme of representation takes place, opens a different prospect and promises the cure for which we are seeking.

See Alexander Hamilton, James Madison, and John Jay, *The Federalist Papers,* ed. Clinton Rossiter (New York: New American Library, 1961), at 79, 80, and 81 respectively (emphasis in the original). For documentation and discussion of how the anti-Federalists favoured a small republic, guided by communitarian sentiments, see Herbert Storing, *What the Anti-Federalists Were For* (Chicago: University of Chicago Press, 1981) and Jennifer Nedelsky, 'Confirming Democratic Politics: Anti-Federalists, Federalists, and the Constitution,' *Harvard Law Review* 96 (1982), 340.

74 Pocock, *Machiavellian Moment,* at 551–2.

75 Tushnet, 'Dia-Tribe,' at 710.

76 See, for example, Alan E. Astin, *Cato the Censor* (Oxford: Clarendon Press, 1978).

77 A lapse lamented in Trubek, 'Where the Action Is,' at 598 n.74. See *supra,* Chapter 3.

78 See Raymond Geuss, *The Idea of Critical Theory: Habermas and the Frankfurt School* (Cambridge: Cambridge University Press, 1981), at 63–4 and Axel Honneth, 'Communication and Reconciliation: Habermas' Critique of Adorno,' *Telos* 10 (1979), 43. And, it might be added, Habermas himself has significantly elaborated and partly changed his position on these questions in the past two decades: for an overview, see William Outhwaite, *Habermas: A Critical Introduction* (Cambridge: Polity Press, 1994).

79 The first comprehensive delineation of his theory was given in Jürgen Habermas, 'What Is Universal Pragmatics?,' in his *Communication and the Evolution of Society,* trans. Thomas McCarthy (Boston: Beacon Press, 1979),

at 1–68. See Thomas McCarthy, *The Critical Theory of Jürgen Habermas* (London: Hutchinson, 1978), at 272–91 for a useful discussion of Habermas's construction and defence of a universal pragmatics.

80 McCarthy, *Critical Theory of Jürgen Habermas*, at 278–9.

81 Geuss, *The Idea of Critical Theory*, at 66.

82 On this topic, see McCarthy, *Critical Theory of Jürgen Habermas*, at 331–2.

83 See W.F.R. Hardie, *Aristotle's Ethical Theory*, 2nd ed. (Oxford: Clarendon Press, 1980), at 46–67.

84 Jürgen Habermas, *Communication and the Evolution of Society*, trans. Thomas McCarthy (Boston: Beaver Press, 1979) at 3. This 'reflexive' account of interaction and mutual understanding contrasts, for example, with early positivist emphases on facts (as against beliefs), objectivity, exactitude, and the writing of scientific knowledge. On the latter see Jürgen Habermas, *Knowledge and Human Interests*, trans. Jeremy Shapiro (Boston: Beacon Press, 1971), at 71–90.

85 And especially would they replace the epistemological presuppositions of liberal theory. As Habermas has more recently noted, the current philosophical moment is strikingly anti-epistemological and anti-foundational in the sense that philosophers, under the influence of pragmatic and hermeneutical inquiries, now tend to: '... emphasize the web of everyday life and communication surrounding "our" cognitive achievements. The latter are intrinsically intersubjective and cooperative. Just how this web is conceptualized, whether as "form of life," "life world," "practice," "linguistically mediated interaction," "language game," "convention," "cultural background," "tradition," "effective history," or what have you, is unimportant. The important thing is that these commonsensical ideas, though they may function quite differently, attain a status that used to be reserved for the basic concepts of epistemology.' See Jürgen Habermas, 'Philosophy as Stand-In and Interpreter,' in Kenneth Baynes, James Bohman, and Thomas McCarthy, eds., *After Philosophy: End or Transformation?* (Cambridge: MIT Press, 1987), 296 at 304.

86 See, for example, Alan Hyde, 'Is Liberalism Possible?' *New York University Law Review* 57 (1982), 1031 at 1038–9; Mark Tushnet, 'Following the Rules Laid Down: A Critique of Interpretivism and Neutral Principles,' *Harvard Law Review* 96 (1983), 781 at 825–6; and Fraser, 'The Legal Theory We Need Now,' at 149 and 183–4. Theorists of both liberal (Bruce Ackerman) and conservative (Michael Oakeshott) persuasions have periodically also framed their political theory in terms of conversation: see Benjamin Barber, *The Conquest of Politics: Liberal Philosophy in Democratic Times* (Princeton: Princeton University Press, 1988), at 120–76.

87 See, for example, Alan Hyde, 'The Concept of Legitimation in the Sociol-

ogy of Law,' *Wisconsin Law Review* [1983], 379 at 399–400 and Tushnet, 'Essay on Rights,' at 1394–5.

88 See Jürgen Habermas, *Legitimation Crisis*, trans. Thomas McCarthy (Boston: Beacon Press, 1975), at 95–110 and the discussion in McCarthy, *Critical Theory of Jürgen Habermas*, at 358–86.

89 On the meaning of 'counterfactual,' in the setting of critical analysis of social norms, see Garbis Kortian, *Metacritique* (Cambridge: Cambridge University Press, 1980), at 78. For a critical, though sympathetic, response to Habermas's goal of a reconstructive science, see Drucilla Cornell, 'Two Lectures on the Normative Dimensions of Community in the Law,' *Tennessee Law Review* 54 (1987), 327 at 333.

90 See John Rawls, *A Theory of Justice*, 2nd ed. (Cambridge: Harvard University Press, 1999), at 102–68.

91 See, for example, Richard Miller, 'Rawls and Marxism,' in Norman Daniels, ed., *Reading Rawls* (Oxford: Blackwell, 1975), 206–30; Michael J. Sandel, *Liberalism and the Limits of Justice*, 2nd ed. (Cambridge: Cambridge University Press, 1998); Stephen Mulhall and Adam Swift, *Liberals and Communitarians*, 2nd ed. (Oxford: Basil Blackwell, 1996); and Elizabeth Frazer and Nicola Lacey, *The Politics of Community: A Feminist Critique of the Liberal-Communitarian Debate* (Toronto: University of Toronto Press, 1993), at 53–60.

92 Benhabib claims that Rawls and Habermas share a 'methodological proceduralism': see Seyla Benhabib, 'The Methodological Illusions of Modern Political Theory: The Case of Rawls and Habermas,' *Neue Hefte für Philosophie* 21 (1982), 47 repr. in Jay Bernstein, ed., *The Frankfurt School: Critical Assessments*, Vol. 6 (London: Routledge, 1994), 285–308.

93 See C. Edwin Baker, 'Outcome Equality or Equality of Respect: The Substantive Content of Equal Protection,' *University of Pennsylvania Law Review* 131 (1983), 933 at 950 and C. Edwin Baker, 'Sandel on Rawls,' *University of Pennsylvania Law Review* 133 (1985), 895. The latter article, it should be noted, argues that it is wrong to attribute to Rawls, though not perhaps to other liberal theorists, an individualist theory of the person. Further astute commentary in this vein is contained in Michael J. Perry, 'A Critique of the "Liberal" Political-Philosophical Project,' *William and Mary Law Review* 28 (1987), 205 at 215–19.

94 See Tushnet, 'Following the Rules Laid Down,' at 825–6. The literature that examines the critical legal use of the techniques of literary and philosophical deconstruction also raises curious questions about the compatibility of these techniques with the normative implications of a communitarian understanding of legal and political action: see, for example, Kenney Hegland, 'Goodbye to Deconstruction,' *Southern California Law Review* 58

(1985), 1203; Drucilla Cornell, 'The Poststructuralist Challenge to the Ideal of Community,' *Cardozo Law Review* 8 (1987), 989; and Joan C. Williams, 'Critical Legal Studies: The Death of Transcendence and the Rise of the New Langdells,' *New York University Law Review* 62 (1987), 429.

95 Roberto Mangabeira Unger, *Politics: A Work in Constructive Social Theory*, 3 vols. (Cambridge: Cambridge University Press, 1987). The individual volumes are Volume 1: *Social Theory: Its Situation and Its Task*; Volume 2: *False Necessity: Anti-Necessitarian Social Theory in the Service of Radical Democracy*; and Volume 3: *Plasticity into Power: Comparative-Historical Studies on the Institutional Conditions of Economic and Military Success.* Hereafter, the texts will be referred to by their brief titles as *Social Theory, False Necessity,* or *Plasticity into Power.* A one-volume selection is available as Roberto Mangabeira Unger, *Politics: The Central Texts,* ed. Zhiyuan Cui (Cambridge: Cambridge University Press, 1997).

96 See Unger, *Knowledge and Politics,* at 236ff.

97 Ibid. at 231–5. This becomes even clearer in his attempt to retrieve what he calls the 'Christian-Romantic image of man,' in Roberto Mangabeira Unger, *Passion: An Essay on Personality* (New York: Free Press, 1984).

98 Unger, *Knowledge and Politics* at 246–8.

99 Ibid. at 159–60.

100 Ibid. at 254–9.

101 Ibid. at 249.

102 The relationship of the universal to the particular is an essential backdrop of all of Unger's attempts to resolve the antinomies of liberal thinking. In many respects Unger adopts an Aristotelian vision of how persons exemplify their species characteristics. He expressly repudiates, of course, the doctrine of intelligible essences that was a leading feature of Aristotle's own account of epistemology and the philosophy of language: see ibid. at 93 and 133ff.

103 See Unger, *Social Theory,* at 23–4.

104 Ibid. at 92–3. See also Unger, *False Necessity,* at 449.

105 Unger, *Knowledge and Politics,* at 273.

106 Ibid. at 245 and 280. Unger's depiction of the conditions of an ideal social group bear some likeness to the type of progressive community envisioned by William Morris: see his *Political Writings,* ed. A.L. Morton (London: Lawrence and Wishart, 1984).

107 Unger, *Knowledge and Politics,* at 297.

108 Ibid. at 281.

109 Ibid. at 274.

110 Ibid. at 260. On Unger's wariness about – though not complete aversion

to – prescriptive or programmatic arguments, see William H. Simon, 'Social Theory and Political Practice: Unger's Brazilian Journalism,' *Northwestern University Law Review* 81 (1987), 832 at 866–7.

111 Unger, *Knowledge and Politics*, at 282–6.

112 Ibid. at 243–4.

113 Ibid. at 262.

114 Roberto Mangabeira Unger, *Law in Modern Society* (New York: Free Press, 1976), at 30 and 127–8.

115 Ibid. at 29.

116 Ibid. at 24.

117 Ibid. at 241–2.

118 Ibid. at 239. Unger has been taken to task for neglecting to learn from ancient Chinese history how this goal of reconciling community with autonomy might be accomplished in ways that do not rely upon mechanisms from advanced Western societies: see William P. Alford, 'The Inscrutable Occidental? Implications of Roberto Unger's Uses and Abuses of the Chinese Past,' *Texas Law Review* 64 (1986), 915.

119 See Unger, *Social Theory*, at 208 and Unger, *False Necessity*, at 10.

120 Roberto Mangabeira Unger, *The Critical Legal Studies Movement* (Cambridge: Harvard University Press, 1986).

121 See ibid. at 39 and Unger, *False Necessity*, at 530–5.

122 See Unger, *Social Theory*, at 163.

123 Ibid. at 5–6 and 154–6.

124 In Unger's view, ibid. at 200: 'The development of an antinecessitarian social theory contributes to the advancement of the radical project – the cause that liberals, leftists, and modernists (those radicals of personal relations) confusedly share. Such a social theory promotes the radical cause because it helps form a social understanding freer from the taints of institutional and structure fetishism.'

125 See Unger, *The Critical Legal Studies Movement*, at 39–40 and Unger, *False Necessity*, 508–39.

126 Unger, *The Critical Legal Studies Movement*, at 36–7.

127 See Unger, *False Necessity*, at 21–3, 130–3, and 196–207.

128 This retrieval again exemplifies one mode of radical insight: the seeking out of alternative programs, structures, or styles of radical will that were suppressed in the triumph of opposing ideologies. On petty bourgeois radicalism, see Unger, *False Necessity*, at 21–31.

129 Ibid. at 104 and 562.

130 *Supra*, at 93–4.

131 *Supra*, at 41 (emphasis added). See also Unger, *False Necessity*, at 588.

132 See C.B. Macpherson, *The Life and Times of Liberal Democracy* (Oxford: Oxford University Press, 1977) for a treatment of the several available different models.

133 V.I. Lenin, *The State and Revolution* (Peking: Foreign Language Press, 1976). On the various political interpretations to which this document has given rise, see A.J. Polan, *Lenin and the End of Politics* (London: Methuen, 1984) and Neil Harding, *Lenin's Political Thought: Theory and Practice in the Democratic and Socialist Revolutions*, 2 vols. (London: Macmillan, 1977–81), II:123–41.

134 See Unger, *The Critical Legal Studies Movement*, at 35–6. It has been argued that the economic aspects of Unger's program will not necessarily do away with problems of large bureaucracy or lack of political access or participation: see Ian R. Macneil, 'Bureaucracy, Liberalism, and Community – American Style,' *Northwestern University Law Review* 79 (1984–5), 900 at 919–29.

135 The article by Andrea Asaro, 'The Public-Private Distinction in American Liberal Thought: Unger's Critique and Synthesis,' *American Journal of Jurisprudence* 28 (1983), 118 predated Unger's essay on critical legal studies, and so fails to deal with his arguments that seek to redeem, rather than to repudiate, liberalism. For a recognition of the changes in Unger's approach to the construction and use of social theory and, in particular, to how social theoretical understanding can be applied to the political uses of legal forms, see Hugh Collins, 'Roberto Unger and the Critical Legal Studies Movement,' *Journal of Law and Society* 14 (1987), 387. In Allan C. Hutchinson and Patrick J. Monahan, 'The "Rights Stuff": Roberto Unger and Beyond,' *Texas Law Review* 62 (1984), 1477 an attempt is made to point out the difficulties that Unger's theory of context-revision confronts. The solution proposed by those authors rests in a reformulated theory of human personality, in which it is recognized that the 'capacity for imaginative reconstruction is also historically situated.' That claim is, of course, caught by the paradox of postponement. A more philosophically adequate approach to the critique of Unger's unfolding project is outlined in Drucilla Cornell, 'Toward a Modern/Postmodern Reconstruction of Ethics,' *University of Pennsylvania Law Review* 133 (1985), 291 at 327–58.

136 Unger, *False Necessity*, at 592. Unger's own experience as a citizen of Brazil, with its chequered history of democracy, and his efforts to influence public debate over constitutional and political reforms in that country are profiled in Simon, 'Social Theory and Political Practice.'

137 Wolin, *Politics and Vision*, at 18–19.

138 See, for example, Raymond Williams, *Culture and Society, 1780–1950* (Har-

mondsworth: Penguin, 1958); Michael Kenny, 'Facing Up to the Future: Community in the Work of Raymond Williams in the Fifties and Sixties,' *Politics* 11 (1991), 14; Stanley Fish, *Is There a Text in This Class?* (Cambridge: Harvard University Press, 1980), at 303–21; and Stanley Fish, *Doing What Comes Naturally: Change, Rhetoric, and the Practice of Theory in Literary and Legal Studies* (Durham, NC: Duke University Press, 1989), at 141–60.

139 For an account of the various orientations giving rise to an appeal to the existence or desirability of a community, see Carl J. Friedrich, 'The Concept of Community in the History of Political and Legal Philosophy,' in Carl J. Friedrich, ed., *Nomos II: Community* (New York: Liberal Arts Press, 1959), 3–24.

140 See Ferdinand Tönnies, *Community and Society*, trans. C.P. Loomis (East Lansing: Michigan State University Press, 1957).

141 See Edmund Burke, *Reflections on the Revolution in France*, ed. Conor Cruise O'Brien (Harmondsworth: Penguin, 1969). For the fears underlying Burke's response to the prospect of revolution, see William Corlett, *Community without Unity: A Politics of Derridian Extravagance* (Durham, NC: Duke University Press, 1989), at 118–41 and Albert O. Hirschman, *The Rhetoric of Reaction: Perversity, Futility, Jeopardy* (Cambridge: Harvard University Press, 1991), at 12–15.

142 For a description of this kind of theory and its chief exponents, see Wolin, *Politics and Vision*, at 412.

143 See Tushnet, 'Following the Rules Laid Down,' at 785.

144 Compare the arguments raised in two sceptical critiques of the contemporary communitarian school of thought generally: H.N. Hirsch, 'The Threnody of Liberalism: Constitutional Liberty and the Renewal of Community,' *Political Theory* 14 (1986), 423 repr. in H.N. Hirsch, *A Theory of Liberty: The Constitution and Minorities* (New York: Routledge, 1992), 241–69 and Amy Gutmann, 'Communitarian Critics of Liberalism,' *Philosophy and Public Affairs* 14 (1985), 308 repr. in Schlomo Avineri and Avner de-Shalit, eds., *Individualism and Communitarianism* (Oxford: Oxford University Press, 1992), 120–36.

145 For an argument that Unger's theory of context-transcendence has difficulty with controlling the implications of perpetual change, see Ernest J. Weinrib, 'Enduring Passion,' *Yale Law Journal* 94 (1985), 1825 at 1835–6.

146 See Ronald Dworkin, *Law's Empire* (Cambridge: Harvard University Press, 1986).

147 See Laurence H. Tribe, 'Structural Due Process,' *Harvard Civil Rights–Civil Liberties Law Review* 10 (1975), 269 and Laurence H. Tribe, *Constitutional Choices* (Cambridge: Harvard University Press, 1985), at 9–20.

148 See, for example, Duncan Kennedy, 'Distributive and Paternalist Motives in Contract and Tort Law, with Special Reference to Compulsory Terms and Unequal Bargaining Power,' *Maryland Law Review* 41 (1982), 563; Jay M. Feinman, 'The Meaning of Reliance: A Historical Perspective,' *Wisconsin Law Review* [1984], 1373; Robert W. Gordon, 'Macaulay, Macneil, and the Discovery of Solidarity and Power in Contract Law,' *Wisconsin Law Review* [1985], 565; and Hugh Collins, *The Law of Contract*, 2nd ed. (London: Butterworths, 1993), at 86–7. The contentious point is how these communal values deviate from 'official' values, to use the term used by Gordon at 576, and are therefore subversive of the dominant ideological images created and sustained by legal doctrine. The nub of the dispute is the sense in which these alternative values disrupt our community as opposed to continuing the normative conversation already entwined in legal dispute.

149 Richard Lewis, 'The Destruction of Community,' *Buffalo Law Review* 35 (1986), 365.

150 Unger, *False Necessity*, at 101.

151 Ibid. at 367.

152 See Unger, *Social Theory*, at 147.

153 Nor is it true that every critical legal writer would see the same implications: see J.M. Balkin, 'The Crystalline Structure of Legal Thought,' *Rutgers Law Review* 39 (1986), 1 at 76: 'I do not believe that our moral and legal consciousness is dialectically structured because it is Liberal consciousness, so that if we could free ourselves from Liberal institutions our moral and legal debates would no longer display a crystalline structure. Our legal institutions and our system of moral values are Liberal, but the contradictions of our thought are not Liberal contradictions, but are only manifested in our Liberalism.'

154 See Martin Krygier, 'Critical Legal Studies and Social Theory – A Response to Alan Hunt,' *Oxford Journal of Legal Studies* 7 (1987), 26 at 34–7 for a socio-historical explanation about the presence and meaning of inconsistency in legal doctrine. A sensitive treatment, from a radical point of view, of the variety of theories of meaning and their implications for accounts of legal practice is contained in the work of Drucilla Cornell: see, for example, her '"Convention" and Critique,' *Cardozo Law Review* 7 (1986), 679 and, 'Two Lectures.'

155 See Jean-Jacques Rousseau, 'Of the Social Contract,' in *The Social Contract and Other Later Political Writings*, trans. Victor Gourevitch (Cambridge: Cambridge University Press, 1997).

156 See Wolin, *Politics and Vision*, at 371–2 and Judith N. Shklar, *Men and*

Citizens: A Study of Rousseau's Social Theory, 2nd ed. (Cambridge: Cambridge University Press, 1985).

157 See Tushnet, 'Anti-Formalism in Recent Constitutional Theory,' at 1508. The foremost example of a non-critical legal attempt to show the contemporary relevance of civic republican ideals to liberal democratic structures is Frank I. Michelman, 'Foreword: Traces of Self-Government,' *Harvard Law Review* 100 (1986), 4.

158 Tushnet, 'Anti-Formalism in Recent Constitutional Theory,' at 1540.

159 For a critique of claims about the actual historical dominance of republican theories, see Don Herzog, 'Some Questions for Republicans,' *Political Theory* 14 (1986), 473.

160 Michael Ignatieff, *The Needs of Strangers* (London: Chatto & Windus, 1984), at 130. See also Unger, *False Necessity,* at 587 and E.J. Hobsbawm, *Nations and Nationalism since 1780: Programme, Myth, Reality* (Cambridge: Cambridge University Press, 1990).

161 Ignatieff himself has more recently meditated over the surge of nationalism in the 1980s and 1990s. He has concluded that nationalism has not been so much the basis for conflict, as the rhetorical rationalization of violence: see Michael Ignatieff, *Blood and Belonging: Journeys into the New Nationalism* (New York: Viking, 1993). For a contrary viewpoint, which treats patriotism as a lively phenomenon still related to the sense of self in liberal communities, and unlikely to disappear soon, see Benedict Anderson, *Imagined Communities: Reflections on the Origin and Spread of Nationalism,* rev. ed. (London: Verso, 1991); Taylor, 'Cross-Purposes,' 174–5; and Yael Tamir, *Liberal Nationalism* (Princeton: Princeton University Press, 1993).

162 Frazer and Lacey, *The Politics of Community,* at 142–9.

163 For a definition of civic humanism that distinguishes it from civic republicanism, see Skinner, 'The Republican Ideal of Political Liberty,' and Charles Taylor, 'Kant's Theory of Freedom,' in *Philosophical Papers,* Vol. 2, *Philosophy and the Human Sciences* (Cambridge: Cambridge University Press, 1985), 318–37 at 334–5. Rejection of civic humanism on this ground is defended in John Rawls, *Political Liberalism* (New York: Columbia University Press, 1993), at 206.

164 Philip Selznick, 'The Idea of a Communitarian Morality,' *California Law Review* 75 (1987), 445 at 457 (emphasis in the original).

165 *Accord* Unger, *False Necessity,* at 587. It is surely wrong to claim that '[o]ppositional ideologies such as classical republicanism and revolutionary Marxism describe a concrete set of arrangements for the state and thus define the utopian goal of a remade social world': James Boyle,

'Modernist Social Theory: Roberto Unger's *Passion*,' *Harvard Law Review* 98 (1985), 1066 at 1079.

166 For an expression of this attitude, see Mark Tushnet, 'The Dilemmas of Liberal Constitutionalism,' *Ohio State Law Journal* 42 (1981), 411 at 424–5.

167 Critical legal writing in this area therefore tends not to differentiate carefully among such contemporary treatments as Rawls, *Theory of Justice*; Robert Nozick, *Anarchy, State and Utopia* (New York: Basic Books, 1974); Ronald Dworkin, 'What Is Equality?' (Two Parts) *Philosophy and Public Affairs* 10 (1981), 185 and 283; Michael Walzer, *Spheres of Justice: A Defence of Pluralism and Equality* (Oxford: Basil Blackwell, 1983); and David Miller, *Social Justice* (Oxford: Clarendon Press, 1976). All these works are assimilable on the critical legal account.

168 Critical legal accounts have not generally approached, in terms of detail or sophistication, the reinvigorating examinations of the rule of law or fundamental rights contained in Paul Q. Hirst, *Law, Socialism and Democracy* (London: Allen & Unwin, 1986); Christine M. Sypnowich, *The Concept of Socialist Law* (Oxford: Clarendon Press, 1990); and Jennifer Nedelsky, 'Reconceiving Rights as Relationship,' *Review of Constitutional Studies* 1 (1993), 1.

169 See Hyde, 'Is Liberalism Possible?' at 1049 and Staughton Lynd, 'Communal Rights,' *Texas Law Review* 62 (1984), 1417.

170 See Anthony Chase, 'The Left on Rights: An Introduction,' *Texas Law Review* 62 (1984), 1541 at 1560–1. Chase's discussion recognizes that 'rights-talk' can be serious and can survive the demise of liberal thought. This is more credible than the claim that the '*logic of rights* is a human invention whose purpose is to preserve us from the notion that we must make political and moral choices': Joseph William Singer, 'The Legal Rights Debate in Analytical Jurisprudence from Bentham to Hohfeld,' *Wisconsin Law Review* [1982], 975 at 1059 (emphasis in the original).

171 For a slightly similar argument in respect of Marx, see Wolin, *Politics and Vision*, at 416–17. On the Platonic attempt to render citizenship unnecessary for moral development, see ibid. at 41–56.

172 See John M. Finnis, *Natural Law and Natural Rights* (Oxford: Clarendon Press, 1980), esp. at 141–56 and John M. Finnis, 'On "The Critical Legal Studies Movement,"' *American Journal of Jurisprudence* 30 (1985), 21 at 35–6.

173 See Dworkin, *Law's Empire*, at 195–216; Ronald Dworkin, 'Liberal Community,' *California Law Review* 77 (1989), 479 repr. in Avineri and de-Shalit, eds., *Individualism and Communitarianism*, 205–23; and Ronald Dworkin, 'Equality, Democracy, and the Constitution: We the People in Court,' *Alberta Law Review* 28 (1990), 324.

174 Aristotle, *Nicomachean Ethics*, trans. Martin Ostwald (Indianapolis: Bobbs-Merrill, 1962), at 1155a22–3. See Bernard Yack, 'Community and Conflict in Aristotle's Political Philosophy,' *Review of Politics* 47 (1985), 92, an article devoted to correcting a common view of the harmony of Aristotle's ideal *polis*. This view is attributed to MacIntyre, *After Virtue*.

175 See Donna Greschner, 'Feminist Concerns with the New Communitarians: We Don't Need Another Hero,' in Allan C. Hutchinson and Leslie J.M. Green, eds., *Law and Community: The End of Individualism?* (Scarborough, ON: Carswell, 1989), 119–50 at 122–5.

176 Ibid. at 128–9.

177 Iris Marion Young, *Justice and the Politics of Difference* (Princeton: Princeton University Press, 1990), at 164–8.

178 See Carole Pateman, *The Disorder of Women: Democracy, Feminism, and Political Theory* (Cambridge: Polity Press, 1989), at 211.

179 See Honig, *Political Theory*, at 162–4 and Frazer and Lacey, *The Politics of Community*, at 192–8.

180 See Frazer and Lacey, *The Politics of Community*, and Honig, *Political Theory*.

181 Charles Taylor, *Hegel and Modern Society* (Cambridge: Cambridge University Press, 1979), at 90.

182 See Thompson, *Studies in the Theory of Ideology*, at 251–2.

183 Charles Lindblom has noted that while convergence of popular opinion might arise on complex social issues, this does not necessarily compel a desire for fundamental change: see Charles E. Lindblom, *Inquiry and Change: The Troubled Attempt to Understand and Shape Society* (New Haven: Yale University Press, 1990), at 119–32.

184 See, *supra*, Chapter 3.

185 Trubek, 'Where the Action Is,' at 592.

186 See Tushnet, 'Truth, Justice and the American Way,' at 1359 and Boyle, 'The Politics of Reason,' at 746.

187 See Trubek, 'The Politics of Reason,' at 608.

188 See Tushnet, 'Anti-Formalism in Recent Constitutional Theory,' at 1527–9.

189 Johnson, *Revolutionary Change*, at 8.

190 Ibid. at 156.

191 Using the term 'politics' here in the sense elaborated in Bernard Crick, *In Defence of Politics*, 4th ed. (London: Weidenfeld and Nicolson, 1992).

192 See generally, Maurice Merleau-Ponty, *Humanism and Terror*, trans. John O'Neill (Boston: Beacon Press, 1969). In the words of Hannah Arendt, who was very clear about the limitations of politics: 'It is because of this silence that violence is a marginal phenomenon in the political realm ... The point here is that violence itself is incapable of speech, and not

merely that speech is helpless when confronted with violence. Because of this speechlessness political theory has little to say about the phenomenon of violence and must leave its discussion to the technicians.' See Hannah Arendt, *On Revolution* (Harmondsworth: Penguin, 1973), at 18–19; Peter Fuss, 'Hannah Arendt's Conception of Political Community,' in Melvyn A. Hill, ed., *Hannah Arendt: The Recovery of the Public World* (New York: St Martin's Press, 1979), 157–76; and Hannah Arendt, *Crises of the Republic* (New York: Harcourt Brace Jovanovich, 1972), at 105–98.

193 Schlegel does not relate the growth of critical legal studies to the upheavals on U.S. campuses in the late 1960s: see John Henry Schlegel, 'Notes Toward an Intimate, Opinionated, and Affectionate History of the Conference on Critical Legal Studies,' *Stanford Law Review* 36 (1984), 391.

194 See Stephen Eric Bronner, *Moments of Decision: Political History and the Crisis of Radicalism* (New York: Routledge, 1992), at 101–23.

195 A brief survey of the rise of the New Left and the emergence of critical legal studies is available in Neil Duxbury, *Patterns of American Jurisprudence* (Oxford: Clarendon Press, 1995), at 428–46. Among the more useful sources are Christopher Lasch, *The Agony of the American Left* (New York: Knopf, 1969); Gianni Statera, *Death of a Utopia: The Development and Decline of Student Movements in Europe* (New York: Oxford University Press, 1975); James Weinstein, *Ambiguous Legacy: The Left in American Politics* (New York: New Viewpoints, 1975); Daniel Aaron, *Writers of the Left* (New York: Oxford University Press, Galaxy Book ed., 1977); Robert J. Brym, *Intellectuals and Politics* (London: Allen & Unwin, 1980); Mark E. Kann, *The American Left: Failures and Fortunes* (New York: Praeger, 1982); Peter Clecak, *America's Quest for the Ideal Self: Dissent and Fulfillment in the 60s and 70s* (New York: Oxford University Press, 1983); Maurice Isserman, *If I Had a Hammer: The Death of the Old Left and the Birth of the New Left* (New York: Basic Books, 1987); James Miller, *'Democracy in the Streets': From Port Huron to the Siege of Chicago* (New York: Simon and Schuster, 1987); and John Patrick Diggins, *The Rise and Fall of the American Left* (New York: W.W. Norton, 1992).

196 As some critical legal writers concede, their visions of a progressive community are utopian and consequently might be subjected to the critique Engels launched against the early European socialists: see Friedrich Engels, *Socialism: Utopian and Scientific* (Moscow: Progress Publishers, 1968) and Vincent Geoghegan, *Utopianism and Marxism* (London: Methuen, 1987). It has been suggested by Michael A. Foley, 'Critical Legal Studies: New Wave Utopian Socialism,' *Dickinson Law Review* 91 (1986), 467 that critical legal studies bears comparison with the work of Fourier and Owen.

197 These are among the 'methodological constraints' of critical legal studies

that arguably duplicate the very constraints radicals criticize as limiting the practice of conventional legal scholarship: see Frank Munger and Carroll Seron, 'Critical Legal Studies versus Critical Legal Theory: A Comment on Method,' *Law and Policy* 6 (1984), 257. Often the debate over 'what is to be done (next)?' takes the form of whether a 'generalising statement of the critical project' can or should be made: see Alan Hunt, 'The Critique of Law: What is "Critical" about Critical Legal Theory?,' in Peter Fitzpatrick and Alan Hunt, eds., *Critical Legal Studies* (Oxford: Basil Blackwell, 1987), 5–19 repr. in Alan Hunt, *Explorations in Law and Society: Toward a Constitutive Theory of Law* (London: Routledge, 1993), 211–26. The answer to this question, though related to the ultimate shape as well as the impact of the movement as a school of legal thought, does not settle questions about the politics of the project.

198 This is one of the problems I have with 'local critiques' as they have been offered by critical legal writers, partly to allow for heterogeneity in critical approaches and partly to compensate for the admitted lack of a total vision. An accessible example of such a local critique, which is conscious of its own limits, is Robert W. Gordon, 'Unfreezing Legal Reality: Critical Approaches to Law,' *Florida State University Law Review* 15 (1987), 195.

199 Duncan Kennedy, 'Rebels from Principle: Changing the Corporate Law Firm from Within,' *Harvard Law School Bulletin* 33(1) (1981), 36 at 39.

200 These conspiratorial possibilities are mentioned as a way of highlighting the active political choices that critical legal writers might face. I do not imply that the horrible things said by opponents of the radical critique about professors often identified as critical legal leaders at élite U.S. law schools are necessarily true: see Jerry Frug, 'McCarthyism and Critical Legal Studies,' *Harvard Civil Rights–Civil Liberties Law Review* 22 (1987), 665.

201 The irony to be found here is also present in the critical legal tactic diagnosed by Don Herzog in which 'CLS authors read legal doctrine politically, but they read liberal doctrine apolitically': see Don Herzog, 'As Many as Six Impossible Things before Breakfast,' *California Law Review* 75 (1987), 609 at 611.

6 Epilogue

1 One version of the obituary for critical legal studies is delivered with some relish in Arthur Austin, *The Empire Strikes Back: Outsiders and the Struggle over Legal Education* (New York: New York University Press, 1998), at 83–111.

2 Searching for a term that comprehends all these approaches, some writers have come up with 'radical multiculturalists': see Daniel Farber and Suzanna Sherry, *Beyond All Reason: The Radical Assault on Truth in American Law* (New York: Oxford University Press, 1997), at 5.

3 For the artist's own sense of his achievements, see the interviews in Peter Schjedahl, *Salle* (New York: Vintage Books, 1987). Salle's work has since been dismissed in Robert Hughes, *American Visions: The Epic History of Art in America* (New York: Knopf, 1997), at 599–600. See also Janet Malcolm, 'Forty One False Starts,' in David Remnick, ed., *Life Stories: Profiles from the New Yorker* (New York: Modern Library, 2001), 505.

4 See Laura Kalman, *Legal Realism at Yale, 1927–1960* (Chapel Hill: University of North Carolina Press, 1986); William Twining, *Karl Llewellyn and the Realist Movement*, rev. ed. (London: Weidenfeld and Nicolson, 1985)); John Henry Schlegel, *American Legal Realism and Empirical Social Science* (Chapel Hill: University of North Carolina Press, 1995); and William Wiecek, *The Lost World of Classical Legal Thought: Ideology in America, 1886–1937* (New York: Oxford University Press, 1998).

5 Richard W. Bauman, *Critical Legal Studies: A Guide to the Literature* (Boulder, CO: Westview Press, 1996).

6 The three editions are: David Kairys, ed., *The Politics of Law: A Progressive Critique* (New York: Pantheon Books, 1982); David Kairys, ed., *The Politics of Law: A Progressive Critique*, rev. ed. (New York: Pantheon Books, 1990); and David Kairys, ed., *The Politics of Law: A Progressive Critique*, 3rd ed. (New York: Basic Books, 1998).

7 See Ronald Dworkin, 'In Praise of Theory,' *Arizona State Law Journal* 29 (1997), 353, at 360.

8 Duncan Kennedy, *A Critique of Adjudication – fin de siècle* (Cambridge: Harvard University Press, 1997), at 9.

9 Ibid. at 10.

10 For partial bibliographies, see Bauman, *Cricial Legal Studies*, chap. 22 (on feminism and the law) and chap. 23 (critical race theory). On postmodernism's arrival and reception in advanced legal studies, see the editors' introduction to Jonathan Hart and Richard W. Bauman, eds., *Explorations in Difference: Law, Culture, and Politics* (Toronto: University of Toronto Press, 1996).

11 As suggested in Ian Ward, *An Introduction to Critical Legal Theory* (London: Cavendish, 1998), at 157.

12 See Victor Marchetti and John Marks, *The CIA and the Cult of Intelligence* (New York: Knopf, 1974).

Index